P9-AOB-190

STUDIES ON THE CHINESE ECONOMY

General Editors: Peter Nolan, Sinyi Professor of Chinese Management, Judge Institute of Management Studies, University of Cambridge, and Fellow of Jesus College, Cambridge, England; and Dong Fureng, Professor, Chinese Academy of Social Sciences, Beijing, China

This series analyses issues in China's current economic development, and sheds light upon that process by examining China's economic history. It contains a wide range of books on the Chinese economy past and present, and includes not only studies written by leading Western authorities, but also translations of the most important works on the Chinese economy produced within China. It intends to make a major contribution towards understanding this immensely important part of the world economy.

Published titles include:

Bozhong Li
AGRICULTURAL DEVELOPMENT IN JIANGNAN, 1620–1850

Alfred H. Y. Lin
THE RURAL ECONOMY OF GUANGDONG, 1870–1937

Nicholas K. Menzies
FOREST AND LAND MANAGEMENT IN IMPERIAL CHINA SINCE THE SEVENTEENTH CENTURY

Ryōshin Minami
THE ECONOMIC DEVELOPMENT OF CHINA

Peter Nolan
STATE AND MARKET IN THE CHINESE ECONOMY

Yuming Sheng
INTERSECTORAL RESOURCE FLOWS AND CHINA'S ECONOMIC DEVELOPMENT

Hong Wang
CHINA'S EXPORTS SINCE 1979

Wang Xiao-qiang
CHINA'S PRICE AND ENTERPRISE REFORM

Shangquan Gao
CHINA'S ECONOMIC REFORM

Xiaoping Xu
CHINA'S FINANCIAL SYSTEM UNDER TRANSITION

Malcolm Warner
THE MANAGEMENT OF HUMAN RESOURCES IN CHINESE
INDUSTRY

Tim Wright (*editor*)
THE CHINESE ECONOMY IN THE EARLY TWENTIETH CENTURY

Yanrui Wu
PRODUCTIVE PERFORMANCE OF CHINESE ENTERPRISES

Haiqun Yang
BANKING AND FINANCIAL CONTROL IN REFORMING PLANNED
ECONOMIES

Shujie Yao
AGRICULTURAL REFORMS AND GRAIN PRODUCTION IN CHINA

Xun-Hai Zhang
ENTERPRISE REFORMS IN A CENTRALLY PLANNED ECONOMY

Ng Sek Hong and Malcolm Warner
CHINA'S TRADE UNIONS AND MANAGEMENT

Studies on the Chinese Economy
Series Standing Order ISBN 0–333–71502–0
(*outside North America only*)

You can receive future titles in this series as they are published by placing a standing order.
Please contact your bookseller or, in case of difficulty, write to us at the address below with
your name and address, the title of the series and the ISBN quoted above.

Customer Services Department, Macmillan Distribution Ltd
Houndmills, Basingstoke, Hampshire RG21 6XS, England

Authority and Welfare in China

Modern Debates in Historical Perspective

Michael Twohey

07/27/2000

HARVARD-YENCHING LIBRARY
HARVARD UNIVERSITY
2 DIVINITY AVENUE
CAMBRIDGE, MA 02138

First published in Great Britain 1999 by
MACMILLAN PRESS LTD
Houndmills, Basingstoke, Hampshire RG21 6XS and London
Companies and representatives throughout the world

A catalogue record for this book is available from the British Library.

ISBN 0–333–72764–9

First published in the United States of America 1999 by
ST. MARTIN'S PRESS, INC.,
Scholarly and Reference Division,
175 Fifth Avenue, New York, N.Y. 10010

ISBN 0–312–21746–3

Library of Congress Cataloging-in-Publication Data
Twohey, Michael, 1962–
Authority and welfare in China : modern debates in historical
perspective / Michael Twohey.
p.   cm.
Includes bibliographical references and index.
ISBN 0–312–21746–3 (cloth)
1. Authoritarianism—China—History.   2. China—Politics and
government.   I. Title.
JQ1510.T95   1998
320.451'01—dc21   98–23638
                                                                              CIP

© Michael Twohey 1999

All rights reserved. No reproduction, copy or transmission of this publication may be made
without written permission.

No paragraph of this publication may be reproduced, copied or transmitted save with
written permission or in accordance with the provisions of the Copyright, Designs and
Patents Act 1988, or under the terms of any licence permitting limited copying issued by
the Copyright Licensing Agency, 90 Tottenham Court Road, London W1P 9HE.

Any person who does any unauthorised act in relation to this publication may be liable to
criminal prosecution and civil claims for damages.

The author has asserted his right to be identified as the author of this work in accordance
with the Copyright, Designs and Patents Act 1988.

This book is printed on paper suitable for recycling and made from fully managed and
sustained forest sources.

10   9   8   7   6   5   4   3   2   1
08   07   06   05   04   03   02   01   00   99

Printed and bound in Great Britain by
Antony Rowe Ltd, Chippenham, Wiltshire

For my parents

Contents

Preface   xi

1 Introduction   **1**
   1.1   Focus of the Study   1
   1.2   Western Perceptions of Chinese Authority   2
   1.3   Post-Mao Perceptions of China's Authoritarian
         Politics   4
   1.4   Themes and Structure of the Book   5

Part I: Ancient Authority and Welfare   **11**

2 Xunzi and Ancient Chinese Authority   **13**
   2.1   Introduction   13
   2.2   Chaos and Confucius   14
   2.3   The Search for Ethics and Order   15
   2.4   Authority and Welfare in the *Lunyu* and the *Mencius*   16
   2.5   Authority and Welfare in the *Xunzi*   19
   2.6   Xunzi's Influence on Chinese History and Politics   24
   2.7   Conclusion   27

3 Kang Youwei   **29**
   3.1   Introduction   29
   3.2   The Challenge to Patriarchal Authority   30
   3.3   Detour Toward Confused Authority   31
   3.4   Authority and Welfare in Kang Youwei's Writings   34
   3.5   The 'Hundred Days of Reform'   41
   3.6   Conclusion   43

4 Liang Qichao   **45**
   4.1   Introduction   45
   4.2   Two Perspectives on Liang Qichao   45
   4.3   Liang's Intellectual Journey to the West   47
   4.4   Enlightened Despotism   51
   4.5   Liang's Critique of the Revolutionaries   53
   4.6   Authority and Welfare in Liang Qichao's Writings   56
   4.7   Conclusion   59

Part II: Revolutionary Authority and Welfare   **61**

5 Sun Yatsen   **63**
   5.1 Introduction   63
   5.2 Sun's Nationalism and Xunzi's *Qun*   63
   5.3 Sun's Democracy and Xunzi's 'Natural Inequality' 67
   5.4 Sun's Socialism and Xunzi's *Datong* 72
   5.5 Conclusion   76

6 Mao Zedong   **79**
   6.1 Introduction   79
   6.2 Sun Yatsen's 'Three Principles' and Mao's Early Years 80
   6.3 Mao's Retreat from Sun's 'Three Principles' 83
   6.4 Explaining Mao's Retreat from Sun's 'Three Principles' 87
   6.5 Sun's Authoritarianism in Mao's China 92
   6.6 Conclusion   94

7 Deng Xiaoping   **97**
   7.1 Introduction   97
   7.2 Sun Yatsen's Influence on Deng's Theory 98
   7.3 Sun's Influence on Deng's Economic Reforms 100
   7.4 Sun's Influence on Deng's Political Reforms 103
   7.5 Deng's Socialism and Sun's *Minsheng* 106
   7.6 Sun's Authoritarianism in Deng's China 107
   7.7 Conclusion   109

Part III: New Authority and Welfare   **111**

8 The 'New Authoritarian' Debates   **113**
   8.1 Introduction   113
   8.2 China's 'Confucian Revival' in the 1980s 114
   8.3 Old Authoritarianism and New Authoritarianism 116
   8.4 The Debate on Institutionalized Confucianism 119
   8.5 The Lessons of the Late Qing   122
   8.6 The Debate on Sun Yatsen's Authoritarian Politics 125
   8.7 The Debate on Mao Zedong's Authoritarian Politics 127
   8.8 Conclusion   129

9 The Impact of Tiananmen **131**
    9.1 Introduction   131
    9.2 The First Phase of the Debates, 1988–9   132
    9.3 The Post-Tiananmen Debates   137
    9.4 Tiananmen's Impact on the People   142
    9.5 Transitional New Authoritarianism?   147
    9.6 Conclusion   149

10 Conclusion **151**
    10.1 Summary   151
    10.2 Authority, Welfare and Democracy in China   158

Notes and References   161

Bibliography   191

Index   217

Preface

The development of this book follows two extended periods of stay in China. I first travelled to Chongqing in 1985, where I taught until 1987. As well as extensive travels in the country, these two years provided an opportunity to observe the effects of economic reforms on China's political situation and stimulated my interest in research on China's political economy. I returned to China for seven months to carry out fieldwork for my PhD in 1992. Much of the book took shape during this time, and is based on research and interviews conducted at Beijing University and the Chinese Academy of Social Sciences in Beijing, as well as at Fudan University in Shanghai. I am grateful to have been granted interviews at Beijing University with two of China's most prominent philosophers, Zhang Dainian and Zhu Buokun. Our meetings sparked questions about traditional Chinese political authority that set the tone for the remainder of my research. John Knoblock's translation and exhaustive exegesis of the Confucian philosopher Xunzi's *Complete Works* became an essential guide along the way. It was through Knoblock's analysis of Xunzi's state theory that I established a connection between ancient and modern authoritarianism in China. I am also indebted to Di Yongjun, Jiang Gangmiao, Li Hong, Wang Zhufeng, and especially Yang Chenqi and Professor Zhang Jiqian of Beijing University, who gave generously of their time in order to assist my research in Beijing.

I would also like to express my great appreciation to Professor Peter Nolan of Cambridge University. Peter set me the task of researching political authoritarianism in modern China. His moral support, his reading of draft chapters, his attention to detail and his challenging questions provided invaluable guidance and motivation. I have also benefited greatly from the support and guidance of Geoffrey Hawthorn and Joseph McDermott at Cambridge. I likewise owe a debt of gratitude to Professor David Lumsden and Professor Bernie Frolic of York University in Toronto. It was David who first drew me to the study of China and Bernie who provided a deeper understanding of Chinese politics. Thanking them and the others noted in no way implicates them or my employer in the views expressed in this book.

This study would not have reached fruition without the support of a Rotary Foundation Scholarship, a Pacific Cultural Foundation

Scholarship, a Canadian Centennial Scholarship, a China–Canada Exchange Scholarship and financial assistance from Jesus College, Cambridge. The encouragement of friends along the way also has been a big help. I extend much appreciation to Marie Källkvist with whom I have shared the challenges and rewards that research can bring. My special thanks to the following people for their assistance, discussions, friendship and good humour, which have all contributed in diverse ways to the completion of this book: Sylvia Chan, David Chennells, Silvana Dean, Kim Ennico, Gerry Fitzpatrick, Rae Fleming, Liz Gordon, Dan Homer, Erling Kagge, Dan and Natalie Kallen, Åke and Ginger Källkvist, Liu Xiaofeng, Yvette Longman, Andrew Mason, Pankaj Mohan, Suzanne Quay, Susan Reva, Luise Rivolta, Steve Saxby and Tim Weston. My gratitude as well to the editorial staff at Macmillan, and namely to Tim Farmiloe, Sunder Katwala, Linda Auld and their colleagues without whom this book would not have appeared.

Finally, I thank my parents, Jack and Rita Twohey, to whom this book is dedicated. They have been a tremendous source of stability, strength and optimism. The book is as much a result of their support, encouragement and patience as it is the product of my own labours. I thank them, my brother Jeff and his wife Nicole for their unstinting loyalty.

MICHAEL TWOHEY

1 Introduction

1.1 FOCUS OF THE STUDY

This book attempts to answer two questions: how do we define traditional Chinese political authority and how has this been adapted to modern China's political economy? These questions have been asked by China specialists many times before, and they have grown in significance as the economic successes of China's post-Mao development strategy have repeated the earlier economic successes of its East Asian neighbours. But China's land mass, huge population and ideological framework seem to confound any comparisons with other countries in the region. Similarly, China has not fallen in line with the post-totalitarian patterns that have swept across Eastern Europe since the collapse of the Soviet state. The single party and its top leadership have continued to be the central decision-making structure in China. That China remains on the periphery of democratic trends embraced by East Europeans and East Asians provokes the need to reevaluate the unique qualities of its authoritarian politics. This book attempts to explain how past systems of Chinese authority have been adapted to China's political institutions this century, and how they have continued to influence policy in the post-Mao years.

Such an undertaking may seem to contradict the idea of a focused study. But a major theme of this book is that 2000 years of history have not altered fundamental definitions and goals of Chinese political authority since China was unified as an empire in 221 BC. Like their Western counterparts, Chinese philosophers and theorists over the millennia have defined authority as a legitimate form of power, whereas power has been defined as an arbitrary, illegitimate use of authority. Where the West and China differ today is in what they see as the foundation of legitimate authority. For Western democracies, authority is most often justified according to liberal and democratic values. This has resulted in extensive debates on the nature and limits of authority. On the one hand it is acknowledged that political rulers must have the authority to perform certain actions, such as the right to make laws, while on the other these actions are criticized if they infringe on the liberty, rights and autonomy of the individual (Miller, 1991, p. 28). In China, discussions on authority have been more one-sided until recently. The crises of acute poverty and conflicts, both

1

military and political, during most of the twentieth century have not afforded Chinese intellectuals and political figures the luxury of western-style political debates. Authoritarian leadership generally was seen as legitimate in China if it could deliver people from conflict and starvation. While defending strong authority for these purposes has had its critics in China, most important Chinese theorists and policy-makers have supported authoritarianism throughout this century. It comprised the major theme of Deng Xiaoping's keynote address at the Eleventh Party Congress in December 1978, which launched China on its current phenomenal economic success. Yet the Chinese leadership's stand on the need for strong authority to achieve this goal is at the heart of its ideological differences with Western democracies. These differences are not new but have existed since greater contact between China and the West began over 300 years ago. The bulk of this study concentrates on these differences as they have been interpreted by Chinese political figures this century.

1.2 WESTERN PERCEPTIONS OF CHINESE AUTHORITY

In the modern era, Western analyses of Chinese political authority began during the European Enlightenment. At the beginning of the Enlightenment, Voltaire spoke with admiration of the strong and orderly character of the Chinese state. However, more frequent exchanges between the capitalist West and China led many European intellectuals to conclude that China's Confucian-based state orthodoxy did nothing more than defend a despotic system of rule that enslaved Chinese subjects, robbed them of their individualism and led to a stationary and unprogressive culture (see Roetz, 1993, Chapter 2). This interpretation gained strength with Montesquieu, whose belief that individual oppression was best curbed by a division of powers among the executive, the legislature and the judiciary was partly influenced by his critique of what he termed China's 'exact observation' of rites (*li*), which he said was the basis of Chinese despotism (Montesquieu, 1989, p. 321).[1] Hegel's writings tended to reinforce this view. He grouped China under the rubric of the 'Oriental World', in which he felt reverence for omnipotent authority was unquestioned, and man only existed in and for himself insofar as his role was related to this authority (Hegel, 1980, p. 190). Hegel also contended that French missionaries' translations of Chinese classical texts had been worthless because there was nothing the West could learn from Confucian writings (Hegel, 1995, p. 121). This image of China was not helped by figures like Marx and Engels. In the first volume of their *Collected Works*, Marx spoke of a Chinese despotism that had become naturally resistant to change (Marx, 1975, p. 126). Engels later described the 'rotting semi-civilization' that was governed by the Chinese state (Engels, 1986, p. 278). But no work of greater influence spoke more negatively of Chinese despotism than John Stuart Mill's *On Liberty*, which was also influenced partly by Mill's fear for Europe's future if the cause of individualism were averted, as he believed had been the case in China. For Mill, China had become a stationary country because thousands of years of despotic rule had instilled a collective conscience that obstructed political and economic development (Mill, 1991, pp. 79–80).

Liberalism and Marxism, the two major political doctrines that had become prominent in the West by the end of the nineteenth century, viewed Chinese political authority as a burden to the state and society. Both doctrines also believed that change and progress could only come to China if the Chinese elite employed Western political and economic practices. Scholars later wrote that our understanding of Chinese state power at this time had been clouded either by the Western liberal tendency to define power according to 'rights' or by the Marxist tendency to place China within the broad categories of the 'Asiatic mode of production' and 'Oriental despotism' (Gernet, 1987, pp. xv–xvi). But these opinions persisted in the West well into the twentieth century. In *The Religion of China*, Max Weber maintained that China's observation of Confucian rites led to a 'relentless canonization of tradition', which was not only despotic but also a barrier to Confucian rationalism (Weber, 1951, p. 164). Perhaps the only major post-Enlightenment, pre-twentieth century Western thinker who spoke about the merits of traditional Chinese authority was Adam Smith. In his *Wealth of Nations*, Smith refers often to the degree of wealth and opulence that China's system of governance had created. Like other Western observers at the time, however, Smith speaks negatively about China's unwillingness to establish greater contact with the West (see Smith, 1990, pp. 46, 102, 119, 178, 185, 238).[2]

It has only been during this century that Western scholars have begun to accept that the basis of Chinese political authority necessitated elements from the Chinese past. This was first argued most forcefully in Levenson's *Confucian China and its Modern Fate*. Levenson claimed that even the Chinese Communist Party (CCP)

could not completely disavow political elements from China's traditional past (Levenson, 1958, p. 135). During the 1960s and early
1970s, much Western scholarship continued to analyze Chinese political authority within a Marxist-Leninist framework. But some scholars
argued that this limited our understanding of Chinese authority
because it emphasized Marxist ideology at the expense of recognizing
continuities with China's pre-Communist period (Johnson, 1973, pp.
v, vii). The need for traditional references proved increasingly useful
in analyses of economic and political anomalies like the Great Leap
Forward and the Cultural Revolution. Schram described the Cultural
Revolution, for example, as '... part of the ongoing effort of the
Chinese people to come to terms with the modern world without
sacrificing their own identity.' (Schram, 1973, p. 3) Schram also said
that the Cultural Revolution and the Great Leap Forward were part
of Mao's conviction that wholesale Westernization in Leninist or
Soviet terms was merely a '... temporary crutch, which had enabled
the Chinese to move forward during a limited period, but could not in
the long run, provide a substitute for walking on their own two feet.'
(Schram, 1973, p. 8) [3]

1.3   POST-MAO PERCEPTIONS OF CHINA'S AUTHORITARIAN POLITICS

In the post-Mao years, and with China's East Asian-like economic
success, scholars are beginning to denounce the relevance of Marxist
schema in explaining Chinese economic development. Research now
seems divided between two schools, the 'political culture' school and
the Leninist school.[4] The culturalists deal with the religious, philosophical and metaphysical elements of traditional and Confucian
authority while investigating less thoroughly the links between these
and contemporary institutionalized Chinese authority. The ideas they
present, such as compliance to familial and collective forms of
authority and the influence of these on the people's acceptance of a
strong state, though useful, do not always answer the bigger question
of how, if at all, modern Chinese statecraft is influenced by traditional antecedents.[5] Johnson criticized the culturalists in the early
1980s, and suggested that a better paradigm for the evaluation of
Chinese authority could be found in Leninism, which he felt had been
inadequately developed for application to the Chinese case.[6]

The Leninist paradigm predominated through the 1980s, and it is still used by important China scholars.[7] It continued to be set against the culturalist argument well into the late 1980s. A question that recurred among experts at this time was whether Deng Xiaoping's post-Mao reforms were '... the inevitable result of a revolution directed by a Leninist one-party state or ... a return to older forms of social organization' (Billeter, 1985, p. 162). This question was at the centre of discussions compiled by Schram about the foundations and limits of state power in China (see Schram, 1985, 1987). Along with its scholarly contributions to the field of post-Mao studies, Schram's work draws together specialists on contemporary Chinese politics as well as on Chinese history and philosophy (ancient and modern) in order to consider both sides of the Leninist-culturalist debate. As might be expected, the discussions yield little consensus. Contributors who relied on a Leninist framework[8] merely touch on possible influences from pre-revolutionary Chinese culture, while the culturalists[9] tended to examine pre-revolutionary historical periods or philosophical concepts without drawing substantive comparisons between these and their influences on the post-Mao period. One critic lamented that although China specialists speak of a relationship between traditional culture and the patterns of authority that have been established in Chinese political institutions, they are reluctant to give their full attention to the true nature of this relationship, choosing instead to focus on either one or the other in their explanations of contemporary Chinese politics (Dickson, 1992, p. 103). This book attempts to fill this gap in the research by examining how ancient Chinese political traditions have influenced modern Chinese conceptions of authority.

1.4 THEMES AND STRUCTURE OF THE BOOK

The overarching thesis of this book is that the ultimate purpose of Chinese political authoritarianism is people's welfare. Strong political authority was considered legitimate authority, both in ancient and in modern China, so long as the Chinese state was able to maintain stability, generate wealth and redistribute this wealth among the people. This outlook is reflected in early Confucian works, in the records of Confucius's own thoughts in the *Analects*, in Chinese philosophical works that succeeded Confucius and in Chinese political theories of the twentieth century. Once again, this thesis is not entirely new. There is a wealth of material that discusses Chinese authority and democracy in the context of Chinese principles of welfare.[10] What this book offers is a new perspective on the philosophical origins of the authority-welfare nexus and on how this has continued to inform the views of twentieth-century Chinese modernizers.

In Part One, the book demonstrates how the pattern of political authority that was followed by important Chinese reformers in the modern era can be traced to political patterns established by the ancient Confucian philosopher Xunzi. Chapter 2 suggests that among the three important Confucian works of the ancient period, the *Analects*, the *Mencius* and the *Xunzi*, only the *Xunzi* presents a clear strategy of how Confucian philosophical concepts could be adapted to state authority. The chapter also claims that Xunzi's transferral of the ancient Confucian virtue *li* ('rite') to a hierarchical system of political rule laid the basis for the authoritarian political structure that twentieth-century Chinese modernizers advocated. This conclusion is central to the book. Compared to Confucius and Mencius, Xunzi has remained a relatively obscure and unimportant figure and one who is rarely cited in modern-day attempts to describe traditional influences on Chinese politics. This was not helped by Bodde's assertion in 1953 that Xunzi presented a 'static' view of history that had little applicability to the historical periods that followed (Bodde, 1953, pp. 28–9). Similarly, important historical surveys like Creel's *The Origins of Statecraft in China* (1970) accord very little space to Xunzi. Even Fairbank's more recent attempt to reevaluate the emergence of Confucian imperial authority in China, though noting the relevance of *li*, does not associate this with Xunzi (Fairbank, 1992, pp. 52–3).

Scholars who discuss traditional authoritarian influences on Chinese politics in the post-Mao years also refer to *li* independently of the *Xunzi*. This is evident in Schram's two volume set, noted in Section 1.3. Here, *li* is described as the 'central axis' of China's societal order (Schram, 1987, p. xi), as the foundation of the Chinese political hierarchy (Billeter, 1985, p. 163) and as the basis of China's opposition to 'individual rights'.[11] But these descriptions assume that modern China's political institutions are direct descendants of the metaphysical *li* from the *Zhouli* (the *Rites of Zhou*) or the *Liji* (the *Record of Rites*)[12] rather than of the political *li* from the *Xunzi*. Schram, for example, says that *li's* origins are '... derived from the cosmic order, which guaranteed [society's] essential oneness [in China]' (Schram, 1987, p. xi). By making such statements, China specialists do not take us much further in our understanding of traditional Chinese political authority than figures like Montesquieu or Mill did. Yet as Chapters 3–9 of this book indicate, the concepts and patterns of political authority that Xunzi established, and which were influenced by *li*, were either borrowed directly or adapted to modern circumstances by Chinese intellectuals and important Chinese political figures of the twentieth century.

Chapter 3 examines how these patterns were reiterated in Kang Youwei's writings in the 1890s. Kang was a Confucian scholar who was influential in the late Qing dynasty's reform movement. He believed that economic and political modernization could take place within a Confucian political and moral framework. His reforms gained the attention of the Emperor Guangxu in what became known as China's 'Hundred Days of Reform' in 1898, but were later halted by a conservative coup. The chapter rejects previous comparisons of Kang's reforms to Western liberal democracy. It suggests that Kang's defence of a hierarchical political system, his support for state intervention in the distribution of wealth and his belief that an advanced material society was the best guarantee of a well-ordered state were influenced by Xunzi's rationale. The chapter concludes that Kang's support for a strong state that was built on indigenous political sources and his emphasis on gradualistic reforms, set the tone for all major Chinese reformers of the twentieth century.

Chapter 4 suggests that Liang Qichao also believed Chinese development required Chinese solutions. Liang was a student of Kang Youwei's. He was exiled to Japan after the conservative coup of 1898 and spent the rest of his life raising support for the reformers' cause among overseas Chinese and foreign governments. The chapter challenges Philip Huang's view that Liang's politics was based on a syncretic union of Western liberalism and Confucianism. It claims that Liang dismissed Western liberal theory in favour of Western statist views that accorded with Xunzi's concepts of *qun* ('grouping') and *gong* ('public-mindedness'). This is evident in Liang's criticism of nineteenth-century English liberalism, his repudiation of Rousseau's *Social Contract* and his rejection of Montesquieu's thesis in *The Spirit of Laws* that political liberty should include the separation of legislative, executive and judicial powers of government. According to Liang, major works that were part of the Western liberal canon were to be faulted because they put individual interests ahead of group interests, individual freedom ahead of national freedom and liberal democracy and laissez-faireism ahead of state authority and state intervention in economics. Even more than Kang Youwei, Liang maintained that it was not a question of preference but of necessity that China adapt a system of state authority in the early reform period, and that this goal was best served not by separating the individual from the state but by grouping the two together for the goal of national wealth and power.

Part II of the book examines China's revolutionary authoritarians. Chapter 5 on Sun Yatsen, who was the father of the Chinese republican revolution, describes how his 'Three People's Principles' (nationalism, democracy and welfare) also strengthen the argument that twentieth-century China's patterns of political authority are influenced by Xunzi. Sun accepted that *li* and *qun* were crucial to the state's ability to shape the conduct of the people. He also accepted that the creation of a wealthy and stable China meant that the nation must be put ahead of the individual. But Sun added four significant innovations to the authoritarian stand of his predecessors. The first was his belief that Chinese political traditions would function best in the modern era if they were united with Chinese nationalism. The second was that in the early stages of development, democratic sovereignty could only reside in a political hierarchy that divided powers and responsibilities among an educated elite (Kang and Liang agreed with this but they did not describe how it was to work as thoroughly as Sun did). The third was that the long-term goal of a wealthy nation must be the equalization of incomes and standards of living. The fourth was that Chinese socialism was to be built on capitalist foundations that emphasized the development of state capital and state control of private capital. Sun was also the first Chinese reformer to claim that the goal of liberty in China was to create wealth. He reasoned that the wealthier the nation became the more a democratic franchise could be extended.

Chapter 6 attempts to contribute to the literature on Mao Zedong by suggesting that his authoritarian rule may have been directed by Sun Yatsen's political principles more than it was by Marxist-Leninist theory. The chapter states that Mao's writings from 1929 to 1949 tend to support Sun's ideological line. It also argues that from the early 1940s to the late 1950s, Mao did not in practice show a definite political orientation toward the Soviet Union, and that he did not treat trade relations with other countries according to Marxist ideology but according to their willingness to do business with China. The chapter maintains that this was because Mao adhered to Sun's argument that foreign capital and investment were essential to building Chinese socialism. The chapter concludes that Mao's radical politics may have been the result of American and later Soviet reluctance to accept this position.

Chapter 7 demonstrates how Deng Xiaoping's politics also seemed to be motivated by Sun Yatsen's theories. The chapter disputes views that refer to 'Dengism' merely as a restoration of 'rational Maoism', or which compare Deng's politics generally to pre-revolutionary discourse. The chapter states that Deng's straightforward response to development, his belief that material gain would best sustain socialism, his acceptance that foreign capital would best assist this process and his views that capitalism must be used but also restricted by a strong state to prevent the polarization of wealth, correspond with Sun's goals in the 'Three Principles'. This and Deng's stress on political stability ahead of democracy, wealth ahead of liberty, and strong central leadership ahead of multiparty politics elicit strong parallels with Sun.

Part III of the book examines the Chinese debates on new authoritarianism (NA). Discussions on NA started in China in 1986, they gathered force by early 1989 and ended in May of that same year during the Tiananmen crisis. The purpose of the NA debates was to seek alternative systems of development to Chinese totalitarianism in the post-Mao period. NA discussions also considered the nature and limits of Chinese authoritarianism and democracy, and the extent to which centralized authority could function legitimately in the absence of democracy. Although considerable research has been done on the NA debates, most of this is descriptive: it explains how and why the debates were initiated, who their principal actors were, in what way divisions existed between the 'democrats' and the 'authoritarians' and when and why the debates ended. Insofar as the research is analytical, it almost entirely examines NA in relation to Western political concepts without exploring the degree to which the debates draw upon long-term Chinese political traditions.[13] These surveys fail to make clear what is 'new' about NA and whether it differs from old forms of Chinese political authority. Chapters 8 and 9 contribute to this research by demonstrating that a full understanding of NA requires an examination of the debates within a wider Chinese political setting. Chapter 8 suggests that the NA debates were influenced by historical precedent, both ancient and modern, far more than existing analyses of NA have indicated. Chapter 9 shows that the main concern of the debates may not have been whether a system of democracy should replace the CCP's authority, but whether this authority could prevent itself from collapsing without exercising greater use of Chinese legality. The chapter reaches the same conclusion in its survey of the post-Tiananmen NA debates and suggests that the events in Tiananmen Square did not alter in all cases Chinese opinion about the need for strong political authority. The book concludes that Chinese traditional concepts of political authority and the way in which these were adapted to Chinese political institutions this century, continued to influence the authoritarian models that NA participants supported in the late 1980s.

Part I:
Ancient Authority and Welfare

2 Xunzi and Ancient Chinese Authority

2.1 INTRODUCTION

> I always recall one line that appears in the Book of Poetry of the Confucian classics. It reads, 'Although [Z]hou is an old nation, it has a new mission.' At the present time, China is an ancient nation which has a new mission and that mission is modernization. My effort is to preserve the identity and individuality of the ancient nation, yet, at the same time, to promote the fulfilment of the new mission. (Fung, 1991, p. 664)[1]

In order to understand how traditional authority could have been adapted to modern China's political economy, it is necessary to examine the philosophical sources that may have informed this authority. This was also the task of China's Confucian scholar-officials in the late Qing dynasty (AD 1644–1912). In their attempts to provide solutions to China's backwardness at the beginning of the twentieth century, important scholar–officials read Western political and economic theory and studied the Western political institutions that they encountered during their extensive travels through Europe and North America. Despite the contrasting world of prosperity, efficiency and political order that they observed in the West, most scholar–officials concluded that China was not ready for the democratic traditions that had inspired these. Many began to believe that answers to China's economic, social and political development could still be found in the Confucian teachings from which they had been groomed for their official positions. More particularly, they returned to the writings of Chinese philosophers from the Zhou dynasty (c. 1122–221 BC). The second half of the Zhou marks what is considered to be the efflorescence of Chinese culture, for it was not only the time when Confucius was alive but the period when all major indigenous philosophies had been established in China. Of equal significance was the unification of China as an empire under the state of Qin at the end of the Zhou in 221 BC. Although the shortest of China's dynasties, lasting only 14 years, the Qin's system of imperial rule was monumental in the way that it continued to influence China's

13

political institutions into the twentieth century. These factors were not far from the minds of Qing scholar-officials who were attempting to reform China's dilapidated state structure. The solutions they offered often have been described in the West and in China under the broad sweep of 'Confucianism' or 'Confucian liberalism'.

But as Chapters 3 and 4 on the Qing scholars Kang Youwei and Liang Qichao indicate, their views about what could be salvaged of the past to serve modern political institutions were far more specific than a broad acceptance of Confucianism. Separate chapters are devoted to Kang and Liang, rather than to other Confucian reformers who were their contemporaries, because Kang and Liang are seen in this book as the principal agents of political transformation between the politics of ancient Chinese authoritarianism and the centralized political system that was advocated by China's revolutionaries. Through an examination of the Confucian *Analects*, the *Mencius*, and the *Xunzi*, this chapter attempts to answer the same questions that Kang and Liang were asking: what is the basis of the Confucian philosophy?; why did the ancient Confucian philosophers believe what they did?; how did this influence the system of imperial authority in the centuries that followed?; how was imperial authority to be transferred to modern political institutions?

2.2   CHAOS AND CONFUCIUS

The first of the above questions is difficult to answer. To argue that the fundamentals of the Confucian philosophy should be understood in a particular way is to invite criticism from specialists on Confucianism. Where there seems to be consensus, though, is in the view that a substantial part of ancient Confucian discourse, and the discourse of other philosophies from the Zhou dynasty, was in response to the tumultuous times in which the philosophers were living. Roetz's study of the Zhou suggests that all major Chinese texts from the period speak of 'chaos' *(luan)* and 'decay' *(shuai)*, of 'worry' *(you)* and 'fear' *(ju)* and of the need for 'deliverance'*(jiu)* from a state of disorder (Roetz, 1993, p. 43). The Spring and Autumn period (551–479 BC) of the Zhou, in which Confucius lived, was also marked by strife and wars between states. Confucius believed that conflict was a manifestation of disintegrating morals. If morals could be improved, he reasoned, military struggles would end and order would be restored. The Confucian *Analects (Lunyu)*, for example, known to be the only text in which Confucius's discussions with his disciples are recorded, is in the main a dialogue about the need for improving ethics and restoring order.[2] Moral regeneration and an orderly society are then fundamental goals of Confucianism, and possibly the basis of the Confucian philosophy. Specialists in Confucian studies have argued that Confucius emphasized two ethical virtues in the *Lunyu* that he believed could improve morals and restore order. These concepts are *ren*[3] and *li*.[4] The philosophical debate on the importance of *ren* and *li* and on which of the two was central to Confucius's thinking, has gone on for centuries. It is not the objective of this chapter to become involved in the debate, but rather to determine whether *ren* or *li*, or both concepts, can help us to understand the relationship between Confucian authority and authoritarian politics in twentieth-century China.[5]

2.3 THE SEARCH FOR ETHICS AND ORDER

Part of the reason that the debate on *ren* and *li* has continued over the centuries is because the *Lunyu* does not state clearly which of the two concepts is more important to Confucius (Shun, 1993, p. 47). One group of scholars has suggested that it is for this reason that the *Lunyu* remains an ambiguous and unsettled document. They suggest that its lack of systematic exposition must be attributed to Confucius's reluctance to define *ren* and *li* precisely, and to his tendency to make them suggestive of the widest possible range of meaning.[6] Indeed no single definition or purpose for either term has been agreed upon in academic discussions up to the present day. *Ren* has been defined as 'humaneness', 'goodness', 'kindness', 'benevolence', 'perfect goodness', 'perfect virtue', 'love for one's fellow man', 'an ethical ideal' and the transcendent basis of an improved humanity.[7] *Li* has been defined as 'rites', 'custom', 'ceremony', 'ritual', 'ritual action', 'rules of propriety', 'decorum' and as the governing basis of good conduct and an orderly society.[8] Other scholars have suggested that the enigma of *ren* and *li* can be partly solved by comparing the *Lunyu* to the classical Chinese texts that antedated it.[9] They claim that while pre-Confucian Classics, such as the *Book of Odes (Shijing)* (850–600 BC), grouped *ren* equally with other classical virtues, Confucius made it the general virtue from which all others were to be understood in the *Lunyu*.

Ren indeed takes a central place in the *Lunyu*, and often seems to represent Confucius's premier virtue. Confucius said that '... It is *[ren]* which constitutes the excellence of a neighbourhood'; or, '... If the will be set on *[ren]*, there will be no practice of wickedness' (see the 1971 edition of the *Analects*, pp. 165–6; hereafter cited as Confucius, 1971). But elsewhere in the *Lunyu*, the cultivation of *ren* merely lays the ground for the higher goal of *li*: '... To subdue one's self and return to *[li]*, is *[ren]*.' In other cases, *li* is the standard by which all actions are governed: '... Look not at what is contrary to *[li]*; listen not to what is contrary to *[li]*; speak not what is contrary to *[li]*; make no movement which is contrary to *[li]*.' (Confucius, 1971, p. 250). The uncertainty that surrounds the definition and ranking of *ren* and *li* in the *Lunyu* will no doubt remain one of the most enduring debates in Confucian philosophical studies. In this book, *ren* will be referred to as 'benevolence' and its derivatives ('beneficent', 'benefits'), and *li* will be referred to as 'social order' because these are the definitions that were used by twentieth-century reformers in China when they applied the terms to modern political institutions. It also should be noted that although Confucian studies usually refer to *ren* and *li* as traditional 'virtues', the terms will be henceforth referred to as 'concepts' to suit their modern applications on which the bulk of this study concentrates.

2.4   AUTHORITY AND WELFARE IN THE *LUNYU* AND THE *MENCIUS*

What is evident in the *Lunyu*, as well as in the writings of Confucius's best-known disciple, Mencius (*c.* 370–290 BC), is the belief that legitimate government should be judged by its ability to create wealth and improve people's welfare. It also appears that these objectives may be linked to a belief in *ren's* ability to effectuate them. When Confucius is asked how a leader should act in order to conduct government properly, he replies,

> When *the person in authority* makes more beneficial to the people the things from which they naturally derive benefit; – is not this being beneficent without *great* expenditure? When he chooses the labours which are proper, and makes them labour on them, who will repine? When his desires are set on benevolent *government*, and he secures it, who will accuse him of covetousness? (Confucius, 1971, p. 353) (Emphasis from text.)

The association between legitimacy, benevolence and welfare appears frequently in the *Lunyu,* almost whenever the 'proper ways' of government are discussed. When Confucius is asked to describe a man who is 'extensively conferring benefits' on all the people, he describes him as a 'sage' *(shengren),* the highest distinction that could be conferred on a person in ancient China. When he is asked about the requisites of government, he stipulates that there must be '... sufficiency of food [in order that there be] confidence of the people in their ruler'; when asked how to maintain wealth in the nation, he says that '... there must be reverent attention to business ... economy in expenditure, and love for men; and the employment of the people at the proper seasons.' (Confucius, 1971, pp. 140, 194, 254)

Mencius also believed that all moral, social and political problems could be solved if the ruler nurtured the welfare of the people (Wong, 1991, p. 41). However, Mencius relied on the utility of *ren* in the fulfillment of these goals to a much greater degree than Confucius. In fact, *ren* is considered by some scholars to be the basis of the entire Mencian philosophy.[10] Mencius even refers to the ideal government as a 'government of benevolence' *(renzheng)* (see the 1988 edition of the *Mencius,* pp. 53, 58, 70, 75, 99; hereafter cited as *Mencius,* 1988). The central place that is given to benevolent rule in the *Mencius* is apparent in the following lines:

> There is a way to win the Empire; win the people and you will win the Empire. There is a way to win the people; win their hearts and you will win the people. There is a way to win their hearts; amass what they want for them; do not impose what they dislike on them. That is all. The people turn to the benevolent as water flows downwards or as animals head for the wilds. (*Mencius,* 1988, pp. 121–2)[11]

Mencius seems to put greater emphasis on the importance of the people than Confucius did. Mencius said, 'The people are of supreme importance; the altars to the gods of earth and grain come next; last comes the ruler' (*Mencius,* 1988, p. 196). These lines have gained much academic attention, and have contributed to Mencius's distinction as China's first humanist.[12] But this may misconstrue the exact nature of the Mencian philosophy. Unlike the development of humanism during the Renaissance in fourteenth-century Europe, in which the authority of the church gave way to the primacy of personality, the Mencian philosophy also continued to see the virtuous leadership of the ruler as the paramount guide to people's actions. As Mencius reminds us: 'The gentleman's virtue is like wind; the virtue of the common people is like grass. Let the wind sweep over the grass, and the grass is sure to bend.' (*Mencius*, 1988, pp. 96–7). From this, it seems that the common people have no real political role in the *Mencius* and that their actions are determined by the authority of the ruler.[13]

Both Confucius and Mencius believed that the end of political rule and the legitimation of political rule was an assurance that the welfare of the people was adequately met. But beyond the clarity of this goal, its attainment, in both cases, is marred by abstractions and contradictions. These manifest themselves in Confucius's contrary statements about the importance of *ren* and *li* to the goals of the state. They are also apparent in Mencius's incertitude about the authority of the people versus the authority of the ruler. Other inconsistencies are conspicuous in both texts. In some cases, Confucius speaks of 'reverent attention to business' and 'employment of people in proper seasons'; in others and much more regularly, he puts virtue – and the virtue of poverty – above the pursuit of wealth. He is often wary of economic or material gain and puts 'truth' ahead of food, comfort and adequate housing. Poverty, whether of a person, a region or of a state is not always seen as calamitous but as the root of happiness (Confucius, 1971, pp. 140, 168, 170, 188, 198, 215–16, 303, 308).

Similar confusion arises in Mencius's writings. Mencius does not ascribe virtue to poverty in the way Confucius does, but a tension does exist in his writings between the need for wealth creation on the one hand and his admonition to officials that the realization of wealth would lead to corruption on the other (*Mencius*, 1988, pp. 50–2, 66, 82). One could argue in defence of these incongruities that their basis was after all philosophical, not political and therefore more reflective than practical. But both philosophers' primary concerns with stability, prosperity and welfare suggest otherwise. The problem rests more in their ambivalence about what the solutions to these concerns should be. It therefore becomes highly questionable whether Confucius in particular can be accurately and justifiably linked with successful development strategies in modern China (as well as in East and Southeast Asia). The *Lunyu* is not only vague in its philosophical renderings but vague on issues which later became so important to leaders in Asia who used Confucius's name to characterize their approaches to development.[14] It cannot be said with accuracy that Confucius is a contributing factor to state-centred economic growth in Singapore, for example, when he frequently shunned the quest for profit.[15] A clearer understanding of the political, economic and social dimensions of Confucianism, and the way in which these prefigured modern Chinese political authority, can be found in the writings of the Confucian philosopher Xunzi, as the remainder of this chapter illustrates.

2.5 AUTHORITY AND WELFARE IN THE *XUNZI*

Despite being considered Mencius's equal as the greatest ancient Confucian philosopher after Confucius, it is only with Knoblock's recent translation of the *Complete Works of Xunzi* (1988–94, 3 vols) that Xunzi's philosophy can be fully appreciated by a Western audience.[16] According to Knoblock, Xunzi's writings have remained less significant than those of Confucius and Mencius because they never received imperial patronage, as the *Lunyu* and the *Mencius* did. In addition to this, the renewed interest in the *Mencius* during the late Song dynasty (AD 960–1279) is said to have eclipsed the relevance of Xunzi's philosophy until the late Qing dynasty (1644–1912), when the *Xunzi* was again given a place of importance by Confucian philosophers. It eventually became integral to Chinese communist theory in the post–1949 years, when Xunzi was recognized as the most progressive of the ancient Confucian philosophers (see *Xunzi*, Vol. 1, pp. vii-viii. All citations from the *Xunzi* are taken from the Knoblock edition).

Xunzi (298–38 BC) lived at the end of the Warring States period of the Zhou Dynasty. Compared to the periods when Confucius and Mencius lived, this was a time of extreme political unrest and disorder. Xunzi encountered states that had become completely divided and demoralized, and that had been annexed by other states because of decades of bad government and weak rulers. He also witnessed, on a much larger scale than his predecessors, the bitter rivalries between warlords who were vying for land. Neither Confucius nor Mencius experienced the continuous prospect of chaos as Xunzi did. One critic has suggested that it may be for this reason that their philosophies are more inclined towards cooperative resolutions than is true of the *Xunzi* (Peerenboom, 1993, p. 133). More generally, Xunzi rejected any philosophy that dealt in abstractions or in ethical intuition. He insisted that ideas and principles that should be discussed are only the ones that have a useful purpose in society (see *Xunzi*, Vol. 1, pp. 7, 9 and Tillman, 1982, p. 25). Although Xunzi recognized that many factors could contribute to disorder, he believed that all of these and all other social and political problems of the state, had their origins in the people's struggle for resources. By resources, Xunzi meant food and other necessities of human existence. He felt that once scarcity was eliminated, chaos would end. Unusually for his time, Xunzi blamed the problem of scarcity on the state's inheritance and acceptance of ideas from his philosophical forefathers. In particular, he condemned the recapitulation of ideas from Mencius and from the Zhou philosopher Mozi (551–479 BC).

Xunzi's Critique of Mencius

Book 23 of the *Xunzi* is an extended critique of Mencius's belief that man is inherently good. 'If man is inherently good', Xunzi queried, 'why does chaos abound in every state?' Xunzi argued that man must be seen as evil and in need of the authority that a strong state could provide. To this end, Xunzi also departs from Confucius and Mencius in his belief that only *li*, not *ren*, should represent the state's conceptual basis of authority:

> How did ritual principles *[li]* arise? I say that men are born with desires which, if not satisfied, cannot but lead men to seek to satisfy them. If in seeking to satisfy their desires men observe no measure and apportion things without limits, then it would be impossible for them not to contend over the means to satisfy their desires. Such contention leads to disorder. Disorder leads to poverty. The Ancient Kings abhorred such disorder, so they established the regulations contained within ritual and moral principles in order to apportion things, to nurture the desires of men, and to supply the means for their satisfaction. (*Xunzi*, Vol. 3, p. 55)

Xunzi felt that *li* was necessary not only to restrict man's desires but also to control the distribution of wealth and goods to meet the state's goal of material existence as generously as possible (Peerenboom, 1993, pp. 124–5). He likewise believed that this process exerted goodness in man because it rescued him from the calamity that could arise in an environment of scarcity (Cheng, 1991, p. 204). Whenever food and goods were in scarce supply, Xunzi contended, man was at his evil worst and rebellions were usual (*Xunzi*, Vol. 3, pp. 55, 155–6).[17] Xunzi also argued that *li's* emphasis on the harmonious development of social organization removed man from his isolation by teaching him to serve other men, as they serve him. He said this would assist the goal of a well-ordered state (*Xunzi*, Vol. 2, p. 121).

This view has been compared to Hobbes's legitimation of a strong state (Roetz, 1993, pp. 68–9, and Schwartz, 1985, pp. 294–6). It has also been likened to Burkian traditionalism, or a system that gives less emphasis to traditional values than to the chaos that could ensue in the absence of such values (Hansen, 1983, p. 80). But more to the point, Xunzi's state theory is rooted in the belief that the elimination of poverty and disorder depended on the state's ability to instil in the people the idea that it was impossible to satisfy fully everyone's needs in an environment of scarcity. This too may have represented Xunzi's rejection of Confucius's philosophy, whose ethical system assumed the possibility of solutions in which everyone comes out ahead (Peerenboom, 1993, pp. 133–4). From this it is evident that the purpose of *li*, as Xunzi described it, is very different from the ritual-ization of *li* that later communicated the standards of etiquette and order to the Chinese court, or the *li* that Western observers described as the basis of Chinese despotism (see Chapter 1).

Xunzi's Critique of Mozi

Xunzi's criticism of Mozi at first seems peculiar because the two philosophers are often compared for their similarities. Both philoso-phers showed a particular interest in the means of government that would provide the greatest prosperity. Both believed that the basis of societal disorder was poverty and that the only way to end disorder was through economic growth. Where the two differed was in the way of achieving this growth. Mozi felt that the answer was to be found in a more egalitarian society, one in which hierarchical differences were removed between members of society as well as between the ruler and his subjects. As these differences were effaced, no task was to be seen as more important or worthy of greater emolument than any other. Mozi incorporated this into what he saw as the best means of wealth creation: frugality, and suggested that the ruler's own example of moderating expenditure and of being personally frugal would influence frugality throughout the country, with the effect of increasing state revenues (see *Xunzi*, Vol. 2, Bks 9 and 10, and Vol. 3, pp. 14, 22).

Xunzi argued that no society could generate wealth on the basis of equal rank and like status, particularly when resources and material goods were scarce. He reasoned that scarcity combined with people's awareness that they were no longer bound according to rank would lead to demands for material goods that would overwhelm the ability of the state to respond to all subjects in equal measure. The result would be contention, civil disorder and poverty:

> When power and positions are equally distributed and likes and dislikes are identical, and material goods are inadequate to satisfy all, there is certain to be contention. Such contention is bound to produce civil disorder, and this disorder will result in poverty. (*Xunzi*, Vol. 2, p. 96)[18]

In addition to this, Xunzi believed that upholding frugality and reduced expenditures as ideals were the worst examples a ruler could set for the people. The economic conscience of the country would be driven not by incentives to labour, which Xunzi felt were the key to producing a surplus, but by a belief that scarcity was so widespread that the only solution was a system of strict budgeting and frugality. According to Xunzi, this was precisely the attitude that led to the deprivation in which the people were living because it failed to produce adequate supplies of food and goods to meet their needs (*Xunzi*, Vol. 2, pp. 128–9). Rather than lowering demands, which Xunzi said was inherent in Mozi's system, Xunzi believed that the goal of the state was to expand supplies:

> ... the Ancient Kings ... caused the various classes of people of the world to realize that what they desired and longed for was to be found with them, and this is why incentives worked.... When incentives work ... then goods and commodities will come as easily as water bubbling up from an inexhaustible spring.... How indeed could the world have the misfortune of inadequate supplies? (*Xunzi*, Vol. 2, pp. 129–30)

Xunzi's hierarchical system was a way to respond to man's desires but also a means by which to redirect these desires into a motive force for further production. As Hsiao notes, damaging this would mean that the motive to produce would disappear and the hope for a condition of plenty would be reversed, hastening the trend toward impoverishment (Hsiao, 1979, pp. 187–8). Xunzi reasoned that a hierarchical state structure, rather than Mozi's egalitarian system, would defend an equality that safeguarded the people equally by delivering them from the fight for resources, and by promising them wealth, regardless of social position (*Xunzi*, Vol. 2, p. 117). If wealth were not redistributed, according to Xunzi, if the lower classes were relegated to a state of poverty, then they would not be able to contribute to the state surplus. The state would not only become poorer but the ruler would lose his legitimacy to rule (*Xunzi*, Vol. 2, pp. 121–2).

Yet Xunzi did not believe that relations between the classes would on their own be so harmonious as to ensure that adequate food, goods and wealth got to all parts of the kingdom. Here too, the state must intervene. Xunzi's system would permit the state's regulatory powers to adjust taxes and finances according to the wealth generated. State regulation would also determine profits, how property was to be distributed, how grains and commodities were to be distributed and taxed, how farmers could be used for state projects during the off-season and how many merchants and traders should be permitted to operate (Xunzi believed that too many of either would impoverish the state) (*Xunzi*, Vol. 2, pp. 102, 123, 134–5). State intervention also fulfilled the kingdom's major imperative of welfare, as Xunzi said, 'This may indeed be described as "allowing the people a generous living through the exercise of government".' (*Xunzi*, Vol. 2, p. 123). Not until all people were fed, clothed and cared for, including all common people, orphans, widows, the poor and the disabled, did Xunzi believe that the ruler's authority was secure (*Xunzi*, Vol. 2, pp. 94, 97). To this end, it has been suggested that Xunzi's interpretation of *li* was taken from the chapter on 'great community' *(datong)* of the Zhou dynasty's *Record of Rites (Liji)* (Chin, 1982, p. 105). *Datong* describes a future period in which all men share the wealth of the state equally.

In one respect, Xunzi does not differ from Confucius and Mencius in his view that the best guarantee of order is a political system that is governed by a single ruler. As Xunzi said, 'Where only one is exalted, there is order; where two are exalted, there is anarchy' (*Xunzi*, Vol. 2, p. 209). But Xunzi did not view a wise leader as omnipotent in the way that Confucius in particular did. Xunzi claimed that just as it is impossible even for a very able person to be 'universally skilled', so too is it impossible for an individual 'to hold every office' (*Xunzi*, Vol. 2, p. 121). Among his most important attributes, a leader's greatest gift, according to Xunzi, should be his ability to choose men of outstanding ability to work under him (*Xunzi*, Vol. 2, pp. 71–2). For Xunzi, a meritocratic political system also emanated from the principle of *li*. Just as *li* represents the 'root of strength in the state' and the 'Way by which ... authority is created', it also is the 'focus of merit' (*Xunzi*, Vol. 2, p. 229). Choosing those of merit ultimately helps to sustain the ruler's own authority. One example of the connection between merit and authority is Xunzi's view that, '[when the ruler] selects the man who is most knowledgeable about ... supervision of state business ... there will be adequate quantities of all useful goods' (*Xunzi*, Vol. 2, pp. 110–11). Under the meritocratic system that Xunzi describes, the ruler remains at the apex of political authority, but he does not command total power. Rather he presides over a system which separates powers and responsibilities, leaving him in a reverential, though passive, role: '... if knights and grand officers divide up official positions and responsibilities ... then the Son of Heaven [the ruler] need do no more than assume a gravely reverent attitude in his person.' (*Xunzi*, Vol. 2, p. 158).

Xunzi argued that without a political system in place as he has here described it, the relationship between ruler and subject would be increasingly oppressive and hostile. But by employing his strategy, he believed that the relationship between the two would be 'increasingly pervaded by liberality' (*Xunzi*, Vol. 2, pp. 110–11). In addition to this, Xunzi seemed to maintain that the strong centralization that characterized his state system was transformative in nature when he said, 'When the techniques of power have reached their end, put into practice the arts of justice.' (*Xunzi*, Vol. 2, p. 244).

2.6 XUNZI'S INFLUENCE ON CHINESE HISTORY AND POLITICS

The unification of China as an empire in 221 BC provided justification for Xunzi's philosophy, and, paradoxically, marked the beginning of its subordination to the *Lunyu* and the *Mencius*. A number of reasons could be cited for this but two appear to stand out as most relevant. One relates to the first emperor himself, Qin Shihuangdi, whose methods of ruling, for centuries condemned as severe, were influenced by Xunzi's teachings. Two of Xunzi's students, Han Feizi and Li Si, who were the founders of China's Legalist school of philosophy, acted as advisers to the first emperor. Li Si became Chief Minister of the Qin and supported the emperor's demand to burn ancient texts. Li Si's association with this event and with the loss of Chinese texts from the period, have left his and, though to a much lesser degree, Xunzi's, reputation tarnished until recently. Some scholars suggest that the Qin emperor was not a tyrant, that he was a farsighted ruler and that he destroyed the forces that divided China by establishing the first centralized Chinese state (see Knoblock's commentary in the *Xunzi*, Vol. 1, pp. 36–7, and Bedeski, 1989, p. 49). The second reason that Xunzi fell into disrepute is his premise that human nature is evil and that goodness is only man-made. This led many Chinese philosophers over the centuries, though drawing on Xunzi's realism, to avoid open identification with Xunzi (Cheng, 1991, p. 71).[19] This, and the great emphasis placed on what are considered the unreasonable demands of Xunzi's authority, rather than on his belief in people's welfare toward which this authority was directed (Rosemont, 1970, p. 48), have contributed to the distorted views of Xunzi over the centuries.

Despite his detractors, Xunzi has not been relegated to a place of unimportance in Chinese history – and even less so in Chinese politics. It is noteworthy that the later Han period (AD 23–*c*.100) was at its strongest and most stable after the emperor Guangwudi exalted the methods and teachings of the *Ru* school of Confucianism (Feng, 1990, p. 38), of which Xunzi was the most important figure.[20] Xunzi's extension of the ritualistic and philosophical *li* to a socio-political order has earned him the distinction of ancient China's great Confucian 'pragmatist'.[21] What is perhaps most attractive about the nature of Xunzi's authoritarianism is his view that institutions, while essential to maintaining order, were not sacred and remained open to change. This suggests that he was less inflexible and dogmatic than might have been thought.[22] It may be because of this that Xunzi's philosophy persisted through the centuries.[23] It also may be for this reason that it again reached its most systematic expression in the last dynasty, the Qing (Tillman, 1982, p. 11), when Chinese reformers began to question orthodox Confucian political institutions.

In addition to this, one need only consider Xunzi's principal concept of *li*, now described by scholars as the key behind the Chinese hierarchical political system, the basis of order and of Chinese 'cultural construction', the rationale that drives Chinese thought and discourse and the barrier to societal chaos to see the relevance of the philosopher to modern Chinese politics.[24] The connection between Xunzi's *li* and the purposes that it was later said to serve can also be explained. Frisina (1989) says that *li* formed the dynamic basis of the Chinese philosophical belief, given great weight by the Ming neo-Confucian scholar Wang Yangming, that there was no such thing as innate moral knowledge unless it could be applied to practical action (see pp. 428–9, 442).[25] This later seemed to provide the dynamic for the politics of Sun Yatsen and Deng Xiaoping and was influential on Liang Qichao. Moreover, other elements of Xunzi's philosophy, such as *qun* ('grouping')[26], found expression in Sun's political theories as well as Liang Qichao's. These adaptations of Xunzi's theories are discussed further in Chapters 4, 5 and 6.

Certainly it seems less than coincidental that Deng Xiaoping's political outlook so closely resembled Xunzi's. Deng began from the same premise that Xunzi did, that only a state-centred society that creates wealth is also capable of creating better human beings:

> It is true that the standards of living and education of our people are not high, but discussion of the value of the human being or of humanism isn't going to raise them. Only active efforts to achieve material, ideological and cultural progress can do that. (Deng, 1987, p. 31)[27]

Like Xunzi, Deng's deepest concern was the elimination of poverty and the provision of food for all the people (see Deng, 1987, pp. 55, 174, 176, 178, 182, 184, 188). Deng rejected the Maoist egalitarianism of the 1960s and 1970s (some aspects of which could be compared to Mozi's egalitarianism), and, in the same way as Xunzi, believed in incentives to labour, in the principle of emolument for work done and in uneven economic growth for the greater goal of common prosperity (Deng, 1984, 163–4, and 1987, pp. 45, 55).[28] Single-party rule was to be followed but not rigid principles that would damage the welfare of the majority of the people. Deng was a pragmatist, as was Xunzi. That Deng was so similar to the ancient philosopher may have resulted from his reading of ancient Chinese historical texts (Salisbury, 1992).[29]

Even more noteworthy is Xunzi's elevation by Chinese scholars as the most relevant of ancient Chinese philosophers in the post-1949 years, which could hardly have gone unnoticed by Deng.[30] In their attempts to inherit ancient philosophical ideas suited to Marxist–Leninist doctrine, many post-1949 intellectuals embraced Xunzi's 'realism'. Xunzi was seen as a thoroughgoing and remarkable materialist for his time. By the early 1960s, he was described by scholars in China as 'the greatest materialist in ancient China.' While criticisms were levelled at Chinese writers of the day who attempted to modernize other pre-Qin philosophers, such as Confucius and Laozi, little criticism was directed at those who wished to modernize Xunzi. One scholar, Yang Rongguo, argued that Xunzi was the most progressive thinker of the Chinese feudal period because he believed that *li's* purpose was 'to satisfy the desires of the people and meet their demands.' Yang concluded that Xunzi was a 'liberator' of the oppressed classes. Confucius and Mencius, on the other hand, were criticized as 'conservatives' because of their desire to promote a *li* that maintained the old slave aristocracy (Louie, 1986, pp. 169–73).[31] Yang Rongguo's advocacy of Xunzi became accepted doctrine by the 1970s:

> Yang's interpretation, in fact, became so popular that by the anti-[Confucius] campaign of the early 1970s, it was the interpretation officially adopted as the 'correct' doctrine.... Once this had been acknowledged, it became difficult to criticize [Xunzi] and unnecessary to defend him in arguments for inheritance. (Louie, 1986, pp. 170, 174)[32]

2.7 CONCLUSION

Like Confucius and Mencius, Xunzi believed that the objectives of state authority were the security and the well-being of the people. But in their discussions about how an ethically based system of authoritarian rule would reach these objectives, the *Lunyu* and the *Mencius* are ambiguous and unclear. If a development strategy in Asia is described as Confucian-inspired, only the *Xunzi* among the ancient Confucian texts proposes an authoritarian system of rule that is similar to that strategy as it has been applied in Singapore, Taiwan and possibly in post-Mao China. What has perhaps been most appealing about Xunzi's strategy in modern China is his uncompromisingly linear view about how to legitimate an authoritarian state. Xunzi believed that if a government could put an end to scarcity and enrich its people, all other social, economic and political problems would disappear. For this purpose, Xunzi defended what he saw as the intrinsic properties of regulation and order in the traditional virtue of *li*. Although a highly ritualized virtue of court etiquette and order at the time, Xunzi believed that *li* also could be used outside the court and that it had multiple applications towards the goals of an ordered and wealthy state. Among these applications, six stand out most clearly. Foremost among them was Xunzi's belief that *li* could constrain man's desires once it was explained to the people that the state must be in charge of apportioning food and goods to everyone when resources were scarce. Once this was understood, the regulatory principles of *li* could also be set in motion to maintain order, to strengthen the state, to enrich the state, to redistribute the wealth of the state and to transform the people to a higher standard of ethical and civil behaviour. The attainment of these goals was reflective of what Xunzi called humane government, or *wang dao* (the 'way of kings') (*Xunzi*, Vol. 3, p. 161). The rest of this book will suggest that Xunzi's outlook was central to China's modern reformers when they justified the necessity of a development strategy that was driven by a strong authoritarian leadership.

3 Kang Youwei

3.1 INTRODUCTION

> The teaching of the last two thousand years has been the teaching of [Xunzi] (Tan Sitong, 1897).[1]

> [Kang Youwei reasoned] that given the habits accumulated during several thousand years of autocratic rule and a people who have no knowledge of democracy, to turn over to them the rights and powers of government would inevitably entail difficulties. Moreover, as the authority of the emperor has gained so much force and strength in the past, it can become a most efficacious instrument of reform in the hands of an enlightened ruler. (Liang Qichao, 1908)[2]

This chapter examines Kang Youwei's influence on the changing pattern of political authority in late nineteenth-century China. The chapter is divided into two parts. The first part surveys Kang's contemporaries, their criticisms of Qing authority and their arguments for and against modernizing this authority. It finds that all agreed on the intrinsic problems of old authority but that none produced a clear programme which would either adapt or eliminate this to suit the needs of modernization, as Kang's proposals did. This is not an entirely new perspective on Kang. The majority of Sinologists inside and outside of China agree that his role as a reformer was, and remains, more significant than that of other Chinese intellectuals from the period.[3]

The chapter contributes to studies on Kang by demonstrating the similarities between his reforms and the rationale that Xunzi put forward over 2000 years earlier. This is an unconventional view of Kang because as a reformer he is usually described as someone who attempted to overturn the autocratic practices that many nineteenth-century Chinese scholar–officials associated with Xunzi. But scrutiny of Kang's writings reveals striking parallels with the ideas of his ancient predecessor. In some cases Kang speaks directly of Xunzi's influences; in others, he supports ideas which reflect Xunzi's thinking. While the chapter concedes that there is to date no conclusive evidence to suggest Kang's full support for a modernized political system based on Xunzi's theories, it emphasizes that what may be more important is the way in which Kang's reform proposals used old patterns of authority to serve new ends.

3.2   THE CHALLENGE TO PATRIARCHAL AUTHORITY

Nineteenth century China was marked by a continual decline of imperial authority. This began at the end of the Opium War in 1842, when the Qing court agreed to the 'Treaty of Nanjing', the first of several treaties that led to the surrender of Hong Kong to the British, Britain's domination of four major Chinese ports and its virtual control of China's imports and exports. Internal matters also contributed to national disintegration and instability. China's population had trebled between 1700 and 1850, greatly outstripping the amount of land under cultivation (Gasster, 1969, pp. 4–5). Poverty, hunger and desperation, combined with an awareness in some quarters of the corruption and profligacy of the Qing monarchy, fuelled national discontent. Uprisings were frequent and further proof of the loss of central control. The Qing army was not able to put down the Taiping Rebellion (1850–64) without the assistance of regional armies, mercenary forces and foreign troops. This, the Muslim rebellions in the southwest (1856–73) and northwest (1862–75), the Nian Rebellion (1852–68) north of the Yellow River and the 'Small Sword Society Uprising' (1853–5)[4] in Shanghai, spanned a quarter century of regional conflict over which the Qing government was often powerless. When Qing troops were able to suppress conflicts, it usually served only to hasten the rise of semi-autonomous regional leaders. The *coup de grâce* was delivered in 1895, when Japan, heretofore considered by the Chinese to be a nation under the shadow of China's superiority, was the victor in the Sino–Japanese War of 1894–5. Insult was added to injury with the 'Shimonoseki Treaty' that ended the war on unfair terms for China in 1895. It was against this background that Confucian scholar–officials were forced to consider the root of China's weakness, and to determine ways to revive its strength.

Some scholar–officials acknowledged that loss of income and of territory, a burgeoning population, the extravagances of the Qing monarchy and regional uprisings were contributing factors to China's disintegration. But the deeper problem, it was agreed by many, had its origins in a traditional pattern of authority that persisted into the modern era. This was known as the *sangang* ('three bonds'), a neo-Confucian concept that was derived from *li*, and which had circumscribed patriarchal authority according to the following designations: 'the ruler guides the subject', 'the father guides the son' and 'the husband guides the wife'. The three major groups that are associated with nineteenth-century Chinese modernization, the Self-strengtheners (or Westernizers), the Conservatives (or Traditionalists) and the Reformers, were critical of the *sangang*, and made recommendations for its elimination or modification. The Self-strengtheners, which included Yan Fu[5] and Li Hongzhang[6], believed that the *sangang* no longer suited the demands of the modern world, that it had caused leaders to become obscurantist, that it had provoked hostility and inequality among the different sectors of society, and that it had prevented those of talent rising to positions of responsibility. Its elimination, they argued, would ensure freedom and democracy (Yan Fu, 1895c, pp. 49–51).[7]

The Reformers agreed with this view, though not consistently and not in all cases. The observance of the *sangang*, according to the most radical reformer, Tan Sitong, was to be blamed directly on Xunzi's teachings, which Tan said had distorted the teachings of Confucius. The reason for this, said Tan, was Xunzi's emphasis on *li*. As Tan saw it, *li* had created a deep-seated patriarchal hold over Chinese society, one that was inhumane, oppressive and intimidating, and which had led to division, resentment, disunity, inequality and a lack of democracy.[8] The Conservatives, by contrast, claimed that a *sangang* that was adapted to modern circumstances was the key to Chinese strength both in the way that it maintained a central control and authority familiar to the Chinese people and in its deflection of democracy, which the Conservatives believed all Reformers to be promoting. How, the Conservatives asked, could China avoid disorder and collapse when the first cardinal virtue, 'the ruler guides the subject', a decree that had been followed for centuries, was suddenly overturned in favour of a foreign idea such as 'people's rights' *(minquan)* (Zhang Zhidong, 1898, pp. 13, 24).[9]

3.3 DETOUR TOWARD CONFUSED AUTHORITY

It cannot be said that the Self-strengtheners or the Reformers suggested reasonable alternatives to the *sangang*, or that the Conservatives put forward a reasonable argument for its renovation. The Self-strengtheners vacillated between the desire to remove the

Qing monarchy, which they felt would also eradicate the *sangang*, and the view that this would lead to disastrous consequences because the Chinese people had grown so accustomed to the *sangang's* authoritarian pattern (Yan Fu, 1895a, pp. 79–80). It is therefore questionable whether the Self-strengtheners truly wished to eliminate, or even to modify, the *sangang* and the pattern of patriarchal authority that it served. This is also evident in their plans for modernization, which did not include an enlarged political role for the people but only the possible economic contributions they could make toward the strengthening of the state. In some cases, the Self-strengtheners believed that the growth of national power would simply require the adaptation of Western technology – at one point they said that China's weakness could be overcome solely through the manufacture of ships and guns.[10] In other cases, they considered the first step toward the creation of wealth to be the raising of tax revenue, at a time when the majority of people were so impoverished that it was impossible for them to take on any added tax burden.[11]

Tan Sitong's arguments are no more convincing than those of the Self-strengtheners. For him, the *sangang* and democracy were polar opposites. Once democratic practices were instituted in China, the class barriers that were an intrinsic part of the *sangang* would be removed, and equality and selflessness would flourish, according to Tan (see Chan, 1984, pp. 72–4, 137, 142–3, 150–2, 183). But one can hardly accept that 'selflessness' is a typical goal of democracy. Tan's inclusion of it seems to be derived more from the *sangang* itself, and from Tan's traditional education generally, than from his knowledge of Western political theory, which has been described at best as 'spotty' and 'limited' (see Chang, 1987, p. 93). Tan did speak of economic reforms in the manner that reformers like Kang Youwei did (for example, the tapping of resources, the development of industry and the redistribution of wealth), but he did so in a superficial way with little sense of an overall political plan that would drive these reforms. He claimed, for example, that a distribution of wealth and a mutual recognition and assistance between erstwhile classes would be the natural result once China had 'regained the rights' that had been displaced by the *sangang* (Chan, 1984, pp. 120–31, and Fairbank and Liu, 1980, p. 300). Whether or not Tan believed that some form of democratic rights pre-dated the *sangang*, his suggestion here that they did contradicts what is usually accepted as historically accurate about China.

The Conservatives' reasons for preserving the *sangang* are also unpersuasive. Its protection was justified, they argued, because it

'... came from Heaven and therefore represented a universal law that could not be changed by the people.' Zhang Zhidong said that the *sangang* was '... the unchallengeable substance upon which China had relied to sustain itself for thousands of years....' To overturn it, would be to betray the country (Zhang Zhidong, 1898, pp. 13–14, 24). This outlook is also evident in the English translation of Zhang's 1898 work, which is titled *China's Only Hope*. In this, the *sangang*, the hierarchical class system and strong centralization are defended, but with no concrete reasons for the inapplicability of alternatives (see Woodbridge, 1900). The Conservatives did indeed want minor changes but, like the Self-strengtheners, these involved the importation of foreign technology without corresponding institutional reforms. In his desire to launch an iron and steel works in Guangdong, for example, Zhang Zhidong sent a message to Germany simply stating, 'Please send one complete smelting plant.' He had no idea of how such a plant worked and no definite plans for obtaining iron ore and coking coal (Ayers, 1971, p. 100). Even though the Conservatives altered their view in a memorial to the emperor in 1901, when they said that 'good government would require the reform of native institutions' (Duara, 1988, p. 58), they seemed to remain, as one critic earlier argued, of a 'traditionalist orientation', which '... militated against any broadly conceived or sustained effort at modernization' (Gasster, 1969, p. 5). This orientation need not have been wrong or misguided (it may have proved its worth during the disorganization that followed the 1911 Revolution). But in addition to maintaining the status quo, such an attitude also reflected complacency, a belief that modernization would take care of itself even if the thinking behind it remained completely unaltered. This view was voiced by one Conservative critic after the 1911 Revolution when he said, '... as long as the emperor had shown benevolence toward the people and ruled the country in a humanitarian and just way, China would have inevitably strengthened its position [without a revolution]' (Li, 1911, p. 2). Of course, this response may have also represented a genuine fear that change would destroy the Conservatives' vested interests, which included considerable landholdings and several provincial governorships (Li Huaxin, 1988, p. 238).

It would be wrong to suggest that none of these figures, or the groups they represented, contributed anything to an understanding of Chinese political authority before and after the 1898 reforms.[12] They may have proved, as Wakeman suggests, that the *sangang* was so fundamental to the nature of Chinese authority that '... political methods alone were insufficient to wreak basic changes', and that any political reform would have to first depend on a 'cultural revolution' to overturn the Confucian norms which had so deeply permeated Chinese society (Wakeman, 1975, p. 205). This argument implies that a modified *sangang*, or its removal, was central to determining a new form of Chinese political authority. But an examination of events during the period suggests that the transformation of political authority was to be determined according to the success of economic and political reforms, regardless of patriarchal constraints from the past. Those who played a central role in the reform process of 1898, the Emperor Guangxu and Kang Youwei, were most deeply concerned with policies that would reform education, the economy and politics for the express purpose of restoring order and making China richer. In addition to this, not only were the Self-strengtheners' and the Conservatives' proposals for modernization piecemeal, when compared to those of Kang Youwei, but they were without corresponding institutional reforms (see Hook, 1991, p. 225). Furthermore, none of their proposals was ever accepted by the Qing court. In most cases they were only addressed to provincial officials, who did not act on intellectuals' advice without approval from Beijing. It was suggested earlier in this chapter that the Conservatives may have resisted change because this would remove the prerogatives to which they had grown accustomed, but the Self-strengtheners also were not above such considerations. Li Hongzhang accepted, for example, the practice of merchants buying official positions, as well as that of officials presiding over enterprises whose workings they did not understand (Spector, 1964, pp. 256–7). This unwillingness to separate political authority from the independent activities of enterprises was roundly condemned by Kang Youwei as a major reason for the poor performance and frequent bankruptcies in Chinese industries. These, along with the other factors noted, prevented the Conservatives and the Self-strengtheners (and Reformers like Tan Sitong) from enunciating proposals that were far-reaching in scope.[13] This distinction rested with Kang Youwei.

3.4   AUTHORITY AND WELFARE IN KANG YOUWEI'S WRITINGS

Sinologists who speak of Kang Youwei's influential role on the late Qing do not normally associate his reforms with Xunzi's philosophy.

Instead, it is generally acknowledged that Kang's most important influence was Confucius.[14] Kang accepted the teachings of Confucius because, as he said, Confucius was a reformer. He added that the true teachings of Confucius had been distorted partly by Xunzi (Hsiao, 1975, p. 79) and partly by the customary values built on *li*, which justified the authority of the patriarchal family and the patrimonial state (Wakeman, 1975, p. 204). As Kang seemed to see it, these factors laid the foundation for a feudal monarchical system that had become so powerful that Confucius's original intentions of reforming institutions, abolishing feudalism and establishing an electoral and legal system were lost (see Kang, 1922, Vols 9 and 13, and Kang, 1988, p. 2). But despite these criticisms, particularly as they were directed at Xunzi, Kang's views draw remarkably near to Xunzi's.

Kang's Revival of Xunzi's Theories

It should be noted that as a Confucian scholar–official who was associated with a system of imperial rule that originated with Confucius, it would be highly unorthodox for Kang to criticize Confucius. What Kang tended to do instead was refer to the compatibility of other Zhou philosophies with his own interpretation of the 'correct' teachings of Confucius that he believed should be inherited by China's reformers. Principal among these was Kang's advocacy of Xunzi's belief that man is inherently evil and that man's desires must be curbed by the state to prevent disorder (Hsiao, 1975, pp. 57–8). Like Xunzi, Kang argued that man's 'goodness' was acquired in society, that it was the product of human effort, that it depended on the restraining influence of *li*[15] and on man's ability to form political communities. Against this, Kang spoke of the chaos that would result if the Qing monarchy accepted either Mencius's belief that man is inherently good, and therefore should be more independent of state regulation, or Mozi's belief in a state-sanctioned system of egalitarianism and frugality. Kang argued that people would not become equal simply because this was ordained by the state. Nor did he believe that frugality was a wise response to centuries of poverty and backwardness (Hsiao, 1975, pp. 57–8, 92, 148–9). Just as he reasoned that man would acquire good morals when he was guided by the state, he also believed that all people would become equal in a state that was guided by an elite hierarchy that conceived methods to generate wealth and share wealth among all the people. Wealth creation and distribution would draw China away from what Kang termed the 'age

of disorder' as people's welfare improved. Wealth was not to be seen
as extravagance but as the 'realization of justice and reason to the
highest point'. Kang claimed that once all people were enriched, once
China had attained its 'great community' *(da tong)*,[16] all people would
also become empowered because authoritarian rule would be transferred to 'people's rule' (Hsiao, 1975, pp. 30, 160–1, 427).

Kang's Support for Constitutional Monarchy (1898–1911)

At the end of the nineteenth century, Kang maintained that these
philosophical precedents must be integrated with a constitutional
monarchy. Between 1898 and 1911 he supported a political system
that gave considerable powers to the monarch during what he hoped
would be a transitional period of modernization. Over time, and if
reforms led to economic and political improvements, the monarch's
powers would be dismantled and transferred to the sovereignty of the
people *(minquan)* under a system of constitutional republicanism,
what Kang called 'full democracy'. To leap toward popular sovereignty, Kang argued, was unreasonable because the majority of
Chinese people were unprepared to manage their own affairs in the
absence of strong authority (Hsiao, 1975, pp. 194, 217, 286, and Xiao,
1992, p. 313). Nonetheless, the road toward fuller political participation could be prepared through a system of local self-government.
Kang felt that participation in local political affairs provided a train-
ing ground for the people to govern themselves as well as the
appropriate environment for them to become responsible citizens.[17]
Voters in each village were to send representatives to a district
'people's assembly' each year, which, with the district administrators
as presiding officers, was to operate according to the principle of
majority rule. This deliberative body would lay down policies; the
administrator would then carry them out (Hsiao, 1975, p. 291). Kang
reasoned that the collective successes of local self-government had
the potential to put greater pressure on the central government's
accountability and efficiency.

   At the central level, Kang's ideal political system would combine, as
he said in his 'Fifth Memorial to the Emperor' (January 1898), the
authoritarianism of Russia's Peter the Great with the governmental
proficiency of Japan's Meiji restoration: '[China should] adopt the
mental attitude of Russia's Peter the Great as the dictate of the mind
and ... take the governmental system of Japan's Meiji as the arche-
type of proficient government' (Hsiao, 1965, p. 20). In fact, each of

the reform proposals Kang sent to the Qing court was accompanied by his two essays, *A Study of the Political Reforms of Meiji Japan*, and *An Account of the Reforms of Peter of Russia* (see Fairbank and Liu, 1980, p. 323). Kang later explained, in his 'Seventh Memorial to the Emperor' (February 1898), why especially Russia provided the political system which China should follow:

> Of all the countries on earth, none is as prosperous and contented as the United States of America, but her republican political system is different from China's autocratic system; none is as powerful and wealthy as England or Germany, but the governments of these, being mixed monarchies ... differ also from that of China. Only in Russia where the monarchical authority is supreme, the political system resembles that of China.... Therefore ... in implementing reform, it would be best for the emperor to adopt the ways of Peter. (Hsiao, 1965, pp. 20–1)

Kang certainly admired statesmen in other Western countries who were able to unify their states into one nation. He praised Cavour for his role in the unification of Italy and Bismarck for his similar role in Germany. The unification of Germany, according to Kang, was brought about not only because of the rapid development of industry and commerce, but because of the strong monarchical authority that was guiding it (Hsiao, 1975, p. 518). Yet he admitted that strong authority on its own would not push China forward without corresponding administrative reforms. He believed that Chinese emperors should accept a more efficient recruitment of talent from below and a leaner bureaucracy if this meant that blueprints for institutional reform could be carried out more quickly (Fairbank, and Liu, 1980, p. 323). A crucial part of this was an assurance from the emperor that communication channels between upper and lower officials would be improved (Zhang Jiqian, 1992, interview). Much like Xunzi, Kang suggested that powers and responsibilities be divided among talented officials, and that they be paid according to their contributions to the state rather than on the basis of their seniority (Hsiao, 1975, pp. 264–6, 269). Kang was familiar with Montesquieu's theory of the 'three powers', but he did not believe that China should immediately adopt a legislature, judiciary or a parliament along Western lines. Instead, he argued that gradual steps be taken toward their full implementation in the future. He urged that this begin with a 'planning bureau' *(zhidu ju)* that was not a legislature or a parliament in the true sense of the word but a government body that would bypass the existing administrative structure for the sake of reforms, and which would initiate the transition from the traditional administrative structure to the modern cabinet (Hsiao, 1975, pp. 266–7).

Kang's Support for a Titular Monarchical Republic (1911–27)

After the 1911 Revolution, Kang warned revolutionary leaders about the dangers of a republican polity because it had never been tested in China. He was in no doubt that republicanism had proved its worth in the United States, but he set this against its disastrous failures in Latin American countries. He concluded that America's youthfulness, its small population and its deep-rooted democratic tradition carried from Britain provided it with ideal circumstances to build its politics on a republican system, but that at this stage in China's history no lessons were to be learned from the American example (Hsiao, 1975, p. 246). His solution was a republic under the guidance of a titular monarch:

> ... a 'presidential republic' ... as exemplified by France or the United States differed from a 'monarchical republic' ... as exemplified by England only in form; they both were 'replacements of absolute monarchy'. For a country like China, which was accustomed to autocratic rule and lacked democratic experience, a 'monarchical republic' offered advantages not found in the 'presidential republic'. In the former, a constitutional (or titular) monarch, standing above political rivalries and competitions, would serve as a working symbol of national unity and stability. (Hsiao, 1975, p. 247)

Unlike Kang's support for constitutional monarchy up until 1911, where the monarch was to have actual, though constitutionally restricted authority, republicanism under a titular monarch meant that the monarch would be a mere figurehead with no real power except in the image of authority and respect that he commanded (Hsiao, 1975, p. 248). To the end of his life (1927) Kang supported this system. He was not against republicanism in principle, but he believed that it must be arrived at gradually through a step-by-step process. Nowhere did this seem more true than in the China of 1911. The revolutionaries had not only toppled the Qing rulers but had ended 2000 years of dynastic rule. In a political environment where the power base was not only new but vulnerable to the regional power bases of competing warlords, Kang questioned how it could be possible to transfer sovereignty to the people without catastrophic repercussions (Chi, 1992, p. 17). What kind of liberty and equality would there be, he asked, when people's rule became mob rule as various groups placed demands on the government it could not meet. He concluded that to '… propagandize democracy … [and] equality … such that an entire country becomes a society of Rousseaus, Voltaires and Montesquieus was nothing but empty words, a utopian dream that helped nothing (quoted in Hou, 1990, p. 22). Kang was also against the revolutionaries' support for what he termed Lenin's doctrine of 'equality of property' *(shehui jun chan yi)* as he made clear in his essay on the 1917 Revolution. Like popular sovereignty, Kang believed that the nationalization of land was a lofty ideal of the 'great community' *(datong)* that could not be realized in his time (Hsiao, 1965, p. 38).

Kang's Economic Reforms

In keeping with Xunzi's belief that man's desires are boundless, and that it was contingent upon government to satisfy these desires through the creation of wealth and the production of material goods, Kang argued that only large-scale industrialization was capable of meeting these needs in modern China. This was confirmed for him by his observations of economic and technological developments in the West (Hsiao, 1975, pp. 307–10). Kang proposed that the success of this strategy would depend on balanced growth in all sectors of the economy. This was a major innovation (and was adopted by the Qing court) because it went against the traditional attitude in China that emphasized agriculture and restricted commerce to one that protected and rewarded industry and commerce. It was to include corresponding legal guarantees that gave greater incentives to industrialists and merchants (Zhu, 1995, p. 122). Agriculture was not to be seen merely as a means of subsistence but as an enterprise in itself, whose production was determined largely by the requirements of the customer rather than the wants of the producer. Along with industry and mining, agriculture was to furnish goods and commodities to the market for a profit, a process that Kang said was to '… enhance the power of the state and promote the welfare of the people.' This outcome was fundamental and was mutually inclusive, as Kang said, again in a way that reflects Xunzi's reasoning, 'When the people are destitute ... there is no means whereby the country can prosper' (see Hsiao, 1975, pp. 304–7).

The role of the state, according to Kang, was to ensure that 'government and business work in smooth cooperation'. Government would be expected to invest in enterprises whose size and financial power made them competitive in foreign markets. These, similar to what was later known as the Japanese *zaibatsu* (the Chinese term is *da gongsi*), were to develop alongside smaller private businesses that were also to be encouraged, advised and protected by the government. A ministry of commerce would be instituted in the capital and was to be in overall charge of the nation's commercial affairs. Chambers of commerce would be set up in all parts of the country, whose primary role was to 'lend strength to entrepreneurs'. Taxes and imposts on businesses would be lightened, commercial laws enacted and insurance made available to businessmen. A nationwide banking system and a suitable currency would hasten capital formation if private banks deposited their silver with the Board of Revenue or provincial treasuries, which would then become the reserve for the paper currency notes to be issued by the Board. In addition to this, Kang saw in the rise of land value both a contributing factor and a consequence of general economic growth. As successful agricultural, industrial and commercial enterprises increased the value of the land, other local businesses could be established and the two could in turn contribute to each other's growth. Although Kang had some misgivings about the influx of foreign capital into China at the time, he also believed that its importation was to be valued if it was invested in undertakings that contributed to the nation's economic growth (see Hsiao, 1975, pp. 311–17).

Hsiao concludes that although Kang supported a market economy that was prompted by government initiatives, he did not believe that government could assist economic dynamism in the long-term (Hsiao, 1975, p. 318). However, more recent research suggests that Kang opposed only certain elements of state-run industry without being against state intervention entirely. Most notably, he believed that once an industry was established, there was no need for court officials who did not have specialized knowledge to supervise the industry's activities. By doing so in the past, officials had prevented shareholders from investing, because the shareholders were wary both of the whims of the Qing court and the, at times, tyrannical behaviour of the officials who were running the enterprises. The lack of separation between the court and the enterprise, Kang argued, was the main reason China's industry and commerce had developed so slowly, and in many cases had failed (Fu, 1984, p. 63).

3.5 THE 'HUNDRED DAYS OF REFORM'

Kang's changing attitude toward political and economic reforms between 1898 and the late 1920s is usually overshadowed by the emphasis studies place on his failure to push through reforms during the 'Hundred Days of Reform' (*Bai Ri Weixin*) in 1898. The Hundred Days marked a period between June and September of that year in which the Emperor Guangxu, on the advice of Kang, issued edicts for reforms that were vast in scope. They included reforms in education, agriculture, manufacturing, trade, administration, the military and the coordination of economic activities, such as the production of goods for export. All of this ended suddenly on 21 September 1898. The Empress Dowager, though retired, continued to hold the real power in China and she staged a successful *coup d'état* after which she stripped Guangxu of his authority and imprisoned him, where he remained until his death in 1908 (see Fairbank and Liu, 1980, p. 327). This chapter will not narrate the specific nature of the policies and events that led to the demise of the 1898 reforms. That has already been done extensively (see especially Cameron, 1931, and Kwong, 1984). What may be more interesting is what Kang himself learned from the failed reforms and how this led him to alter his reform programme.

It is important to make it clear that Kang believed with hindsight that the Reform Movement of 1898 was a mistake because it attempted to accomplish too much too quickly at a time when national conditions were not suited to such changes (Tan, 1980, p. 288). Various reasons have been stated for China's unpreparedness, conservative reaction and fear of the disintegration of Chinese ethics being the most common among them.[18] But these tend to generalize the failings of a reform programme that may have worked if it had been implemented gradually. Fairbank and Liu claim that the Hundred Days was running smoothly while it stayed within the boundaries of educational, military and economic reforms. But once Guangxu showed a readiness to discuss political reforms (which he hesitated to do initially), he was seen as increasingly radical, and as someone whose views ran counter to the ideological stand of almost the whole of officialdom (Fairbank and Liu, 1980, p. 327). What was most important to the Qing court, as well as to Kang in the years following 1898, was the creation of a strong and efficient government rather than one that was democratic. This was also Guangxu's stand in the years preceding 1898, and is evident in an edict he issued shortly after the Shimonoseki Treaty was signed with Japan in 1895. In this, Guangxu said, in words that echoed his ancient Confucian predecessors and foreshadowed the views of Sun Yatsen (see Chapter 5), that strength would only be returned to China if the government could provide beneficial effects for both the national economy and the people's livelihood (*minsheng*) (see Lü, 1995, p. 51). Here too, Guangxu agreed with what would become a political mainstay of his successors, that only strong central authority could ensure these benefits (see Tan, 1980, p. 288, and Gasster, 1968, p. 80). One critic even suggests that the 1898 reforms did not work because so much of Qing central authority had been lost to regional Manchu tribesmen (Mu, 1982, p. 141).

Kang's turn toward a reform programme that was guided by strong authority strengthened the argument among Chinese Conservative reformers that he never sincerely believed that Confucius was a reformer and a democrat and that he used this argument merely to ward off his opponents (Ye, 1898, p. 1). This could be true, and could lend support to the argument that Kang was a follower of Xunzi rather than of Confucius. But it is also important to note how Kang's thinking changed over time. He did indeed believe between 1888 and 1898 that administrative reforms could act as a prelude to a democratic system that transformed itself from aristocratic politics to constitutional government. But the failure of the 1898 reforms, and especially the further disintegration that followed the 1911 Revolution, proved to him that restoration on such a large scale was not possible. From 1911 onward, Kang believed that only a powerful central government was capable of dealing with China's problems; that every possible measure should be used to maintain China's political unity; and that the autonomous polity of warlords must be curbed in order to prevent further disintegration at the political centre (see Xiao, 1992, pp. 321, 336–40). It is significant that Kang's solution of a titular monarchical republic as the best assurance that these goals could be met was not reached in China, but during 16 years of exile (after 1898) in which he studied the political, economic and social conditions of the 31 countries he visited (Chi, 1992, p. 14).

3.6 CONCLUSION

Liang Qichao said in 1921 that Kang Youwei was the first Chinese thinker to provide China with a system of modern authority that would gradually transform itself to democracy (Hsiao, 1975, p. 207). Kang's solutions for this transformation were highly practical in outlook. They concerned themselves little with adapting the patriarchal *sangang* to the modern era, which represented a major hurdle to change for the majority of Qing intellectuals. Instead Kang concentrated on a reform programme that adapted what he saw as the best of the past in order to serve the needs of modernization. Kang claimed that his ideas were influenced by Confucius and that Confucius was a reformer and a democrat. Yet so much of Kang's thinking, as well as the reasons behind the political and economic reforms he introduced, draw on the patterns that Xunzi established. A strong state, a rich country guided by a professional elite whose main goals were the protection and welfare of the people, and an evolutionary progression toward greater equality and justice are all goals of Kang's system, as they were of Xunzi's. Kang has been described as a bearer of practical statesmanship (Chang, 1971, p. 67), a distinction also given to Xunzi by specialists on ancient China, as was noted in Chapter 2.

The desire for practical solutions was no doubt influenced by the environments in which both men lived. Not since the late Warring States period, when Xunzi lived (298–38 BC), had China become so badly divided and so dangerously exposed to collapse as it had during the late Qing and early republican periods (Bedeski, 1989, pp. 47–8). The political choices Kang made demanded as their primary goal the restoration of order. That Xunzi made similar choices in similar circumstances 2000 years earlier may have confirmed for Kang the necessity of such choices. The argument that Kang's politics was influenced by Xunzi is given added weight by the fact that Kang devoted a separate essay to *li* (entitled *Liyun Zhu*) because he believed the concept still had the potential to sustain authority, create wealth and transform society in modern China. In the *Liyun Zhu*, Kang wrote that *li* was indispensable to society, and that its evolution must precede the evolution of *ren* if China were to reach the final advent of the 'great community' *(datong)* (Chang, 1987, p. 53). Kang's comparison of *li* to *ren* is also notable for what it says about the abiding importance of the ancient Confucian virtues to Chinese modernizers. In choosing indigenous sources to meet the goal of welfare in the modern era, and in choosing *li* over *ren*, Kang was obviously attuned to the rationale that Xunzi had put forward. This also seemed to be true of other Qing scholar–officials, for by July 1907 an office for the study of *li* had been created in Beijing 'as one of the preparatory measures taken for the establishment of constitutional government' (Bastid, 1987, p. 181). But Kang was under no illusion that the route towards constitutional democracy would not require basic changes to China's ancient political system. He felt that political authoritarianism should neither be maintained in its patriarchal form nor that it should be overturned. He stressed that it could be transitional, and that it could be transferred to the people in the form of democracy once the state had become wealthy. The people could prepare themselves for constitutional government by participating in local political affairs. Kang also argued that strong authority on its own without corresponding administrative reforms would not achieve the long-term wealth and democracy that China sought. In addition to this, he believed that authoritarian principles could also be transferred to large-scale industrialization that was promoted and protected by the state. Finally, Kang said that the failure of the Hundred Days of Reform proved the value of incremental reforms that were governed by successful economic growth. Kang's conclusions set the tone for all major reformers in China who succeeded him.

4 Liang Qichao

4.1 INTRODUCTION

> Seeking classical models ... reformers like Liang [Qichao] recalled
> that the ancient Chinese philosopher [Xunzi] had distinguished
> man from other creatures by virtue of his ability to create voluntary
> communities. If all social units were thus a consequence of human
> effort to band together, then no single unit was more 'natural' (ie.,
> legitimate) than any other. (Wakeman, 1975, p. 201)

Kang Youwei confirmed the necessity of maintaining Xunzi's philosophy if China were to implement a modern authoritarian strategy.
Liang Qichao seemed to support this view. But beyond this, Liang
argued that authoritarian rule would not function successfully in
China until the people were taught why an emphasis on collective
interests was a better guarantee of their own welfare than an emphasis
on individual interests. Liang also justified this argument according to
Xunzi's principles. This chapter examines these principles and shows
how they informed and confirmed Liang's political conviction that
Chinese development required Chinese solutions. Liang did not reach
this position without seeking Western alternatives. No other mainland
Chinese scholar this century has given more serious attention to
Western political theory or written more prolifically about it than has
Liang. But his readings of figures like Mill, Rousseau, Montesquieu
and Bentham convinced him that Western liberal democracy would
sow dissension and disorder in China, and that it would hamper
Chinese rulers' abilities to push development forward.

4.2 TWO PERSPECTIVES ON LIANG QICHAO

It was not until the 1970s that the West came to an understanding of
Liang Qichao's influences on Chinese political theory. At that time,
two key works were written about Liang. Philip Huang's *Liang Ch'i-
ch'ao and Modern Chinese Liberalism* (1972) argues that Liang had a
syncretic political orientation, one that sought a new epistemology
and ethics that combined classical political liberalism and
Confucianism and which led to Liang's support for *minquan* ('political

rights').[1] According to Huang, Liang believed in his early years that
minquan's absence was the cause of China's weakness and that its
establishment through a liberal democratic polity, which adopted a
constitution, a parliament and a system of representative constituencies, would contribute to China's strength (see Huang, 1972,
pp. 28–31, 59, and Chap. 7). Huang concludes that the main reason
Liang supported *minquan* lay not in protecting 'people's sovereignty',
but in shoring up support for a 'national sovereignty' whose main goal
was Chinese development (Huang, 1972, pp. 65, 70, 73). However,
Huang's argument that Liang reached these conclusions through a
syncretic combination of Western and Chinese ideas, and that, in
Liang's pre-1903 years, John Stuart Mill's writings influenced this
thinking (Huang, 1972, pp. 72, 80), may neglect Liang's emphasis on
political elements from Xunzi's philosophy that he saw to be best
suited to defining and legitimating a new Chinese state.

Hao Chang's *Liang Ch'i-ch'ao and Intellectual Transition in China,
1890–1907* (1971), argues that Liang's political thought was driven by
Xunzi's concept of *qun* ('grouping') and by *gong* ('public-mindedness')[2], and that these justified Liang's support for statism rather than
a syncretic union of liberalism and Confucianism (see Chang, 1971,
Chaps 4 and 8). Chang does not offer unqualified support for the view
that Liang was a modern-day Xunist. He draws our attention to the
fact that Liang was critical of Xunzi and of the School of Han
Learning that Xunzi influenced, which continued to hold sway over
Chinese scholars in the late Qing. Chang adds, however, that given
the state China was in at the time, it was natural that scholars like
Liang would see Xunzi '... as the fountainhead of [the] deplored late
development of Confucianism', that Xunzi's emphasis on the central-
ity of *li* and the consequent authoritarianism of Confucianism was to
blame for this and that practical statesmanship therefore required the
discrediting of Xunzi. Nonetheless, according to Chang, almost all of
Liang's writings rely particularly on *qun* as the basis of a new Chinese
practical statesmanship (Chang, 1971, pp. 75–6, 95). Liang's questions
about political integration, political participation and legitimation,
and the scope of the political community all return to the primary
question of 'how to group or integrate the Chinese people into a
cohesive and well-knit political community' (Chang, 1971, pp. 75–6,
95–6).[3] Chang argues that Liang not only rejected English liberal
thought of the late nineteenth century but also the intellectual trends
of Nietzschean individualism and Marxian socialism. Liang believed
that all three represented a ridiculous nineteenth-century outlook

that either emphasized populism or an ideology that gave no consideration to the future.[4] As he maintained, '[o]nly for the future does the present take on meaning and value.' And only by emphasizing *qun* and *gong*, Liang added, could China have any future (Chang, 1971, pp. 95–100, 105–6, 177). The remainder of this chapter will show that Chang's perspective on Liang is more true to Liang's long-term development goals than is Huang's. Before examining the way in which Liang transformed *qun* and *gong* into a modern political ideology, the next section investigates his reading and eventual rejection of Western liberal theory.

4.3 LIANG'S INTELLECTUAL JOURNEY TO THE WEST

The Problem with a 'General Will'

It also has been claimed that from 1894 to 1902 Liang's political thought was influenced to a great degree by Rousseau's *Social Contract*, and that it was a document which Liang felt was suited to the political needs of China at the time (Hou, 1990, pp. 24–6). But Liang eventually dismissed Rousseau's belief that the 'general will' made self-rule a goal to be sought. Liang asked, 'Is there really such a thing as a general will?; does the general will reflect what the majority of the people want?; is it true to say that if a majority of people hold the same view, it is a good thing and that it is a view worth enforcing?' These were among the arguments that Liang used in his debates with Sun Yatsen's revolutionary party while the two men were living in Japan. The revolutionaries believed that 'racial revolution', the deposing of the non-Han monarchy in China, was a necessary prelude to political revolution. Liang argued that not all people wanted to overthrow the Manchu emperor, and that this was proof of the general will's inapplicability in China. He added that even if there were a consensus that the emperor should be ousted, there was no guarantee that this would lead to an improvement in China's situation. Liang cites the French Revolution as evidence of this, saying that although regicide was supported by large numbers of French people, its eventual realization merely led to one despot being replaced by another (Liang, 1906d, pp. 202–6).

Liang believed that even in times of peace if a government endorsed the idea of a general will when people did not understand its basic nature, anarchy and mob rule would be the outcome. This too could be proved, according to Liang, by considering the problems that followed the French Revolution. In a joint article written with Kang Youwei, Liang argues that the French Revolution failed to deliver the French people from oppression because Lafayette was too willing to meet the people's demands for civil rights *(minquan)*. Liang goes on to say that the French creation of a 'less-than-perfect' parliament that, unlike Britain's parliament, relied only on a lower house, led not to people's sovereignty but to 'people's autocracy' *(minquan zhuanzheng)*, which prevented the government from carrying out its duties effectively. What was needed in France in the post-Revolution years, according to Liang, were not civil rights but 'social rules' *(li)* that would guide the largely uneducated people, that would lighten their taxes and that would alleviate poverty. Why, Liang asked, did people in France demand freedom and equality when the main problems were poverty and hunger? To this he adds, in words reflective of Xunzi, that without strongly enforced social rules, poorly educated men's desires would turn ferocious and would destroy the nation. Liang concludes that the main lesson of the French Revolution is that freedom and equality would only come peacefully to China once it had met its most important goal of improving its material civilization (Kang and Liang, 1906, pp. 295–7, 318–22, 327–30). If the Chinese people were well educated and prepared for such political changes at the time, on the other hand, Liang was in no doubt that Chinese leaders would welcome their role in a constitutional process (Liang, 1906d, pp. 222–3). But he felt that in early twentieth-century China participatory consensus was useless. Its implementation would lead to confusion and to abuse of new-found, but badly understood, rights at all levels (Liang, 1906b, p. 192). The solution was not to seek an identity of interests between the individual and the state, but to seek ways to release the innate energy of the community (through *qun* and *gong*) and turn it into a source of national strength (Nathan, 1976, pp. 23–4).[5]

The Problem with a Constitution

Liang gave a number of other reasons why China was not ready for a constitution. For one, a constitution required the establishment of a congress. This would make Chinese political officials accountable and enforce the idea that the people could unseat the president if he did not effect successful changes. Once again, Liang asked whether granting such rights to the people would not inhibit a government's ability to get things done and lead to further instability? To which he answered these were not rights but a burden that China could do without (Liang, 1906b, p. 192). Liang also disagreed with Rousseau's view that legislative and executive functions should be divided. According to the *Social Contract*, the people would comprise the legislative assembly, or the true source of state authority, while the government's role would be largely that of executing the people's laws (Rousseau, 1938, pp. 11–14, 18). Again, this simply could not work in China, according to Liang. For one, there existed no administration in the modern Western sense. Therefore, there were no administrative laws established to outline and separate the duties of the judiciary and the administration. Secondly, there were relatively few tax laws and criminal laws and no sizeable police force to control them. Thirdly, there were no constituencies, nor could there be in the short-term because the Chinese territory was too vast and transportation too inadequate to facilitate the process. Moreover, Liang asked who would lead local elections when even the most basic fundamentals of such a process were unknown to anyone in China (Liang, 1906b, pp. 194–5). By 1903, Liang completely rejected Rousseau's theories as untimely, unsuited and 'fatal' to China. The only solution was strong political authority:

> Freedom, constitutionalism, republicanism: these are but the general terms which describe majority rule.... Were we now to resort to rule by this majority, it would be the same as committing national suicide.... In a word, the Chinese people must for now accept authoritarian rule; they cannot enjoy freedom.... Those born in the thundering tempests of today ... – *they* will be my citizens, twenty or thirty, nay, fifty years hence. *Then* we will give them Rousseau to read, and speak to them of Washington. (Grieder, 1981, p. 167)

While in Japan, Liang also read a Japanese translation of Montesquieu's *Spirit of Laws*. Hou argues that Montesquieu's ideas represented a model of reform for Liang in the 1894–1902 period because Liang believed that a 'division of powers' among the executive, the legislature and the judiciary would prevent corruption in representative political regimes (Hou, 1990, pp. 24–6). But in a similar fashion to his repudiation of Rousseau, Liang eventually retreated from accepting Montesquieu, saying that if China were to carry out a system that separated powers, each would become rigid and self-seeking and would be in constant conflict with the others, which would lead to disunity in the state and in society and between the two (Liang, 1906d, p. 209).

Utilitarianism and the 'Public Interest'

Liang also became familiar with Jeremy Bentham's theories of social utility and economic growth while in Japan. He introduced Bentham's concept of utilitarianism to China in 1902. Both Huang and Chang discuss Liang's understanding of utilitarianism. While each agrees that Liang disregarded Bentham's 'science of legislation', which was based on a precise calculus of pain and pleasure, each also perceives Liang's interpretations of Bentham from different angles. Huang states that the Benthamite formula came nearest to the Confucian idea of *ren* (which Huang defines as 'humaneness') for Liang because '... what impressed Liang was not the utilitarian "science" of morality but simply the category "the greatest majority"' (Huang, 1972, p. 71). Chang, on the other hand, says that Liang's acceptance of Benthamite principles also reflected his disavowal of the Mencian distaste for profit and utility. To hold such views, according to Liang, was not only idealistic and impracticable but wrong. In words that seem to support Bentham and possibly Xunzi, Liang added that 'The search for profit was inherent in human nature; to disregard it would be unrealistic' (Chang, 1971, p. 206). Liang never subscribed to Western utilitarian values in their original form. It has been argued this was because of the difficulty the idea of self-interest posed to his central concern that profit and utility should have collective goals. Likewise, utilitarianism, if rightly understood, according to Liang, meant devotion to the *qun* and the *gong* as the higher common interests that were embodied in the state (see Chang, 1971, pp. 207–9).[6]

The Problem with 'Individual Interests'

It was Liang's seven month stay in America in 1903 that laid to rest any favourable inclinations he may have held toward Western democratic ideas. Like Kang Youwei, Liang reached the conclusion that the successful outcome of American democracy was historically unique while also ill-suited to the majority of nations.[7] Both Huang and Chang comment on the effect Liang's observations of America had on him. But while Huang merely suggests that Liang believed American politics and industrial development to be so advanced that it was not a model for China to follow (Huang, 1972, pp. 77–80), Chang delineates more explicitly what it was about America that caused Liang to turn to an unquestioned allegiance of *qun*. For one, Liang claimed that what he was seeing in the day-to-day activities of the American people and the massive expansion of American industry was both a short-term strength and a long-term weakness. Over the long-term, the gradual displacing of group interests in favour of individual interests, or what Liang saw as a prevalent trend in America, would only lead to an uncooperative, conflicting and disunited nation that, Liang believed, would be unable to compete with other nations. In the short-term, he conceded that the American system had the power to make America immensely strong, but he felt that there would be a price to pay for other nations, especially because of the threat of American imperialism, increasingly evident in American foreign policy. On this basis, Liang roundly concluded that group dynamism was more important than individual dynamism, and that authoritarianism and government intervention were far superior to liberal democracy and laissez-faireism in the long-term.[8]

After his trip to America, Liang's writings reflected his central concern with statism. He grew to believe that the divergent nature of different classes made any kind of consensus impossible. What Liang sought, and what Rousseau's social contract could not provide, was a way to reconcile contrary interests and divergent social groups. Was it not in the best interests of the nation, Liang asked, for the state to rise above societal conflicts for the sake of maintaining order? In answer, he asserted that there could be no compromise for China at this stage in her history: strong leadership and a strong state were the major signposts to be followed along the Chinese road to development (see Chang, 1971, Chap. 8). Much like Kang Youwei, Liang's perceptions of America led him to conclude, for a time, that the best political model for China to follow was to be found in Russia (Grieder, 1981, p. 167).

4.4 ENLIGHTENED DESPOTISM

After returning to Japan from North America, Liang's main Western inspirations became those of the German jurists Johann Kaspar Bluntschli (1808–81) and Conrad Bornhak (1861–1944) and their theories of state-building. Although not important for their theoretical influences in Europe, Bluntschli's and Bornhak's writings were extremely influential on Japanese constitutionalists of the late nineteenth century.[9] Bluntschli criticized the idea of a social contract, and what he saw as the trend in nineteenth-century Europe to place an inordinate emphasis on the individual. He argued that '[i]nstead of deriving its existence from the citizens, the state is actually the source from which individuals derive their status *as* citizens and all their legal rights (quoted in Nathan, 1986a, p. 61). Bluntschli's theory[10] helped to corroborate Liang's own criticisms of his main rival, Sun Yatsen, and the main political trend in China to which Liang was opposed at the time, republicanism. In his critique of Sun, and following on from his rejection of Rousseau's theories, Liang felt that the rights granted to the people under a republican regime meant that the state really had no independent rights over the people. If people's rights were to become the highest priority, this would go against what Liang saw as China's primary goal of strengthening the state (Liang, 1906b, p. 167).

Bornhak's apprehensions about the dangers of establishing a republic by revolution in nations that had not previously nurtured the idea of self-government confirmed for Liang Bluntschli's view that the state was a supreme rational body. Bornhak argued that a republic was inherently unable to fulfill the main function of the state, which he held to be the resolution of conflicts of interest among different segments of the population, because there existed no authority outside the people themselves. Since the people, especially those who were not accustomed to self-government, could not always be counted on to resolve their own conflicts peacefully, a republic would only sink into strife from which absolutism was likely to arise. Liang also believed that absolutism, or what he saw as its opposite, a complete breakdown of authority, would manifest itself in different ways under a republic. Either sovereignty would become the sole preserve of a parliament, which could come to dominate the executive and establish a 'parliamentary absolutism', or a system that included a separation of powers would be instituted, which would violate the indivisibility of sovereignty (Gasster, 1969, pp. 110–12). These problems convinced Liang that sovereignty neither rested in the ruler nor in the general will of the people but in the state itself under a system of enlightened despotism (Liang, 1906b, p. 165). He held that enlightened despotism was not a question of preference but of necessity in China, or in any other country where weak and ineffective government had prevailed or been toppled, where levels of literacy were low and where the population was ethnically diverse (Grieder, 1981, p. 168).

4.5 LIANG'S CRITIQUE OF THE REVOLUTIONARIES

Social Reform or Social Revolution?

Socialist theory arrived in China in the early 1900s. There was considerable confusion over its precise definition, with state socialism and social democracy often viewed synonymously (Bernal, 1968, pp. 104–6, 108, 112). However, Liang was unambiguous in his descriptions of what he considered the different branches of socialism. He divided these into two broad types: the social reformers, or those who agreed with Bismarckian theory, and the social revolutionaries, whom he saw as Marxist in orientation:

> One type was the social reformer; he recognized the contemporary social system, but wished to make reforms in it. This type was represented by men like Adolf Wagner, Schmoller, and others who agreed with Bismarck. The second type was the social revolutionary. He did not recognize the present social order, wishing to overthrow it and build anew. This type was represented by Marx and Bebel among others. (quoted in Scalapino and Schiffrin, 1959, p. 337)

For Liang, socialism represented a 'lofty and pure principle', a noble response to the problems that China was facing at the time, but also the least practical response (Liang, 1906c, p. 339). In the interim, he believed that social reform, or a state socialism comparable to the development strategy he had encountered in Japan, one that nationalized crucial industries and introduced government initiatives to underwrite the entrepreneurial risks of innovation in other economic areas, was best suited to a transitional polity under enlightened despotism (Grieder, 1981, p. 192). To this end, he rejected the applicability of European socialism in China. As he saw it, the industrial revolution and unregulated laissez-faire capitalism, combined with a long history of an exploited peasantry and massive inequalities, made revolution necessary in Europe. But since neither massive industrialization nor laissez-faireism on a nationwide scale had ever taken place in China, Liang argued that social revolution was inappropriate to the Chinese situation.

Even if China had industrialized and introduced capitalism at the same time that the Europeans had, Liang went on, he did not believe that these would have been permitted unrestricted development, or a development that led to injustices. Why this was so was attributable to *li* itself, which Liang said had remained too firmly in place in China to allow the cataclysmic outbursts that occurred in Europe (Kang and Liang, 1906, pp. 318–20). Because social revolution was linked to industrial revolution and because China had not had an industrial revolution, Liang believed that the problems that existed in China need only be repaired, not overturned. Rather than revolution, he maintained that the nation should concentrate its energies on the goal of prosperity and that every effort should be made to advance new means of production. Capitalists were to be relied on to create wealth and to improve people's livelihoods. If Chinese capitalists were encouraged, Liang suggested, they would become strong and more numerous, and the means of production would be increasingly in the hands of the Chinese rather than the sanctuary of foreign investors. Ultimately, this would mean a stronger China, one that could resist foreign aggression (Liang, 1906c, pp. 333, 339–40, 343).

Manchu Rule or Partition?

Liang also worried that revolution and the implementation of social-ist policies in China was a step in the direction of a complete foreign takeover. He gave several reasons for this claim. One was that the Manchu regime had gained the support of the foreign powers, some-thing that a revolutionary party would not be able to do in the short-term. Under the new and unfamiliar policies of a revolutionary party, the foreign powers would inevitably become anxious about safeguarding their territory and investments. This would require the positioning of foreign troops on Chinese soil and the likely scenario of clashes between them and the Chinese military. The Manchu government would not have the strength to suppress a spiralling conflict, and would have to rely on at least one foreign power's assis-tance to do so. This power's influence would increase, and there were bound to be further disputes between it and the other powers for territory and influence.[11] Liang also felt that republicanism could mean further clashes among the Chinese people, and the possibility that one revolutionary army would be displaced by another, or by several others, making disunity the norm (Liang, 1906a, p. 282).

These problems would hasten the decline of foreign investment, according to Liang. Without this investment, what he saw as a vital component of Chinese unity, the nation was sure to be further divided (Wang, 1906, p. 464). He added that disorder would erupt once a republican regime had established itself politically. Struggles would arise between the army and the people, between labour and the upper classes, between the different political parties that were instituted under republicanism and between the provinces. Moreover, given that China was unaccustomed to rule by law, the chances of a republican government turning into a military dictatorship would be greatly heightened, according to Liang. Like Kang Youwei, Liang cites the examples of Central and South American countries in support of his fears (Liang, 1906a, p. 284).[12] Therefore, Liang argued, the Han Chinese must not attempt to separate themselves from the ruling Manchus. A far better option, to his mind, would be to try to absorb the Manchus, along with the Muslims, Tibetans, Mongols and other groups in China (Gasster, 1969, p. 82). Liang's main point was that any form of disturbance in China would give the foreign powers an excuse to intervene, divide the nation and declare war.[13] He saw the preservation of the Manchu regime as the lesser of two evils. Against Sun Yatsen's views, Liang reasoned that what China needed was not socialism or a nationalism that drove the Manchus out, but an absolutism that strengthened the already decentralized Qing government. He referred to the plan of Japan's Meiji restorationists in support of this claim, which said 'absolutism first, capitalism second' (Liang, 1906c p. 359). Liang concluded that if the political situation in China remained steady, the foreign powers, though still a dominant force, would also assist in the generation of national capital, which he asserted remained the chief source of China's strength (Wang, 1906b, pp. 463–4).

Land Nationalization and Henry George's 'Single Tax'

Liang used this same argument to criticize Sun Yatsen's plans for the nationalization of land. Liang insisted that the private ownership of land was a product of history that had for the most part proved itself successful. By leaving it in the hands of private owners, he went on, its value would rise steadily in accordance with social progress. To nationalize land, Liang contended, would not only take incentives away from farmers but would also decrease state revenues (Liang, 1907, pp. 581–2). In response to the revolutionaries' claim that land would not be confiscated but bought, Liang argued that it would still be confiscation, because the price of the land would be artificially lower than if it were sold using real market prices. If the revolutionaries were to follow this policy through, Liang claimed that it would lead to nothing more than 'one large landlord and one large industrialist', or what he referred to as 'one big public enterprise'. How in these circumstances, he asked, can officials serve the people's needs? (Liang, 1907, pp. 592–4). Furthermore, Liang took issue with the revolutionaries' assumption that private landholdings would naturally mean the exploitation of labour in all cases. He said that the majority of landlords in China did not hire workers and that the big landlords who did were generally not exploitative. The system had also proved itself in the way that it enabled many farmers to become landlords, not through the toil of others, but through their own hard work (Liang, 1907, pp. 581–2, 586–90).

Liang also criticized Henry George's theory of the single tax on land values, which was of great interest to Sun Yatsen. Liang alleged that one tax from the nationalization of land could hardly provide the government with enough state revenue for further development. How could it, he asserted, when the majority of those who were asked to contribute were so impoverished that the tax would have to be set artificially low? (Liang, 1907, pp. 591–2). The prospect of building a modern state, he added, required vast sums of money generated through a variety of taxes combined with an accumulation of capital that the government must be willing to reinvest in domestic industries and businesses (Liang, 1907, pp. 592–3). For Liang, the real concerns for the Chinese government at this stage were not the nationalization of land or the single tax but the problem of production. As was true for Kang Youwei, Liang believed that this would be best handled by a government that was willing to set up new enterprises and save those that were failing by 'bringing big capitalists together with smaller ones in a close working relationship that also protected the workers' (Liang, 1907, p. 595). Liang concluded that the revolutionaries could not achieve this because their annexation of land would only serve to widen the gap between the rich and poor (Liang, 1907, pp. 600–1, 606).

4.6 AUTHORITY AND WELFARE IN LIANG QICHAO'S WRITINGS

Liang's debate with the revolutionaries ended in 1907. In the summer and autumn of 1908, the Qing government's efforts to crack down on groups that claimed the right to assemble openly for democratic purposes included Liang's Political Information Institute, angering

Liang to the point that he too began to believe that it may be in China's best interests to overthrow the government. But he never joined the revolutionaries' cause (Fairbank and Liu, 1980, pp. 495, 510, 513). Once the national assembly was established in late 1911, Liang took his place among the moderates in opposition to Sun Yatsen's Revolutionary Party (Fairbank and Feuerwerker, 1986, p. 102) and Liang never conceded a theoretical defeat.

There may not have been a great enough theoretical difference between Sun and Liang for Liang *to* concede defeat. Each man advocated a similar development programme for China.[14] The issue in the debate between the two men was not so much one of capitalism versus socialism, but the implications for China's national development of controlling capitalist growth. In its origins, therefore, Chinese socialism was as much a product of capitalism as it was of socialism. And from what we understand of Liang's interpretations, and Sun's in the post-1911 years, it is more accurate to define the socialism they advocated as state socialism. This is probably because an understanding of socialism first came to these men not from Lenin but through their own observations of capitalism at work in Japan, Britain and the United States (see Dirlik, 1988, pp. 134–5, 138, 143). As such, their solutions for China did not bear the sort of revolutionary elements found in Leninist doctrines. Rather, their primary concerns were how to gather individuals together for the purpose of economic prosperity, and how to ensure that this did not in turn lead to an unbridled capitalism that infringed on the welfare of the Chinese people. For Liang, this necessitated an authoritarian political framework based on enlightened despotism, one which promoted the development of a capitalism that was regulated by the state. This was to be a mixed system where private enterprise played an important role in the larger ends of the nation's socialist policies. Liang felt that this approach would prevent the internal social conflict and oppression that might occur under an unrestricted capitalist system and also facilitate the pooling of national resources in order to compete successfully on the international scene (Chang, 1971, pp. 270–1).

Despite his reading of Western political theorists[15], and his observations of the wealth and strength that had been built on a politics that emphasized individualism and laissez-faireism in the United States, Liang never wavered from his view after 1903 (and perhaps even before) that development in China should be guided by indigenous concepts like *qun* and *gong*. Even in the wake of the failed 1898 reforms, Liang, who was described at the time as a 'liberal', a 'democrat' and even a 'revolutionary' (Feng, 1990, pp. 32–57) spoke with fear of the chaos and 'troubled times' *(ju luan si)* that the absence of an authoritarian leadership and the proliferation of regional leaders that revolution could bring to China. Like his predecessors, Liang believed before and after 1898 that a strong authority that was able to eliminate poverty would hold the key to sustained Chinese unity, and to peace and tranquillity *(shen ping si)* (Liang, 1896, pp. 11–12, 17, and 1898, pp. 27–8).

The remainder of Liang's writings also reflect the same problems that concerned Xunzi and Kang Youwei. Liang speaks of the state's struggle for survival, of survival's dependency on the ruler's establishment of a hierarchical system that puts those of superior talent in command and that absorbs the desires (here described as 'rights' and 'privileges') of man for the greater good of the nation. He speaks of liberty not as a prelude to but as the terminus of a nation that has become militarily and economically strong (Nathan, 1986b, p. 157, and Levenson, 1959, pp. 116–17). In his later years, Liang's patronage of these views increasingly relied on his interpretation of ancient China's philosophers.[16] All, including Xunzi, were critically evaluated by Liang in relation to China's political and economic needs at the time. But, as was true for Xunzi and Kang Youwei, a major point of Liang's criticism was Mozi, a criticism which extended to book length (see Liang's *Mozi Xue An*, 1922). In addition to this, Liang found fault with Mencius's opposition to economic gain in national affairs, but he also renounced the Mencian belief that recurrences of order and disorder were a natural part of human history that man was ill-equipped to prevent (Liang, 1930, pp. 4, 58, and Chap. 4).[17] By contrast, Liang cited the strength of Hobbes's theories of the absolute power of the monarch to maintain order in his comparisons of Hobbes to Xunzi (Levenson, 1959, pp. 124–5, 148). Scalapino and Schiffrin have compared Liang's outlook to Edmund Burke's, that of a willingness to rely on cultural traditions, rather than on revolution, to propel new developments on the basis of old customs or institutions, a comparison that also has been made with Xunzi, as noted in Section 2.5 (Scalapino and Schiffrin, 1959, pp. 339–40). Finally, like Xunzi, and as was later the case for Sun Yatsen, Mao Zedong and Deng Xiaoping, Liang Qichao subscribed to the idea that any epistemological system that China used must be action-oriented, that it must follow the old 'knowledge-for-action' dictum that had gained in importance through the theories of the neo-Confucian philosopher Wang Yangming (Chang, 1971, pp. 284–8).

These conclusions add weight to Chang's view that Liang's thinking was driven by components of Xunzi's political system (Chang, 1971, p. 151). They also strengthen the argument that criticisms Liang had of Western liberalism were in every case part of his concern with maintaining Xunzi's idea of *qun*. Further to this, Liang's wish to go beyond what was seen as orthodox Confucian economic thinking, that of limiting man's desires and discouraging consumption to harnessing these desires in order to accumulate capital, create a surplus profit and encourage consumption (Chang, 1971, pp. 157, 213–14, 292), could not be drawn, it would seem, from any Chinese source (apart from Kang Youwei) other than Xunzi. In the modern period, these views were validated for Liang through his reading of German statist theories (Chang, 1971, pp. 256, 258).

For these reasons, Huang's argument that Liang's politics relied on a syncretic combination of liberalism and Confucianism seems to misinterpret the politics that Liang truly was pursuing for China. To be sure, Huang does not describe Liang as a liberal in the classical sense, speaking more of a liberty that falls within the domain of national sovereignty. But the fact that Huang continues to refer to Liang as a liberal, as a 'liberal-Confucian', as someone who in his early years was deeply influenced by John Stuart Mill and whose thoughts should be seen firmly in the context of modern Chinese liberalism (Huang, 1972, pp. 65, 69–73, 80–1, 160–5), complicates a political philosophy that ultimately relied on few, if any, basic sources other than *qun* and *gong*. In point of fact, Liang never wrote a separate essay on Mill and only referred to him in passing, as Huang himself states (Huang, 1972, p. 72).

4.7 CONCLUSION

Like Kang Youwei, Liang Qichao concluded that authoritarian rule must remain in China. Like Kang, Liang accepted and discarded certain elements from the ancient Chinese world that he felt would suit the demands of a modern authoritarian state. Like Kang, Liang believed that the modern state must continue to be guided by the regulatory principles of *li*. What Liang added to these arguments was the view that the common people themselves must be taught why authoritarian rule remained the only choice for China when the goal of the Chinese revolution seemed to be the removal of centralized authority. Liang argued that the way to teach the people about the need for authoritarian rule was by emphasizing *qun* and *gong*. He did not doubt the value of *li* to China's industrialization but he did seem to question whether *li* could work on its own when the people, who were after all the productive force of industrialization, did not understand why such an undertaking was necessary, and why it needed to be guided by an authoritarian leadership. But if they could be taught the economic value of 'grouping' *(qun)* and if they could accept the idea that 'public-mindedness'*(gong)* brought benefits to everyone, Liang reasoned that authoritarian rule would be more effective. What was later described by Sun Yatsen and Mao Zedong as the need for the 'psychological mobilization' of the people is largely attributable to Liang's use of *qun* and *gong*. Where Kang Youwei's support for authoritarian rule primarily centred on state institutions, Liang's authoritarianism articulated a harmonization of interests between the individual and the state. Kang can be rightly called the Qing's bearer of a practical statesmanship that championed strong authority. But Liang was responsible for giving this broad support. He achieved this by writing essays in simple prose that could be understood by larger numbers of people in China than Kang's writings, which were more inclined towards the high-flown style that was expected of Confucian scholars. Although Liang's essays were written during his exile in Japan and though they were banned by the Qing monarchy, they were smuggled into China and read by a very large audience. His view that China could not adapt Western constituencies, because China was so vast and its transportation so inadequate that very few people could get to the constituencies, was one of several views that enabled the average person to understand the problems that democratic institutions could bring to China.

It was noted at the beginning of Chapter 2 that Kang Youwei and Liang Qichao were the principal agents of transformation between the politics of ancient Chinese authoritarianism and the centralized political system that was advocated by China's revolutionaries. Kang's and Liang's influences on Mao Zedong, for example, have been well documented. And the success of Deng Xiaoping's post-Mao reforms has led to a growing industry of enquiry into whether Liang might have been Deng's most important pre-revolutionary inspiration.[18] But as Part Two of this book demonstrates, China's revolutionaries differed from Confucian scholar–officials in their belief that Chinese political traditions could only apply to modern authoritarian politics if they included an emphasis on Chinese nationalism.

Part II:
Revolutionary Authority and Welfare

5 Sun Yatsen

5.1 INTRODUCTION

> Sun Yat-sen pointed out that *wealth* was to modern Chinese what *liberty* was to the Europeans of the eighteenth century – the supreme condition of further progress. (Linebarger, 1937, p. 77)

In order to understand how traditional authoritarian principles were transferred and used after China's 1911 Revolution, this section of the book examines modern China's most important revolutionary figures: Sun Yatsen, Mao Zedong and Deng Xiaoping. This chapter describes Sun Yatsen's support for authoritarian rule in China by analyzing his ideas about nationalism, democracy and welfare in his lectures on the 'Three People's Principles' (*Sanmin Zhuyi*).[1] Much has been written about the *Sanmin Zhuyi* and critics agree that it represents Sun's most important work.[2] In this chapter, an attempt is made to contribute to this research by suggesting that the fundamental elements that comprise Sun's nationalism, democracy and welfare can be traced to Xunzi's philosophy. Much more than Kang Youwei or Liang Qichao, Sun seemed to have built his political ideology on patterns that Xunzi established. The *Sanmin Zhuyi* also marks a turning point in the definition and legitimacy of authoritarian politics in China. Its importance as a text during Sun's life, and later for figures like Mao Zedong, meant that the Chinese state was legitimated on socialist foundations, as they were defined by Sun's welfare principle. This seemed to inform Mao's authoritarian stance and major policies of the Chinese Communist Party in Mao's early years[3] and may have continued to influence Deng Xiaoping's political outlook, as Chapters 6 and 7 indicate.

5.2 SUN'S NATIONALISM AND XUNZI'S *QUN*

China specialists tend to agree that Chinese nationalism did not replace, but continued to be driven by elements of traditional Chinese culture. For this reason, they define the Chinese nation-state as an 'ethnic-state'.[4] Yet few who support this definition have also defined the traditional Chinese elements which comprise its basis.

Additionally, few discuss the ethnic-state thesis in connection with Sun Yatsen's concept of nationalism *(minzu)*. This seems a peculiar omission because it was Sun's *minzu* that established the foundation for modern Chinese nationalism. While research on Sun Yatsen has yet to draw connections between his political outlook and the ancient doctrines of Xunzi, Sun's defence of Chinese nationalism makes use of ancient Chinese concepts that were also important to Xunzi's defence of a strong state. It has been suggested that five ancient concepts figure prominently in Sun's political doctrines. These are *li* ('social order', 'stability'), *qun* ('grouping'), *gong* ('public-mindedness'), *wang dao* ('way of kings'), and the idea that knowledge must be action-oriented.[5] If this argument is accepted and if it is also accepted that Sun's *minzu* accurately characterizes the Chinese ethnic-state, then it is an ethnic-state whose conceptual antecedents must be derived from Xunzi's philosophy. This is not to suggest that the concepts noted were the exclusive domain of Xunzi. But Sun's use of them, both directly and according to the political and social norms that the concepts had established, is highly reflective of the thinking that was intrinsic to Xunzi's rationale.

There is indeed much to suggest a theoretical consistency between Sun and Xunzi. Like Xunzi, Sun believed that *li* was crucial to the state's ability to shape the conduct of the people. This was just as true for Sun during a period of incipient Chinese nationalism under a republican government as it had been during the Chinese dynastic period, with which *li* was usually associated. The difference was that through nationalism the people's thinking was to be shaped by their loyalty to the nation rather than by their loyalty to the emperor (Sun, 1928, Vol. 1, pp. 144, 213–14). Similarly, like Liang Qichao, Sun may have adopted *qun* and *gong* because of what he saw as their capacity to unite the people and the leadership for the sake of shared nationalist goals.[6] To these, he added *wang dao* in defence of his position that a modern Chinese nation must be organized and governed by a capable leadership (Sun, 1928, Vol. 1, p. 1). This, likewise, draws parallels with Xunzi's perspective that only a political system governed by *wang dao* could prevent anarchy, eliminate poverty and create wealth (Chap. 2). As succeeding parts of this chapter will illustrate, this position accorded with Sun's rejection of popular sovereignty in the early development phase of Chinese modernization. *Wang dao* was also preferable to *ba dao* ('the way of might') because *ba dao*, in Sun's opinion, had established the basis for the defence of laissez-faire policies, which he believed brought about adverse economic conditions and unjust international economic relationships (Sun, 1928, Vol. 1, p. 1).[7] Theoretically, all of these concepts were to work in conjunction with Sun's revival of the 'knowledge-for-action' dictum, or his reversal of the ancient Chinese expression that said 'knowledge is easy and action is difficult.'[8] Sun said that development in China *must* be based on the view that true knowledge was action-oriented and was to have the good of the nation at heart (Sun, 1928, Vol. 1, p. 227)[9], a stance which can be traced to Xunzi (Chap. 2). It is also a position that Sun's successors, Chiang Kaishek and especially Deng Xiaoping, felt was vital to Chinese development (see Chiang, 1947, pp. 185–6, and Chapter 7 of this book). Although the concepts *li, qun* and *gong* had already been explicitly discussed by Kang Youwei and Liang Qichao, Sun broadened the definitions and utility of these concepts for the sake of nationalist goals. This was particularly the case with *qun. Qun* still meant 'grouping' for Sun, but it also referred to 'equalization', or Sun's long-term goal of improving the welfare *(minsheng)* of all the people. As such, there exists a direct connection between the *qun* of *minzu* and the *qun* of *minsheng*. This has also been seen as Sun's justification for his rejection of a laissez-faire economy and his acceptance of state capitalism as the only way to guarantee distributive justice in economic life (see Yü, 1989, pp. 96–7). This conclusion lends support to the argument that Sun's ethnic-state and the goal of Chinese nationalism generally, correspond with Xunzi's reasoning that only a strong unified state is capable of sustaining the wealth and welfare of *all* the people (Chap. 2).

Sun's long-term aim of equalizing wealth according to Han nationalist principles may have been the most divisive issue in his debate with Liang Qichao in Japan at the beginning of the twentieth century. Although Liang accepted the need for a system of state capitalism whose goals were the same as Sun's *minsheng*, Liang also felt that the fulfilment of these goals depended on a Han alliance with the ruling Manchus. The revolutionaries countered this by saying that the Manchu's elite position combined with its small numbers meant that the Manchu aristocracy could not possibly share the collective interests of the entire Chinese nation. For the revolutionaries, the continuation of Manchu rule would mean the continuation of national oppression and national inequality.[10] This conclusion also links the purpose of Sun's *minzu* with his long-term objectives of democracy *(minquan)* and livelihood *(minsheng)*. The objective of *minquan* was to eliminate national oppression, and the internal and external forces that Sun believed constituted its presence (the

Manchus and the Imperialist powers). The objective of *minsheng* was to eliminate national inequality and to ensure 'complete democratic rights' through greater equalization of incomes and standards of living. Because the Han people comprised the largest 'group' in China, Sun's revolutionaries argued that only they could have such collective interests at heart and that therefore Han nationalism was the most direct route to *minquan* and *minsheng* (Wang, 1907b, p. 638, and Chen, 1905, p. 125).

Gasster has suggested that the Chinese revolutionaries' adherence to the idea that the largest ethnic group was the only group that could rule legitimately in China was derived from the Confucian classic *Zuozhuan* (*Tradition of Zuo*), which states, 'If he be not of our kin, he is sure to have a different mind' (Gasster, 1969, p. 77). But the revolutionaries' concerns that national oppression and national inequality would be aggravated under a minority government seem more likely to have been derived from their acceptance of Xunzi's concept of *qun*. An examination of extracts from the *Xunzi*, which were brought together in the *Qunshu Zhiyao* (*Book of Group Regulations*),[11] indicates just how consistent Sun's link between the establishment of *minzu* and the goals of *minsheng* is with Xunzi's objective. For Xunzi, the state's accumulation of wealth and power were highly dependent on the leader's ability to unite 'the Hundred Clans'. This unity was to ensure greater 'strength' and 'accomplishment'. And unity would remain constant so long as the people were '... allow[ed] ... a generous living ...' Once a certain stage of wealth was reached, '... the Hundred Clans ... [would not] presume to transgress the prohibitions of ... superiors' (see Books 11.12, 12.5, 18.1, 10.2 and 24.2 of Knoblock's edition of the *Xunzi*). How important the *Qunshu Zhiyao* was to Sun is difficult to determine, but the writings of Sun's revolutionaries on nationalism in Japan, where the *Qunshu Zhiyao* was of considerable importance, frequently associate the goal of Chinese nationalism with 'grouping'. Modernization of the Chinese nation was to be built on 'the manifestations of the psychology of group', and in a political environment in which there were common characteristics of 'consanguinity', a common spoken and written language and common customs.[12]

This thinking also seemed to influence Sun's deep fear of 'cosmopolitanism'. He felt that cosmopolitan influences could have an adverse effect on China's ability to unify, strengthen and enrich itself. Sun said that it was cosmopolitan thinking that enabled a minority race like the Manchus to conquer the Han people and bring the Ming dynasty to a close [in 1644]. He and other revolutionaries, believed that the same consequence was in store for China in the twentieth century if economic and political influences from foreign countries continued because of the absence of Han nationalism (Sun, 1928, Vol. 1, pp. 83–4 and 90–1, and Wang, 1906b, p. 462). This position may have also revived Xunzi's rejection of heterodoxy, or his belief that the influence of more than one school of thought on the ruler would have a debilitating effect on the state (Chap. 2). It also anticipates Deng Xiaoping's condemnation of what he believed were the dire effects of 'spiritual pollution' and 'bourgeois liberalization' on Chinese economic reforms in the 1980s and 1990s (see Deng, 1994, p. 245, and 1987, pp. 35–6). Perhaps more than anything else, it is Xunzi's theories on state guidance and state unity, and the proven ability of these to unite all of China in 221 BC, that have left an indelible impression on Sun's and Deng's views about what the imperatives of Chinese nationalism should be.

5.3 SUN'S DEMOCRACY AND XUNZI'S 'NATURAL INEQUALITY'

Although the Chinese revolutionaries held debates about democracy with Liang Qichao in Japan in the early 1900s, their opinions remained tentative and unclear until the post-1911 Revolution years. The main reason for this was because the revolutionaries did not believe that full-scale discussions on democracy were necessary in the pre-1911 years while the more urgent issue of 'national oppression' had still to be resolved.[13] It was not until the May Fourth Movement got under way in 1919 that Sun began to consider on a more serious level how Chinese democracy should be defined and in what way it should be instituted. This section suggests that Sun produced a unique democratic system which took shape after he had rejected the applicability of Western democratic models to China. It also suggests that the constituent elements of Sun's democracy reflect philosophical antecedents from Xunzi.

Although it was the activities of the May Fourth Movement that provoked Sun's own questions about Chinese democracy (see Sansom, 1988, p. 16), he was critical of May Fourth students and intellectuals who protested against government policies. He claimed that the students' demands for 'liberty' were excessive, and that too much freedom and too many opinions would break the much needed solidarity of the Chinese people. He was especially troubled by what he saw as an indiscriminate acceptance among May Fourth participants of Rousseau's idea that human beings are born with 'natural rights'. Surely, Sun argued, it was more in keeping with the Chinese situation at the time to say that people were born with 'natural obligations' toward the material and cultural development of society. In fact, this viewpoint coincided with Sun's own interpretation of Rousseau's *Social Contract*. Sun said the main argument of the *Social Contract* was that man gave up such rights as freedom and equality for socioeconomic reasons in the social contract for establishing the state (Sun, 1928, Vol. 1, pp. 187–8).[14] Sun's emphasis on natural obligations and on the importance of China's material development led him to conclude that liberty had only one purpose – the creation of individual wealth over the long-term. He argued further that although European wars from the early seventeenth century onward had been a struggle for individual liberty, the war that had been waged in China was a struggle against individual poverty. To be eradicated from poverty, and to get rich, *was* freedom for the Chinese people (Sun, 1928, Vol. 1, pp. 199, 204). Representative democracy and individual rights could not ensure this, according to Sun. He reasoned that the goal of enriching the individual first necessitated the presence of a strong state. If a representative system were introduced, it would defeat this goal because of what he saw as democracy's inherent ability to weaken the state (Sun, 1928, Vol. 2, p. 46).

Sun acknowledged that the liberty he described would be viewed in the West as a greatly restricted liberty, but he also argued that Western theorists themselves had never supported an unconstrained liberty. He said that John Stuart Mill's greatest contribution to political theory was not the concept of liberty, but the necessity of limiting certain freedoms.[15] Sun felt that May Fourth participants had also come to accept the idea that liberty was not sacrosanct, and that it needed to be put within boundaries for the good of the individual as well as the state (Sun, 1928, Vol. 1, p. 213).[16] Sun did not doubt that the political trend of democracy was a world trend and unstoppable (Chang and Gordon, 1991, p. 108). But he also believed that it was more in the interests of the Chinese people at this time to curb what was already a greater sphere of liberty than was recognized by Western critics. Sun described the people of China as a 'strip of scattered sand' that needed to be united for the nation's goals (Sun, 1928, Vol. 1, pp. 213–14).

Like Liang Qiqiao, Sun claimed that the great fault of the post-French Revolution period was the extreme emphasis placed on 'natural equality' in Europe and America. As Sun saw it, to embrace natural equality in China would also be to undermine progress: 'If you want uniformity of equality then there will be no progress in the world ... equality is man-made and not of nature....' (Sun, 1928, Vol. 1, pp. 228–9). Sun went so far as to say that 'natural equality' as it came to be known after the French Revolution was a 'false equality' because it did not have 'public welfare' at heart (Sun, 1928, Vol. 1, pp. 240, 252).[17] But he also felt that the more the developing nations concentrated on 'public welfare', the more equal the people would eventually become, politically and economically (Sun, 1928, Vol. 1, p. 240).[18] The best way to fulfill this goal was to accept the necessity of a 'natural inequality' in the early stages of development that was based on a system of elite political rule. Sun said that development in China depended on the people's acceptance of a government run by men of special talent and skill (see Leng and Palmer, 1961, p. 147). Along these lines, he divided society into three relatively distinct groups: (1) those who are '... endowed with unusual intelligence and ability ... [and who] think in terms of group welfare ... are the promoters of progress [and therefore] are the best equipped to rule'; (2) those capable of managing or supervising programmes formulated by a gifted leadership[19]; and (3) those who have little more than the capacity to work for the fulfilment of such programmes and who are destined to serve the nation in that manner (see Gregor and Chang, 1989, p. 127, and Linebarger, 1937, pp. 104–5).[20]

Sun's hierarchical system divided those who fell into Groups One and Two according to two further categories. Those in Group One were defined as the men of *quan* ('authority'); those in Group Two as the men of *neng* ('ability'). He argued that this conceptual division marked a fundamental shift in the nature of Chinese authority. He claimed that until this time the main hindrance to Chinese development had been the overwhelming and uncompromising level of *quan* that was invested in Chinese emperors. By introducing *neng*, those who were responsible for the control of political authority were to work with, and be advised by, those with abilities in different fields, and who were to exercise political responsibility. Sun reasoned that the separation of political authority and political responsibility and the entrusting of government administration to experts, had the potential both to end the autocratic practices that were an adjunct of imperial rule and to foster higher levels of political participation in the future (Sun, 1928, Vol. 2, pp. 47–58, and 85–6).

Quan and *neng* also give us a clearer idea of where political sovereignty resides in Sun's political system. Linebarger notes that when *quan* is applied to the exercise of political functions, it means 'sovereignty' or 'political proprietorship' (Linebarger, 1937, p. 107). This applies to Group One, those who are 'best equipped to rule'. *Neng*, on the other hand, and its definitions of 'ability', 'competency' or 'capacity', applies to the individual. But it does so according to two criteria: in the first instance, to those who are capable of administering public affairs; in the second instance, to those who have the ability to have political rights in a democracy. At an early stage of development, the latter of these two does not apply because the majority of the people, those in Group Three, have not yet the 'ability' to have such rights (Linebarger, 1937, p. 107). Therefore, any 'rights' that are conferred on the individual can only go to those in Group Two. Linebarger concludes that,

> In arguing for the political acceptance of inequality and the guarantee of government by a select group, Sun was continuing the old idea of leadership modifying it only to make it consistent with democracy. Under the system he proposed, the two great defects of democracy, untrustworthiness and lack of continuity of policy, would be largely eliminated. (Linebarger, 1937, p. 109)[21]

Sun's justification for an elite democracy is also based on the long-term goal of *minsheng*. As Sun said, so long as the abilities of the more intelligent were not curbed, social progress would move forward more quickly and all people would benefit (Sun, 1928, Vol. 1, p. 245). Sun's democracy worked on the principle that an elite hierarchy must first create democracy and then give it to the people (Martin and Shui, 1972, p. 156). To adapt liberty and equality as they were advocated by Western governments would lead to a 'state of anarchy', according to Sun. For this reason, he viewed a hierarchical society based on intellect as a society of 'true freedom' and 'true equality' (Sun, 1928, Vol. 2, p. 46, and Metzger, 1992, p. 18).

Sun said in 1924 that China must *de novo* 'think out a [democratic] method' (Sun, 1928, Vol. 2, p. 44). While acknowledging the huge differences in the worlds that Sun and Xunzi inhabited, Sun's views on democracy, as was true of his proposals for Chinese nationalism, bear many similarities to Xunzi's notions of authority. For Sun, the primary goal of democracy was the nurturing of the nation's material development and the creation of wealth. A wealthy society would also become a more liberal society. Similarly, Xunzi said that '[Once there are] adequate quantities of all useful goods ... the relation between ruler and subject ... is increasingly pervaded by liberality' (see Section 2.5). For both Xunzi and Sun, this could only be effected through an elite hierarchy which relied on the most intelligent to contribute to the needs of the state. As Xunzi said of the ruler, '... [He] selects the man who is most knowledgeable about handling official tasks and delegates to him supervision of state business.' (Section 2.5). Neither Xunzi nor Sun agreed that authority or equality could be shared; such a proposition would lead to anarchy: 'When power and positions are equally distributed ... there is bound to be contention' (Chap. 2). Sun's *quan* and *neng* and his belief in the need to divide those who hold political authority from those who have political responsibility, also correspond to Xunzi's thinking. Sun's designating the men at the top of his hierarchical system as the men of *quan* because of their ability to improve the welfare of the people is seen here in Xunzi's words: 'The state is the most powerful instrument for benefit in the world. The ruler of men is the most influential position of authority for benefit in the world.' (*Xunzi*, Vol. 2, p. 149). The differences Sun draws between *quan* and *neng* also correspond with the Xunist political outlook: '... if knights and grand officers divide up official positions and responsibilities ... then the Son of Heaven [the ruler] need do no more than assume a gravely reverent attitude in his person' (Section 2.5). Both men believed that this system would only serve the foremost consideration of 'welfare' if it were initiated on the basis of a 'natural inequality'. Xunzi said that the way to reach the goal of great harmony *(datong)*, or what one might term the ancient approximation of Sun's *minsheng*, was to accept the '... fundamental principle by which to nurture the empire', that 'There is equality only insofar as [the people] are not equal.' (*Xunzi*, Vol. 2, p. 96). As early as 1907, this point was confirmed for Sun's revolutionaries. They said the great lesson they learned from their study of the French Revolution was that the 'economic rights' of the people could only be improved by granting sovereignty to an elite leadership, rather than to the people themselves (Wang, 1907b, p. 642).

But perhaps nothing brings Sun nearer to Xunzi than Sun's analysis of the debate on democracy that followed the American Revolution. Sun's rejection of Jefferson's belief that man's nature is good and that every man should have liberty, equality and full political power and his acceptance of Hamilton's belief that man is evil, that man required the guidance of a strong centralized state and that the people should be granted only a limited sovereignty, is reminiscent of Xunzi's critique of the *Mencius*. Xunzi's criticism of Mencius's view that man is inherently good in Book 23 of the *Xunzi* justifies the opposite, that man is evil, for the same reasons that Sun justifies his critique of Jeffersonian democracy. Just as Xunzi said that without strong governmental authority, man's evil nature would lead to selfishness, disorder and rebelliousness (Section 2.5), Sun said of people's rule in a stage of underdevelopment, 'When those evil men have got hold of the great power of the state, they will handle the interests of the country for their own selfish ends ... provoke riotous governing and trigger anarchy *(da luan)* (Sun, 1928, Vol. 2, pp. 3–6).

5.4   SUN'S SOCIALISM AND XUNZI'S *DATONG*

The main priority of Sun's *minsheng* ('people's livelihood', 'welfare') was to ensure that the '... economic well-being of all the people was raised beyond subsistence level.' Sun did not accept that revolution in China could be said to be complete until the menace of poverty was eliminated (Sun, 1928, Vol. 2, p. 115). On this basis, *minsheng zhuyi*, rather than the conventional term for Chinese socialism, *shehui zhuyi*, defined the objective of Sun's socialism. This section suggests that Sun's *minsheng* is a wholly independent approach to socialism, which relied on Western political theory only insofar as it accorded with the prerogatives of *minsheng*.

Sun did not treat the utility of any political doctrine with as much criticism as he did Marxism. In particular, he was repelled by Marx's idea of 'class struggle', saying that it was a political activity from which only a 'sick society' could benefit. The reason that class struggle had arisen, according to Sun, was because the emphasis on survival as the goal of social progress had been neglected: 'Man seeking survival is the cause of social progress; class warfare is not the cause of social progress. Class warfare is a ... [result] of ... man's inability to survive' (Sun, 1928, Vol. 2, p. 141).[22] Sun likewise objected to Lenin's idea that a political elite's means to power, and its ability to persist once in power, rested on its ability to exploit mass political discontent. Sun countered that mass mobilization for political purposes should be the state's lowest priority. He said this for two reasons. One was that although he did not dispute the existence of the social injustices that

Lenin's mass mobilization was confronting, he felt that social injustices in themselves could only be dealt with rationally by administrative policy from above *after* the establishment of a strong government. The second reason was Sun's claim that a politically-based mass mobilization would interfere with the important goal of attracting foreign investment (Leong, 1987, pp. 69–70, 86).[23] Mobilization from above was warranted only if it had the purpose of '... mobiliz[ing] energies in pursuit of the gains already achieved in wealthier industrialized societies' (quoted in Friedman, 1974, p. 19). This position adds weight to the argument that Sun held a utilitarian attitude toward both labour and peasants (Sansom, 1988, p. 127)[24] and that he viewed their primary role to be participation in economic reconstruction under an elite government, not political movements. As Sun said, without the guidance of 'friendly intellectuals' and 'good leadership', the workers '... would open their mouths only to blunder' (Chan, 1987, p. 129). In addition to this, Sun maintained that the goal behind Leninist industrialization, the strengthening of the proletariat, fell short of his own revolutionary goal as it was ordained by *minsheng*, that of bringing benefit to the *whole* nation (Linebarger, 1937, p. 247). These views also reinforce the position, often repeated by Sinologists, that Leninism was of little, if any, relevance to Sun Yatsen's socialism.[25]

By the 1940s, it was believed that Sun's thinking was based on the theories of the American scholar Maurice William's *Social Interpretation of History*, whose central theme, that humanity seeking survival and not conflict was the real centre of gravity of history, was said to have greatly appealed to Sun (see Zolotow, 1948, Chap. 5). From the late 1950s through to the 1980s, scholars claimed that Sun's *minsheng* was influenced by German and Japanese social reformism and particularly by Bismarckian reformist policies and the national protectionist theories of Friedrich List.[26] Scholars also argued at this time that Sun was an ardent disciple of the American Henry George, who influenced the theories of the American 'Progressivists'. Sun was similar to the Progressivists, it was suggested, because he advocated moderate reform instead of radical revolution, promoted a nationalist movement that did not wish to overthrow capitalism, end private incomes or abolish private property but rather to reform these for the sake of human progress (see Chang, 1982, pp. 4, 6, 11, 13, 15). One consensus, which was reached at a symposium on Sun Yatsen studies in Germany in 1982, was that Sun's theories relied on a synthesis of Chinese and non-Marxist Western ideas (see Kindermann, 1982).

None of these views need be challenged as wrong. Sun speaks at some length and with admiration, about figures like Bismarck and his ability to 'harmonize interests' between capitalists and labourers, to nationalize land and railroads, to prevent the monopolization of wealth by large landlords and large capitalists, and to make capitalism serve state socialism (Sun, 1928, Vol. 2, pp. 24–5). Similarly, almost two decades before Sun presented his *minsheng* lectures in 1924, his revolutionaries said that Henry George's idea of the single tax on land complied with the first phase of the *minsheng* programme, that of mediating conflicts between the rich and the poor. They also agreed that the state socialism that was practiced in Germany and Japan, and especially in Germany, had proved successful when compared to rival political systems (see Feng, 1906, pp. 425, 430–2, and Hu, 1906, p. 378). But long before these views were expressed, Sun had already settled on the independent value to China of the 'Three People's Principles', as he said in 1896:

> ... [In 1896] I went to Europe to study the methods of its political administration.... I understood that although the foremost European countries had achieved power and popular government, they could not accord complete happiness to their peoples.... I conceived the idea of the simultaneous settlement, by means of revolution, of the questions of national economy, national independence and popular freedom. Hence arose my so-called [*Sanmin Zhuyi* – 'Three People's Principles']... (Sun, 1918, p. 193)

Some years later, Sun said that Western socialism would not suit this goal because he believed that all Western socialist theory was anarchic by nature. It had to be this way, he claimed, because Western nations had neglected *minsheng*, making revolution the only solution (Sun, 1905, p. 82). By 1906, Sun's revolutionaries were already speaking of *minsheng's* main objective of equalizing accumulated wealth in China. They did so without referring to comparable theories from the West (see Zhu, 1906, pp. 433, 436, 445–6). In 1907, they suggested that the indigenous character of *minsheng* was particularly suited to this goal because its basic mandate of creating prosperity for all did not have to contend with the problems to which European socialism was responding: the disparities in wealth and position that were a consequence of both the European system of nobility and the industrial revolution (Minyi, 1907, p. 667, and Wang, 1907b, p. 638).

Sun's independent approach to socialism through *minsheng* may also be derived from the Chinese word *min* ('people') and its cognates. *Min li*, for example, refers to both the 'strength' and the 'wealth' of the people; that of *mintian*, to the 'heaven of the masses'. Heaven, in this context, can also refer to adequate amounts of food, as in the expression *min yi shi wei tian* ('the masses regard sufficient food as their heaven'). Likewise, *minsheng* is seen to have failed if the following is expressed: *minsheng bu sui* ('the people are not prosperous') (see Mathews, 1943, pp. 631–2). In other words, the variations on *min*, in many cases, reflect the combined objectives of Sun's *minsheng*: sufficient food and sufficient wealth. All of *minsheng* devolves to these objectives. Sun did not accept that socialism would prove itself in China until poverty was eliminated, and China's 400 million people had enough food to eat (Sun, 1928, Vol. 2, pp. 164–5, 169, 198). Moreover, Sun felt that his emphasis on these objectives and his approach to achieving them, marked a unique contribution to socialism, as he said, 'We must put back as the heart of every government's social and economic problem of history, the problem of welfare' (Sun, 1928, Vol. 2, p. 156). Sun's successor, Chiang Kaishek, later said that the goal of the 'Three People's Principles' [that of *minsheng*] was the same as that in the chapter on *Datong* ('Great Harmony') in the ancient *Book of Rites (Liji)* (Chiang, 1947, p. 289). As noted in Chapter 2, it was also the *Liji* and particularly the chapter on *Datong*, that provided the foundation for Xunzi's philosophy.[27] This again adds weight to the view that Sun's theories were influenced by Xunzi's philosophy.

Sun's development programme was ambitious in scope. It included comprehensive plans for communications systems, commercial harbours, modern cities with public utilities, water power development, iron and steel works, mineral development, agricultural development, irrigation work and reafforestation (see Sun, 1944, p. 12). It also included a provision for the practice of local self-government at the county *(xian)* level, in which members of local councils and local officials would be elected by the people while the central government retained control over national affairs. It is beyond the purpose of this chapter to discuss Sun's plans fully.[28] Of greater interest here is Sun's view of what should drive this programme. He believed that the goal of socialism would first require a period of capitalist development and industrialization.

Sun said that there was no reason why China could not build socialism on capitalist foundations. He argued that both Chinese and foreign capitalists would not exploit but enhance the labourer's level of *minsheng*. For this to work successfully, it was vital that leaders emphasized the development of state capital and state control of private capital. State regulation would prevent the expansion of private capital and an unequal distribution of wealth (Sun, 1928, Vol. 2, pp. 140, 184–5). New nationalized industries would be built on the taxation of earnings from private capital and on future advances from land values after land had been nationalized (Sun, 1928, Vol. 2, pp. 137, 178–81). These measures would prepare China for what Sun proposed would be a new market in the country that was open to goods and investment from abroad. He described China as an 'economic ocean' capable of absorbing all surplus capital as quickly as industrial nations could produce it (Sun, 1944, pp. 10–12, 14). But opening China's doors to foreign capital also depended on the existence of a strong state. Sun's revolutionaries said in 1907 that a strong state was the only means capable of both handling the abundance of foreign capital they expected would 'pour' into China after the revolution, while also ensuring that foreign control was kept out (Minyi, 1907, pp. 674–5, and Wang, 1907b, p. 638). Sun's view that a strong state that was buttressed by state capital and state industry would prevent the inequalities that existed in capitalist countries (Sun, 1928, Vol. 2, pp. 186–7)[29] calls to mind Xunzi's view that state intervention was the best way to provide the people with a 'generous living' (Chap. 2). For Xunzi, this also required a strong state, an emphasis on large state projects, state supervision over the regulation of land and capital, and state control over profits, taxation and the number of merchants and traders. Both men believed that state regulation would enhance *minsheng's/datong's* central objective of ensuring that the people share everything in the state (Sun, 1928, Vol. 2, pp. 186–7, and Gangulee, 1945, p. 91).

5.5   CONCLUSION

James Gregor said in 1981 that judgments which had been tendered by specialists on the specific relationship between Sun Yatsen and the Confucian tradition would remain speculative because Sun never stated how the philosophy of China's ancient sages entered into his political doctrines (Gregor, 1981a, p. 55). This chapter has suggested that Sun's connection with the Confucian tradition can be most clearly seen in the philosophy of Xunzi. Important principles that compose Sun's 'Three People's Principles' correspond in virtually every aspect with dictates that were central to Xunzi's philosophy. Both men believed that state unity was the basis of a wealthy and strong state, that this unity depended on state orthodoxy for guidance, that wealth was the foundation for greater liberty and equality, and that an authoritarian political system built on an elite hierarchy was best suited to creating this wealth. What also comes to light from the study of Sun is that as the early twentieth century progressed, Chinese theories about political authority did not, despite much greater contact with the West, move toward Western theories but nearer to Chinese traditional patterns. Kang Youwei and Liang Qichao at least accepted that there was a Western political system which China could model itself on at the time, that of the Russia's under Peter the Great (see Chapters 3 and 4). But Sun never advocated fully any non-Chinese political system for China.

Sun's adaptation of the principles and patterns that Xunzi established was fundamental to Sun's perspective on Chinese socialism. It is patently clear that the prescriptions of Marx and Lenin had no bearing on this perspective. It is also questionable whether Western social reform theories influenced Sun, or simply confirmed his opinions. In a statement that anticipated Deng Xiaoping's outlook by nearly six decades, Sun said that the method of Chinese socialism '... must take [Chinese] facts as the raw material ...', and that the basic fact that this socialism must address was 'poverty' (see Sun, 1928, Vol. 2, pp. 164–5, and Chapter 7). An end to poverty was the supreme goal of Sun's 'Three Principles', a goal that was also a prime concern for Xunzi (Section 2.5). All other economic developments were contingent upon the eradication of poverty. This can be noted in Sun's challenge to those who questioned his unwillingness to fashion Chinese modernization on capitalist principles: '... if a great famine should come and destroy all the people of Shanghai or Canton do you think that the price of a piece of land in Shanghai or Canton would be as high as the price is at present or not?' (Sun, 1928, Vol. 2, p. 169).

Sun added a number of significant innovations to the authoritarian stand of Kang Youwei and Liang Qichao. But all of these seemed to hinge on Sun's belief that the long-term goal of Chinese socialism would be augmented by a period of state capitalism that welcomed foreign investment.[30] In this respect, Sun retained the non-ideological outlook that would become the preserve of future revolutionaries in China, when he said in 1924, 'if we use existing foreign capital to build up a future communist society in China, half the work will bring double the results' (quoted in Godley, 1987, p. 116). This outlook has influenced the development strategy of Taiwan but also that of China under both Mao Zedong's and Deng Xiaoping's leadership.[31] In Taiwan, the *Sanmin Zhuyi's* main goal of 'parallel achievement of equality and affluence' requires '... a tolerance that affluence must be based on unequal distribution.' This is to be guided and adjusted toward uniform distribution and equality through national planning that allowed a commingling of individual economic activities alongside public economic activities (see Ma, 1975, pp. 152-3, and Shih, 1977, p. 79). Mao and Deng also seemed to agree with this strategy and with the hierarchical system that was preordained to direct it, though this changed for Mao by the late 1950s. As Chapters 6 and 7 below illustrate, their solutions may have been influenced more by the patterns that Sun had established than by the theories of Marx or Lenin.

6 Mao Zedong

6.1 INTRODUCTION

> Contemporary China has grown out of the China of the past.... We should sum up our history from Confucius to Sun Yat-sen and take over this valuable legacy. This is important for guiding the great movement of today. Being Marxists, Communists are internationalists, but we can put Marxism into practice only when it is integrated with the specific characteristics of our country and acquires a definite national form. (Mao, 1938, Vol. 2, p. 209)[1]

Since 1949, when the Chinese Communist Party (CCP) took power in China, the theoretical basis of Chinese political authority has been designated by the CCP as a combination of Marxism–Leninism and Mao Zedong Thought. Whether each ideology influenced Mao's politics, or whether one did so independently of the others, has been the subject of much discussion and academic debate. Conclusions vary considerably. These either isolate and argue in favour of certain Marxist or Maoist principles, or they integrate the two on the basis of Confucian precedents.

Critics who have devoted considerable research to the study of Mao tend to side with the view that Mao was more strictly Leninist than he was a follower of Marx, Confucius or even of his own theories.[2] Others defend the importance of Marxist guidelines in Mao's writing that emphasize the theory and practice of revolution (Fann, 1979, p. 156). Still others claim that Mao was not precisely Marxist or Leninist but that he was Leninist-Stalinist. They argue that only through Stalin's views was Lenin's theory confirmed for Mao, that in colonial nations where no socialism was to be expected, a bourgeois democratic revolution should be built on a peasant base, but should be led by a Chinese proletariat (Chang, 1992, pp. 25–6). Some also dispute this. They argue that Mao's leadership was '... neither "the vanguard of the proletariat" in the Marxist–Leninist sense, nor a "peasant party" in the orthodox Communist sense, but was made up of professional revolutionaries based on peasant discontent.' Because they lacked an understanding of communism, it is maintained, the peasants relied on certain features of traditional Chinese authority to direct their movement (Chao, 1990, p. 43). This emphasis on nativistic elements in Maoism is a growing field of enquiry. It generally follows two directions, one theoretical, the other structural. Those who support the structural argument suggest that Maoist political organization was nothing more than a manifestation of traditional Chinese imperial authoritarianism (see D. W. Chang, 1990, p. 56). Those who follow the theoretical argument hold that there is a direct connection between Confucianism and Mao's Marxism. They add that though Mao rarely spoke of the affinities between the two creeds, his nurturing on the one at a young age would have prepared him to grasp the dialectical materialism of the other at a later age (Dow, 1979, p. 99). These contrasting theories suggest that the essence of Maoism remains open to debate (Knight, 1990, pp. 104–5).

While most of the aforementioned studies have put great store in a Marxist–Leninist framework, none of them refers to Sun Yatsen's influence on Mao.[3] This is peculiar, especially because in his early years (until about 1949) Mao wrote about Sun's influences with a deeper commitment than he did to the theories of Marx, Lenin or Stalin. The chapter suggests that what was most significant about Sun's theories for Mao was the view that foreign capital and investment were essential to building Chinese socialism. This is a view that Mao promoted in the 1930s, 1940s and well into the 1950s, although he did not always acknowledge Sun in doing so. The chapter also suggests that American and Soviet reluctance to accept this position was highly influential on the autarkic development path and the consequent radical politics that Mao adopted in the late 1950s.

6.2   SUN YATSEN'S 'THREE PRINCIPLES' AND MAO'S EARLY YEARS

Mao said in 1937 that it was in keeping with the historical requirements of the Chinese revolution to revive and restore Sun Yatsen's 'Three People's Principles':

> Does the Communist Party agree with the Three People's Principles? Our answer is, Yes, we do.... The revolutionary Three People's Principles of Dr. Sun Yat-sen won the people's confidence and became the banner of the victorious revolution of 1924–27.... Consequently, it is completely in keeping with the historical requirements of the Chinese revolution that the essence of the

Three People's Principles should be revived and restored.... (Mao, 1937, Vol. 1, p. 270)[4]

It could be argued that Mao held this belief only to placate Sun's successor, Chiang Kaishek. Chiang and top members of China's Nationalist Party, the Guomindang (GMD), were wary of Mao's overtures toward a CCP–GMD coalition government after the war because of what they saw as Mao's support for the importation of Marxist–Leninist theory to China. But even by the autumn of 1949, when the CCP had defeated the GMD in China's civil war, Mao continued to speak of the relevance of Sun's principles (Mao, 1949, Vol. 4, p. 457).[5] That Mao cited Sun Yatsen as justification for the ways and means of the CCP in the post-revolutionary period says a great deal about his admiration for his predecessor. What Mao referred to as 'new democracy' from 1940 onward was, by Mao's own admission, identical to Sun's doctrines.[6] This was particularly true in economic terms. Mao said, 'The economy of the New Democracy which we advocate is likewise in accord with Dr. Sun's principles ...' (Mao, 1945, Vol. 3, p. 231). Mao referred to Sun's ideas on land nationalization and the regulation of capital as proof of his commitment to Sun's principles, and to show his advocacy of Sun's theory of *minsheng*:

On the land question, Dr. Sun championed 'land to the tiller'. On the question of industry and commerce, Dr. Sun stated in the Manifesto [of 1924] enterprises such as banks, railways and airlines, whether Chinese-owned or foreign-owned, which are either monopolistic in character or too big for private management, shall be operated and administered by the state, so that *private capital cannot dominate the livelihood of the people: this is the main principle of the regulation of capital*. (Mao, 1945, Vol. 3, p. 231) (Emphasis added.)

Many other elements that were central to Mao's writings also seemed to be drawn from Sun Yatsen. Like Sun in the post-1911 years, Mao was a gradualist until the mid-1950s. He opposed the idea of turning China into a nation that practised socialism immediately after the revolution. Similarly, Mao believed that China had too little capitalism and that a prolonged stage of capitalist development was necessary for the more important goal of socialism:

Strangely enough, some spokesman of the Chinese bourgeoisie fight shy of openly advocating the development of capitalism.... There are other people who flatly deny that China should permit a necessary degree of capitalist development and who talk about reaching socialism in one stride and 'accomplishing at one stroke' the tasks of the Three Principles and socialism. (Mao, 1945, Vol. 3, p. 233)

Capitalism was not to be combined with Western democracy to attain this goal (Mao, 1929, Vol. 1, pp. 108–9). Mao was also against liberalism, which he said arose from 'petty-bourgeois selfishness'. He believed that support for liberal views would 'corrode unity', 'undermine cohesion', 'cause apathy' and 'create dissension'. Liberalism and democracy would also alienate Party organizations from the masses, according to Mao, because under democratic policies these organizations would give greater weight to popular interests than to carrying policies through (Mao, 1937, Vol. 2, p. 32).

The alternative to liberal democracy and to an immediate transformation to socialist democracy was to be a Chinese system of 'democratic centralism' (Mao, 1937, Vol. 2, p. 57). Strength at the centre was not to be built from the grassroots but from the highest levels to the localities. Mao thought it imperative that minority interests be subordinated to majority interests for the sake of organizational discipline in the Party and in all other governmental and societal affairs (Mao, 1929, Vol. 1, pp. 108–9, and 1942, Vol. 3, p. 44). At the same time, democratic centralism was not to hamper the development of individual initiative, the growth of private capital and the protection of private property (Mao, 1945, Vol. 3, pp. 230–1). So long as these developed within the framework that the state had established, and did not hamper the livelihood of the people, they were considered acceptable. Only through a consensus that minority views would submit to majority views, as well as an understanding that democratic centralism should not stunt individual initiative and meritocracy, both within the Party and the government and among the people, did Mao believe that democracy could be extended and discipline and unity maintained.[7] Mao was also against what he termed 'absolute equalitarianism', as Sun was, not only in the bourgeois democratic phase of the revolution but also under socialism: '... even under socialism there can be no absolute equality....' (Mao, 1929, Vol. 1, p. 111). Additionally, Mao accepted the idea of local self-government, as it had been described by Sun Yatsen, and of convening people's congresses at county, municipal and provincial levels, and in border regions, to elect the governments at corresponding levels (Mao, 1948, Vol. 4, p. 187). Mao feared what he saw as the ravages of foreign imperialism while also blaming certain elements of Chinese feudalism for allowing richer nations to overrun China (Mao, 1945, Vol. 3, p. 233). The way of combating this for Mao, as was true for Sun, was to unify the people according to strong nationalist principles, to promote education and to eliminate illiteracy (Mao, 1945, Vol. 3, pp. 243–4, 250).

The creation of wealth would also follow the economic structure that Sun advocated. The economy was to comprise the state sector, the private sector and the cooperative sector (Mao, 1945, Vol. 3, p. 231). State industry was to constitute the 'leading force' in the national economy and the main body for the regulation of capital. But capitalist private property was not to be confiscated. Equalization of land ownership would follow Sun's 'land to the tiller'. Rent reduction would be enforced but landlords would not be eliminated (Mao, 1940, Vol. 2, p. 353). According to Mao, this had the purpose of building a rich peasant economy that in its initial stages would not be socialist in nature, but would '... contain elements of socialism' and would lead to '... various types of cooperative enterprises ...' (Mao, 1945, Vol. 4, pp. 71–3). The eventual socialization of agriculture would be '... coordinated with the development of a powerful industry, having state enterprise as its backbone.' This was expected to establish the basis of a 'complete, consolidated socialism' in the future, which was manned by peasants and workers but run by experts (Mao, 1949, Vol. 4, pp. 419, 423).

6.3 MAO'S RETREAT FROM SUN'S 'THREE PRINCIPLES'

Teiwes has referred to the years between 1929 and 1949 as the period of 'stable Maoism' because of the remarkable political stability of the CCP at this time (Teiwes, 1984, pp. 99-100). This point also lends weight to the importance of Sun's principles even in a Chinese political regime that was officially guided by Marxism–Leninism. Despite the similarities between Mao and Sun in Mao's early years, by 1940 Mao insisted that only parts of Sun's 'Three Principles' were of use to the CCP. Mao's selective interpretation of Sun's theories also coincided with what is generally seen as Mao's increasingly ideological political stance. Mao's retreat from the 'Three Principles' was never total, but became increasingly ambiguous by the mid-1950s. More explicitly, it rested on Mao's belief that the CCP's programme for the democratic revolution was only in agreement with Sun's Manifesto from the First National Congress of the Guomindang in 1924:

> The so-called democratic system in modern states is usually monopolized by the bourgeoisie and has become simply an instrument for oppressing the common people. On the other hand, the [Guomindang's] Principle of Democracy means a democratic system shared by all the common people and not privately owned by the few. (Mao, 1940, Vol. 2, p. 409)

Mao saw the Manifesto of 1924 as demarcating two historical periods in the application of Sun's principles: the old 'Three Principles' reflected the demands of the bourgeois-democratic revolution while the new reflected Mao's 'new democracy', or a 'joint dictatorship of several revolutionary classes'. This included an alliance with Russia and a key authoritative role for Chinese peasants and workers (Mao, 1939, Vol. 2, p. 364, and 1940, Vol. 2, p. 409). This became known in CCP circles as Sun Yatsen's 'Three Great Policies'.

Chan has argued that Sun never enunciated or even vaguely supported the 'Three Great Policies' as the CCP described them (Chan, 1987, p. 129). In addition to this, Mao's interpretation of the 1924 Manifesto exaggerates the need to dislodge one-party dictatorship, which Sun believed should stay in place until increased wealth and higher levels of literacy forced a change in the nation's political structure. Although Sun spoke of a democratic system shared by the common people, he did not believe that this could come about until a sufficient period of political tutelage had run its course. But Mao began to speak of a more immediate and thoroughgoing democratic plurality. Government was not only to be *of* and *for* the people (as Sun too had wished), but also *by* the people. Mao simply did not accept that this goal would be an inevitable outcome of political tutelage. He reasoned that attempts at unification by a dictator in modern China had from the time of Yuan Shikai [8] only served to weaken and divide the nation, and thereby aggravate the problem of foreign aggression (Mao, 1945, Vol. 3, p. 244). He concluded that the choice was one of autocratic unification by a dictator (and by this he was referring to the Guomindang) versus democratic unification by the people and through a coalition government.

While Mao believed in his early years that the principles and practices of democracy and socialism were determined historically, he exhibited much less certainty of this in the years that followed liberation in 1949. This is especially evident between 1954 and 1955, following the publication of the first CCP draft constitution in June of 1954. Initially, Mao continued to argue that democracy and socialism fell into a consecutive ordering that was confirmed by China's historical circumstances. He said that if socialism were introduced before China had adequately prepared itself, then the nation's overall goal of socialism would be pushed headlong towards failure (Mao, 1954, Vol. 5, p. 143). But a year after stating this, in a report presented to Party committees from across the nation, Mao spoke of the imminence of a 'nation-wide high tide of socialist transformation in the countryside', which was to commence with a 'socialist mass movement'. He chastised Party members who complained of the pace of such measures. Their reluctance to hasten progress toward socialism seemed only to provoke his new conviction in the need for its immediacy. By December 1955, Mao spoke of a socialist transformation that was to be completed ahead of schedule (Mao, 1955, Vol. 5, pp. 184, 202, 239).

Similarly, while Mao reiterated and supported, in the pre-1949 years, Sun's views on the importance of a national bourgeoisie, on capitalist private property, capitalist production and the equalization of land ownership based on rent reduction rather than on the elimination of landlords, he equivocated over these beliefs by the early 1950s. In June of 1953, he argued that individual ownership was an acceptable part of the transition to collective ownership and socialism. But later that same year, in speeches given in October and November, he spoke of the contradiction between private and public ownership and between capitalism and socialism (Mao, 1953, Vol. 5, pp. 93–4, 135–6). Even before this, in 1952, the CCP had confiscated all land from landlords and redistributed it to the peasants, leaving the landlords who had not been executed without a significant role to play (Mao, 1952, Vol. 5, p. 77). This went against Mao's earlier acceptance of Sun's view that landlords could make important contributions to economic growth. Radical cooperative policies in rural areas followed the confiscation of land from landlords by 1956. And by 1958, China witnessed the establishment of a vast agricultural commune system. Even the magnitude of these changes was negated, at least theoretically, in 1956 when Mao said that '[e]very unit of production must enjoy independence ... if it is to develop more vigorously.' This was seen to be true not only for the communes but for individuals, factories and all other units of production (Mao, 1956, Vol. 5, pp. 289–90, 292, 294–5).

When Mao recanted these views after the CCP victory, he did so by setting his achievements against what he thought to be Sun Yatsen's failings. Mao said that as a result of Sun's reliance on the petty bourgeoisie and national bourgeoisie '... forty years of revolution ... end[ed] in failure' (Mao, 1949, Vol. 4, pp. 421–2). It was nonetheless a bourgeois democratic revolution that Mao claimed to be waging in the early 1940s, which culminated in the CCP's victory. Whereas this line worked during the war years, Mao seemed loath to accept its efficacy in times of peace. His new direction, it has to be conceded, may not only be linked with an ideological shift. Mao *did* seem to believe that in practical terms the advent of a greater socialization of productive relations would lead to a higher degree of productive output. To his own rhetorical question of whether ownership should be individual or collective, capitalist or socialist, he replied: 'Abundant supplies and the relations of production under individual ownership are utterly incompatible with each other' (Mao, 1953, Vol. 5, p. 134). Whether this view was inspired by practical or ideological considerations, one critic has suggested that Mao's increasing emphasis on the importance of productive relations over productive forces, especially following the Eighth Party Congress of 1956, is seen today by many in China as a 'radical leftist mistake' (Rong, 1992, Interview).[9]

By far the most radical of Mao's departures from the pragmatic line that he had held earlier was his view that the collective decision-making of democratic centralism should be transferred to a system of mass democracy. Meisner has described this as Mao's 'pristine Populist-type belief' in the 'general will and innate socialist consciousness' of the people. Meisner adds that this phenomenon was built not on the political and intellectual influences of the Bolshevik Revolution or on traditional Chinese intellectual sources, but from within the Chinese historical environment in which Mao as its principal functionary was attempting to map a new course for Chinese politics (Meisner, 1982, pp. 94, 112). What this amounted to, at least in theory, was a reverse in the dynamics of political authority from the leadership to the led, from democratic centralism to mass democracy. By 1955 Mao spoke positively of the people's varied opinions and criticism of the leadership. By the end of 1957, he encouraged the people to struggle against those in command. The people were to 'speak out freely, air their views fully, and hold great debates.' Any disorder that followed was not to be feared by the leadership, according to Mao.[10]

6.4 EXPLAINING MAO'S RETREAT FROM SUN'S 'THREE PRINCIPLES'

In the 1980s, some scholars agreed that Mao's pragmatism was broken in the late 1950s once he assumed a more direct relationship with Marxist–Leninist ideology.[11] With time, and the uncovering and analyses of CCP documentation from the period, scholarship shifted to an examination of particular historical events and their influence on Mao. Ruan suggests that a number of circumstances surrounding the Eighth Party Congress in 1956 changed Mao's views. He argues that Mao was prepared to begin a period of de-Stalinization in the 1955–6 period in order to prepare the way for opening up relations with the West,[12] but Khrushchev's condemnation of Stalin, combined with calls for greater democracy and liberalism in Poznan and Budapest in 1956, forced Mao to consider the consequences of similar demands in China if domestic reforms were to be carried out (Ruan, 1994, pp. 2–3). Ruan also cites other tensions within the CCP at the time as influencing Mao's change in political direction. Mao's 'anti-rightist' campaign against figures like Liu Shaoqi, Zhou Enlai, Chen Yun and Deng Xiaoping, and their corresponding retort against 'leftist errors', are held up as one example. Another is Mao's unwillingness to legalize the household contract system that would improve economic incentives for the Chinese peasants, something which Zhou Enlai, Liu Shaoqi and especially Deng Xiaoping believed was necessary (Ruan, 1994, pp. 2–5).

Clearly these events contributed to the tumultuous years that followed. But they may not have been key factors in Mao's ideological turnabout. This section suggests that Mao changed political direction because his attempts to form better relations with the United States, and later the Soviet Union, on what might again be termed Sun Yatsen's principles, had failed. Like Sun, Mao was not initially inclined to let ideological differences with capitalist nations, particularly the United States, obstruct his all-important goal of generating capital in post-war China. It was when the United States repeatedly rejected the idea that it could be possible to build a 'national socialism' on capitalist foundations, when it refused to acknowledge what Deng Xiaoping later termed the 'building of socialism with Chinese characteristics', that Mao began to follow an autarkic development path that eventually failed. The situation was made worse in the early 1960s when the Soviet Union refused to recognize China as an equal partner with mutual interests.

John Service's[13] interviews with Mao between 1941 and 1945 reveal just how interested the Chinese leader was to pursue relations with capitalist nations, especially the United States, despite his talk of an alliance with the Soviet Union in 1940 (see Esherick, 1974). Service concluded from his interviews that Mao believed the United States could play a vital role in the trade and investment that China would need in the post-War period. Mao also felt that these relations would prevent Chinese isolationism (a view Deng Xiaoping later held. See Chapter 7). But what is most startling are the revelations that Service recorded during his interviews with Mao in 1944 and early 1945 at China's revolutionary base camp in Yan'an. In these interviews, it became obvious to Service that Mao had no definite political orientation toward the Soviet Union, that he had worked to make his programme realistically Chinese and that he was seeking the sympathetic approval of the United States. Mao hoped that economic development in the post-war years would rely on a programme of rapid industrialization that was based on capitalism and large-scale foreign assistance. The United States, not the Soviet Union, was seen as the best country to assist with this (Esherick, 1974, pp. 293, 298, 308, 314-15). Mao's views, as recorded on 13 March 1945, confirm this:

> [Mao] then rather mildly observed that America did not yet have a clear view of the issues involved in China, that it did not yet fully understand the Communists, and that although American policy as recently shown in China was still an enigma, he could not believe that it was fixed and unchangeable.... [Mao then points out to Service how he sees America and China cooperating in the future, saying] China's greatest postwar need is economic development. She lacks the capitalistic foundation necessary to carry this out alone.... America and China complement each other economically; they will not compete. China does not have the requirements of a heavy industry of major size. She cannot hope to meet the United States in its highly specialized manufactures. America needs an export market for her heavy industry and these specialized manufactures. She also needs an outlet for capital investment.... America is not only the most suitable country to assist this economic development of China, she is also the only country fully able to participate. (Esherick, 1974, pp. 372–3)[14]

It is easy to see the similarities between Mao's proposal for China's economic development at Yan'an and what Sun Yatsen proposed in

The International Development of China (Chapter 5). Mao did not dispense with such views even after the Communists defeated the Guomindang, and in effect the United States, in 1949. He persisted in the hope of improving ties with the United States '... to the point of the closest friendship' (Mao, 1949, Vol. 4, p. 443). More generally, Mao, like Sun, continued to view trade relations with other countries on the basis of their willingness to do business with China, rather than according to political ideology. As Mao said, 'We want to do business. Quite right, business will be done. We are against no one except the domestic and foreign reactionaries who hinder us from doing business ...' (Mao, 1949, Vol. 4, p. 416) – a remarkable view when one considers the radical and isolationist ideology in which China was immersed during the Cultural Revolution. One can hardly imagine the priorities of business being major determinants in Mao's thinking.

But these views prevailed, and they did so in an environment that remained non-ideological and flexible (Sheng, 1993, p. 135). Mao even went so far as to refer to President Roosevelt as an 'enlightened bourgeoisie'.[15] His reason for describing Roosevelt in this way evinces the importance Mao placed on friendly, non-ideological relations between nations at the time. Mao liked Roosevelt because of what he saw as the American President's cooperation with the Soviet Union's programme of 'domestic democratization', despite the great difference in political outlook between the two countries (Sheng, 1993, p. 150). From this, it can be inferred that Mao might have believed if Roosevelt could hold a conciliatory view toward a nation that supported a rival political ideology, there should be no reason that he would alter such a view when dealing with China.[16] And Mao was determined to maintain this relationship with the United States, even if the US abandoned China during the Sino-Japanese War. This is evident in Mao's statement of early December, 1944: 'If the United States abandons us, we shall be very, very sorry, but [we] will ... accept your help with gratitude any time, now and in the future.' (Sheng, 1993, p. 154)

Sheng contends that such statements from Mao could not always be trusted to be genuine. He suggests that in the pre-1945 years, Mao shifted his views to suit different circumstances (Sheng, 1993, p. 154). To a certain extent, this may be true. But when it came to foreign investment and trade, Mao did not abandon hope that these should continue with America, even once relations between Beijing and Moscow were at their very best. This was evident during Mao's first trade talks with Stalin in Moscow in December, 1949. At the time,

Mao sent a cable back to other Party members in Beijing saying that although trade with the Soviet Union should be seen as important, Chinese modernization also required that the CCP '... get ready to do business with Poland, Czechoslovakia, Germany, Great Britain, Japan, the United States, and other states' (Goncharov, *et al.,* 1993, p. 240). The words 'to get ready to do business' indicate that Mao had not given up on the capitalist nations in his hopes of securing trade and investment from them. Indeed, Mao's attitude at this time does not differ from the thinking behind Deng Xiaoping's economic reforms, which have proved themselves so hugely successful. Recent evidence suggests that it was this attitude that first led to divisions between Stalin and Mao. In a top secret document to Stalin in January, 1950, a Soviet adviser in China reported that Mao's policies on foreign investment and foreign-owned enterprises were no different from those of Sun Yatsen's successor, Chiang Kaishek. The document indicates that Mao and top CCP members were in favour of maintaining all foreign capitalist enterprises, concessions and trading companies under the clauses of the previous agreements of the Guomindang authorities. Mao himself argued, on 9 January 1950, that the CCP would nationalize only those foreign capitalist enterprises that harmed China and would limit themselves to raising taxes on the rest. The document concluded that '[s]uch behavior ... can only be explained by nothing else than pressure on the government of China from the right wing of the national bourgeoisie, which has pro-American inclinations.... (Goncharov, *et al.*, 1993, pp. 247–8).

Not even the tensions that escalated between the United States and China during the Korean War dampened Mao's hopes of better economic relations with the US and the other large capitalist nations. In fact, Mao did not allow a presumably shared ideology with North Korea get in the way of his criticisms of North Korean leader Kim Il-sung's persistent threats to attack South Korea. It seems Mao was more concerned that a US–North Korea military engagement would destroy plans for domestic economic recovery than he was that a North Korean victory would contribute to the worldwide struggle against imperialism (He, 1994, pp. 149–50). In the wake of the Korean War, Mao's desire for better economic relations with capitalist nations matched his earlier views, as noted in a speech that Mao gave in 1956: '... [o]ur door is open. In 12 years, Britain, America, West Germany and Japan will all want to do business with us' (He, 1994, p. 151).[17] Here too, Mao seems to be repeating Sun Yatsen's view as it is found in Sun's *International Development of China*, that

China could provide an 'economic ocean' for the capitalist nations to dump their overproduction (see Chapter 5). It is also noteworthy that Mao makes no reference in the above quotation to the obstacles to trade that may have been posed by differences in political ideology, or that he thinks it relevant to mention the contributions of the capitalist nations to China in conjunction with similar contributions by the Soviet Union or the Eastern Bloc countries, as he did in 1949 (see (Goncharov, *et al.*, 1993, p. 240).

What became a radical posturing might not have been because of deeply held Marxist convictions on Mao's part, but because the United States government would not involve itself in trade relations with a communist country. This was part of the US three principles toward China, which were articulated by US Secretary of State John Foster Dulles in 1958. Dulles stated that 'the United States would not recognize the PRC, would not admit it to the UN and would not lift the trade embargo [against China]' (quoted in He, 1994, p. 152). To this, Mao responded, also in 1958, 'We should take the advantage of the American three principles to lock our door and carry out socialist construction with our own efforts' (He, 1994, p. 152).[18] Relations between the CCP and Dulles may have been strained beyond repair as early as 1954. It was during the Geneva conference of 1954, which temporarily halted the Vietnam war, that Dulles humiliated Zhou Enlai in public by refusing to shake Zhou's proffered hand. Theodore White, an American journalist who had lived in China from 1938 to 1945, described Dulles's actions as '... probably the most expensive display of rudeness of any diplomat anywhere, ever' (White, 1983, p. 164). The trade and recognition that the CCP sought were refused. Mao's 'radicalism' might have been a choice that was forced upon him more than it was a position of his own choosing. In addition to this, though his writings from the period exhibit confidence in an independent socialist strategy, his words with foreign visitors to China at the time belie this confidence. He is reported to have said to a foreign delegation to Beijing in early July of 1959, '... please give us ten years time, and then you can come again to see if we have been correct' (Tan, 1995, p. 40). These words could be taken to suggest that Mao was seeking approval for his new programme as much as he was resigning himself to the fact that there was no alternative programme.

Even the short-lived friendly relations with the Soviet Union are now seen as second best, as far as Mao was concerned (see Xiang, 1995, and Deckers, 1995, p. 222). And, as Goncharov notes, the differences in attitude and aspirations between Mao and Stalin and the Soviet advisers stationed in China during this period also marked the beginning of the end of friendly relations between the two sides (Goncharov, *et al.*, 1993, pp. 110–29). The situation was not helped when the same factors of mutual recognition and trade that China sought with the United States were also withdrawn from China by the Soviet side. In 1959, Moscow unilaterally abrogated the Sino-Soviet Technological Defense Agreement, signed in October, 1957. By 1960, Russia withdrew all its technicians and abrogated every commercial contract with China (Chang, 1984, p. 131).[19] But even the severing of ties with the Soviet Union did not mean that Mao closed China's door to the world completely between the late 1950s and 1976. Comparisons have been made between this phase of Maoism and the theories of the nineteenth-century German economist Friedrich List. Although List did not believe in state ownership to the extent that Mao did, he argued in favour of a pervasive policy of state-led development in which protectionism, investment in infrastructure and a strong emphasis on education were crucial. This, and an internally-based industrialization, which included protection for infant industries that could not survive competition from more efficient foreign rivals, was expected to develop productive powers to the point that a country could open to and compete with other countries on equal footing. But, according to Deckers, Mao went beyond the first stage of the Listian strategy (the autarkic stage) by following a programme of 'selective delinking'. That is, although China adhered to a policy of state-led development and protectionism between 1958 and 1976, it also continued to exchange products and resources with other countries, albeit on a relatively small scale. This too may have been the result of Sun Yatsen's influence on Mao. From this perspective, Deckers suggests that we should not see the post-1976 changes as indicative of Mao's failure, but a sign of Mao's success, because they prepared the way for Deng's 'open-door policy' (Deckers, 1994, pp. 218–24).[20]

6. 5   SUN'S AUTHORITARIANISM IN MAO'S CHINA

Mao's authoritarianism shifted to a more radical orientation, but he never renounced totally certain elements of Sun Yatsen's theories.[21] This was particularly the case with Sun's idea that foreign capital could be used to build Chinese socialism, which Mao enunciated in his interviews with John Service. Although Mao did not acknowledge

Sun directly in this respect and although he referred to Sun less in his writings as the years went on, one is hard-pressed to determine from what other theorist he could have taken the idea. Mao adhered in practice, at least until 1949 (and perhaps well into the 1950s), to the same development strategy that he articulated in his interviews with John Service in 1945. And there is much else that suggests a kind of theoretical accord between Sun and Mao from the time that Mao first took an interest in politics. As early as 1911, at the age of 18, Mao began to read translations of the works of Mill, Montesquieu, Rousseau, Spencer and Kant. Like Sun, Mao rejected these theorists. He also stressed the unacceptability of their ideas several years later, when he said that the Western constitutional systems in countries like Britain, France and the United States were ill-suited to the needs of China (see Mao, 1940, Vol. 2, p. 412, and Spence, 1990, p. 303). These needs, as they were expressed in Mao's first known article, published in the Chinese journal *New Youth* in 1917, recapitulated the views not only of Sun but of Kang Youwei and Liang Qichao as well. According to Mao, China's main priorities at this time were the maintenance of unity and stability, and the prevention of foreign domination. Mao's justification for such views, again like his predecessors, was based entirely on indigenous sources and most notably on his acceptance of Xunzi's pragmatism (see Fairbank and Feuerwerker, 1986, pp. 790–1). Mao also accepted the need for elite government at this time.[22] He felt that a system of elite political authority could play the dual role of being educative and transformative, the same reasons that Kang, Liang and Sun supported a similar system. Marx's ideas did not suit this goal for Mao, as he wrote in 1919, because Marx's strategy 'expected rapid results' to the neglect of long-term goals and it was a strategy that was 'too violent' (Fairbank and Feuerwerker, 1986, pp. 795–7).

Even after the establishment of the CCP in 1921, Mao did not accept what he termed an 'abstract Marxism'. He believed that if Marxist principles were to apply to China at all, they must acquire a nationalist form.[23] In the early years of the CCP, this nationalism bore many similarities to Sun Yatsen's politics. This was evident in 1927, when the Central Committee criticized Mao's strategy for the Autumn Harvest Uprisings[24] because it relied on military force rather than on faith in the strength of the masses. Mao defended himself by referring to the value of Sun's legacy: 'In the past, we criticized Sun Yat-sen for running a purely military movement, and we did just the opposite [by] … concentrating on the mass movement.… We must be aware that political power grows out of the barrel of a gun' (quoted in Fairbank and Feuerwerker, 1986, p. 822).[25] By referring to Sun in this context, Mao also showed that, like Sun, he did not accept Lenin's theory of exploiting mass political discontent as a means to power (see Chapter 5). It was Mao's stand on the Autumn Harvest Uprisings that led to his first split with the Russian Communists in 1927. It was also what would assure his leadership of the CCP when Chinese Party members who first sided with the Russian Communists in 1927 later admitted that Mao was right (White, 1983, p. 257). Marxist classics can hardly be said to be a guiding force for Mao even at a later stage of the Chinese revolution. Marx's *Das Kapital* did not appear in a Chinese translation until the mid-1930s and there is no evidence that Mao ever read it. Mao's secretary, Chen Boda, reported that Mao did not have any opportunity to read Stalin's works until the late 1930s (see Li, 1989, p. 23). But this was the same time that Mao was formulating his theories about 'new democracy', which this chapter has suggested were motivated by Sun Yatsen's 'Three People's Principles' (also see Li, 1989). In the post-1949 years, Mao's personal study in Beijing was said to be notable for its wealth of Chinese classics and the almost complete absence of Marxist classics (and not a single book by Stalin). Mao did not request that this situation be changed. It was done so by others 'for the sake of appearances' (Salisbury, 1992, pp. 8–9, 11, 50).

6.6 CONCLUSION

It would be wrong to reduce all of Maoism to Sun Yatsen's theoretical antecedents. But as this chapter has attempted to illustrate, there is compelling evidence to suggest strong theoretical links between the two men.[26] Once Mao's efforts to apply Sun's principles to post-1949 China were frustrated by American and Soviet resistance to their application, Mao became more ideological. This led to enormous failings and terrible costs to vast numbers of the Chinese population, for which Mao must be criticized.[27] But Mao's belief in the early 1940s that American willingness towards greater trade and openness with China would prevent Chinese isolationism, while at the same time make China more self-reliant (a view later echoed by Deng Xiaoping) (see Deckers, 1994, p. 224), makes one wonder just how different the post-1949 situation would have been, had such a goal been met. When this goal again seemed attainable with the imminence of Nixon's visit to China in the early 1970s, the Marxist–Leninist ideology, to which Mao had seemingly turned, was rendered nonsense once Mao realized that increased trade and investment prospects were at hand, as Kissinger notes in his meeting with Mao in 1971:

> ... Mao reverted to a recurrent theme of my meetings with [Z]hou [Enlai]: 'I think that, generally speaking, people like me sound a lot of big cannons. That is, things like "the whole world should unite and defeat imperialism, revisionism, and all reactionaries, and establish socialism."' Mao, seconded by [Z]hou, laughed uproariously at the proposition that anyone might take seriously a decades-old slogan scrawled on every public poster in China. (Kissinger, 1979, p. 1062)

Kissinger's observation of what was for huge numbers of people in China a lethal contradiction may also help to characterize who Mao was as a revolutionary. Although rarely considered today in the West as anything other than a radical politician, Mao differed little in his early years from China's harbingers of change that have been discussed in previous chapters. But one major difference that separated Mao from Kang Youwei, Liang Qichao and Sun Yatsen was his tremendous success at meeting the goals that they had articulated. As a soldier who was immersed in a revolution of larger scale and greater length than Sun Yatsen had commanded, Mao's task was to recruit, train and organize a huge military not only to wage war over a 20 year period but to prevent the poverty, anarchy and famine that existed in China at the time from ravaging and demoralizing the troops and civilians in the territory that he controlled. Mao did this with tremendous success. By 1944, it was estimated that the areas the CCP controlled in China protected some 90 million people (White, 1983, p. 248), about a quarter of China's population at the time. These areas were orderly, and the people in them well-fed. The success of this strategy, when set against the failure of the Guomindang to prevent famine and anarchy in other parts of China, might have convinced Mao that his victory in the Revolution also was an ideological victory that could be utilized successfully in China's post-war development programme. History has shown how tragically misguided this thinking was. The outcome of Maoist radicalism helps to confirm Sun Yatsen's view that a hastened socialism in an environment of poverty also leads to anarchy (Chapter 5). The next chapter examines Deng Xiaoping's theoretical outlook. It suggests that Deng's 'Four Modernizations' programme is also influenced by Sun's 'Three Principles'.

7 Deng Xiaoping

7. 1   INTRODUCTION

> Although Deng Xiaoping's 'pragmatic, "whatever works" kind of socialism' ... has often been adduced to support the contention that as political leaders go, he is not very 'ideological', it would be a great mistake to infer from this that ideology plays no role at all in the shaping of his policies. The fact is, Deng's reforms are guided by a very potent ideology – we may call it an ideology of 'authoritarian modernization' – and it is precisely this ideology that Deng shares with his non-Communist predecessors. (Cohen, 1988, p. 535)

The nature of Deng Xiaoping's developmental socialism is said to be difficult to pin down (Dittmarr, 1993, pp. 3, 21).[1] Scholarly discussion generally divides itself into two groups. The first group maintains that Deng's politics represents a restoration of rational Maoism, though there is disagreement over which Maoist elements laid the foundation for Deng's policies. One position within this group, especially prominent in the early 1980s, argued that the principal difference between the two men was to be found in the ideological debate between 'redness' and 'expertness' long present in CCP discussions. It said that while neither man questioned the importance of communist ideology, Deng also believed that bolstering Chinese communism required economic growth and that economic growth required the influence of technical expertise, not political ideologues (see Moody, 1984, pp. 34–44, and Womack, 1979, pp. 768–92). Another position relied on a Weberian framework to compare Mao and Deng. It suggested that Deng had all but dispensed with Mao's use of charismatic authority in favour of rational–legal authority and a greater emphasis on socialist legality. However, not all scholars who hold to this line agree that Deng himself has been completely immune to the use of charismatic authority.[2]

The second group defines Deng's politics without depending as strongly on comparisons with Mao. One position within the group distinguishes Deng from Mao by claiming that Deng's politics is based on a power structure of elite–party politics while Mao's was built on mass–line politics. This view is also apparent in works that analyze post-Mao China within a Leninist framework.[3] A second proposition states that all of Dengism can be reduced to Deng's belief in pragmatism, and that the fundamental aim of this pragmatism is positive economic results.[4] Others compare Deng's reforms to the economic strategies of Friedrich List and to the politics of Bismarck as well as to the Burkian advocacy of despotic government.[5] As was indicated in previous chapters, these comparisons also have been made with Sun Yatsen and Mao, and Xunzi and Liang Qichao in the case of the Burkian comparison. Another position, one which reflects a growing field of research, attempts to explain Deng's authoritarianism through comparative analyses with China's pre-revolutionary period. Certain aspects of Deng's Four Modernizations programme have been likened to the Self-strengthening Movement of the 1860s, the Reform Movement of 1898 and the Revolution of 1911. Deng himself has been compared to figures like the Empress Dowager, Yuan Shikai and Chiang Kaishek.[6]

None of these views could be challenged as incorrect. All evidence from 1978 to the present indeed suggests that, when compared to Mao in his later years, Deng does put more faith in expertise, that his politics does rely to a greater degree on rational institutions than on personal power, and that he does favour an elite government that is more pragmatic in its policy making than was the case under Mao. It is also indisputable that Deng's reform programme mirrors similar reform measures that were proclaimed as early as 1861 (the beginning of the Self-strengthening Movement), and which were reiterated by prominent Chinese figures at different times well into the twentieth century. This chapter demonstrates, however, that among the various theories of Deng's forerunners, those found in Sun Yatsen's *Plans for National Reconstruction* (1918), and especially in Sun's *Three People's Principles* (1924), come nearest to describing the development strategy that Deng has followed. The chapter suggests that it is not enough to simply group Deng's policies together with similar policies that were put forward by leading figures from the pre-revolutionary period. Nor is it enough to associate Deng only with Sun Yatsen's 1911 Revolution. It is rather the mature theories of Sun (from 1918 onward), in some cases as they were adapted by Mao Zedong during the new democratic period (see Chapter 6), that have provided much of the inspiration for Deng's post-1978 reforms.

7.2   SUN YATSEN'S INFLUENCE ON DENG'S THEORY

It was noted in Chapter 5 that Sun Yatsen believed that useful knowledge was 'action-oriented' knowledge that had the good of the nation at heart. This represented Sun's challenge to the pre-Confucian philosophical dictum that said 'knowledge is easy and action is difficult'. Sun felt that this dictum posed the gravest threat to his plans for national reconstruction, because it had left the Chinese people passive and incapable of 'knowing' their role in China's development programme:

> This theory is my sworn enemy, a thousand times more powerful than the Manchus ... [it] not only destroys the iron will of my comrades, but it also robs the millions of the Chinese people of their reasoning faculty ... [this] dictum 'Knowledge is Easy and Action is Difficult' ... [is responsible for] the abandon[ment] ... of reconstruction.... I now write this counter-dictum 'Knowledge is Difficult, Action is Easy' ... to prove that my plans [for reconstruction] are far from being a mere mass of words. (see Hu and Lin, 1931, pp. 46–7)

This rationale may also reflect the basis of Deng Xiaoping's development programme. Deng rejects any sort of knowledge in the abstract, or Marxist theory that is unrelated to Chinese conditions. As he said, Marxist theory would only apply to China if it represented 'a guide to action' (Deng, 1987, p. 134). To enforce this line, Deng has stated repeatedly that all work in all fields must 'seek truth from facts' *(shishi qiushi)*.[7] As was true of Sun's 'knowledge-for-action' motto, 'truth from facts' purported psychological mobilization for the objective of national reconstruction: 'Only if we emancipate our minds, seek truth from facts, proceed from reality in everything and integrate theory with practice, can we carry out our socialist modernization programme smoothly....' (Deng, 1984, p. 154). The main goal of modernization for Sun and for Deng was to fend off poverty. This was reflected in Sun's words, which were often reiterated by Deng, that Chinese socialism must take as its basis the main fact that the Chinese nation was impoverished (Chapter 5).

Deng did not acknowledge Sun's influence on his 'truth from facts' motto. Nevertheless, there exist salient parallels between Deng's reasons for introducing the expression and the objectives of his forerunner. Sun made known his 'knowledge-action' argument before publishing his *Plans for National Reconstruction* in 1918 in order that the motto be absorbed by the people as the fundamental basis of national reconstruction (see Hu, and Lin, 1931, pp. 44–5). Similarly, the relationship between 'truth from facts' and rebuilding figures prominently in virtually all Deng's speeches that precede his keynote address in December 1978 that launched China's current economic reform programme.[8] The link between Sun's and Deng's thinking can also be upheld by Deng's assertion that the restoration of 'seeking truth from facts' at the end of the Cultural Revolution was a restoration of the policies from Mao's new democratic period, or the time when Mao's policies seemed to correspond with Sun's theories (see Deng, 1994, pp. 249–50, and Chapter 6).

Both Sun's and Deng's deep concern with a simple, straightforward response to development was undoubtedly influenced by the lack of development and disorderly circumstances that the opposite way of thinking had perpetuated in China. Each man was aware of the stagnation and destruction that an allegiance to abstract cultural and ideological thinking could cause. Each had witnessed the disunity, disorder and warlordism, as well as the humiliation, subjugation, poverty and widespread famine that manifested themselves because of this thinking. Both were convinced that the mobilization of the people's energies for the common goal of prosperity first required a reversal of such thinking. That Deng chose to stress 'truth from facts' for this purpose suggests at the very least his commitment to a theoretical pattern that Sun had established as early as 1918.

7.3 SUN'S INFLUENCE ON DENG'S ECONOMIC REFORMS

It has been suggested that the collapse of communist regimes in Eastern Europe in the 1989–91 period convinced Deng that only material gain could save socialism (Shambaugh, 1993a, p. 410). As true to Deng's policies that this assertion is, it also implies that Deng's outlook was altered only as a result of the cataclysmic changes that took place in the communist world in the early 1990s. It seems more accurate to suggest that Deng accepted since the 1940s the positive connection he saw between material gain and a sustained socialism. Deng's support for Mao's new democratic revolution [1940–56][9] tends to confirm this argument (see Deng, 1994, 284–5, and 1984, p. 277).[10] This section proposes that two factors need to be considered when discussing Deng's economic reforms. One is, as noted, the importance to Deng of economic principles from Mao's new democratic period. The other is Deng's belief in what will be termed 'uneven economic development' for the sake of long-term prosperity. In each case, the driving force behind these factors is seen to be the principles of Sun Yatsen.

As was indicated in Chapter 6, it was during the period of New Democracy that Mao spoke of Sun Yatsen's influence on CCP policy most favourably. It was also at this time that Mao attempted to convince American and Soviet leaders that foreign capital could be used to build an independent Chinese socialism. This too was a goal that coincided with Sun's thinking (see Chapter 5). That it was frustrated during Mao's time and eventually halted by 1958 taught China its gravest lesson, as we infer from Deng's words in 1985: 'Our experience in the 20 years from 1958 to 1978 teaches us that poverty is not socialism, that socialism means eliminating poverty' (Deng, 1987, p. 107). As early as 1978, Deng argued that the CCP's goal of eliminating poverty through improved trade relations and joint ventures with capitalist nations was not a new one, but a revival of what Mao himself would have pursued had he not been stopped by the American embargo in the post-1949 years (Deng, 1984, p. 142). Since, according to Deng, the aim of socialism was to eliminate poverty, he did not believe that the resumption of trade with capitalist nations in the post-Mao years conflicted with basic communist principles. As he said, a communist society is one in which there must be 'vast material wealth.' (Deng, 1987, p. 107)

Deng has stated that China's period of new democracy was the time at which Mao completed his most valuable theories (Deng, 1984, p. 277). In a talk with Mikhail Gorbachev in May, 1989, Deng also claimed that new democracy was not based on Mao's reading of Marx or Lenin (Deng, 1994, pp. 284–5). Considering the profound historical importance of Gorbachev's visit to Beijing in 1989, which effectively normalized relations between the two countries after 30 years of animosity, one is struck by the boldness with which Deng rebuked the theoretical basis that had purportedly united the world's two largest socialist states since 1949. His words are, however, another indication of the relevance of Sun Yatsen's theories to China's present modernization programme. This was evident as early as 1983, when Deng said that the goal of 'socialism with Chinese characteristics' was to contribute to '... national prosperity and the welfare and happiness of the people' (Deng, 1987, p. 13), the precise goals Sun articulated when he said that '... foreign capital [could be used] to build up a future communist society in China ...' (Chapter 5). Like Sun, Deng believed that emancipation from poverty, and not liberty as it is defined in liberal democratic theory, represents true freedom for the Chinese people. More often than any other concern in his speeches through the 1980s and 1990s, Deng stressed the view that socialism meant eliminating poverty and creating wealth.[11]

It was noted in Section 7.3 that Deng had adhered to these views since the 1940s. This can be seen in the 1992 publication of Deng's *Selected Works*, which includes his speeches from 1938 to 1965. Many of Deng's speeches from the new democratic period emphasize the utility of capitalism, the need to develop industry and commerce and a 'flourishing market' and the urgency of distributing food and redistributing wealth. In several instances, the speeches also stress the main objective of meeting the 'people's livelihood' (Deng, 1992, pp. 76, 83, 87, 105, 114), and, in one instance, the importance of developing the economy in accordance with '... the path that Dr Sun Yatsen pointed out to [the Chinese leadership].' (1943) (Deng, 1992, pp. 122–3). Support for the assumption that Deng's reforms are a revival of views put forward in Mao's new democratic period have gained recognition in the 1990s (see Schram, 1993, pp. 410–11, and Su, 1993, p. 11). But these conclusions only go part of the way to explaining the basis of Deng's politics because they ignore fundamental components of Mao's new democracy which were built on Sun Yatsen's influences.

During an interview in 1979, Deng stated that the long-term goal of advancing socialism in China would be best served if the development of productive forces and the creation of wealth progressed unevenly. When pressed that such a view would have profound implications for socialism, particularly because of the inequalities it could produce, Deng responded that so long as the state remained strong, inequalities that were a consequence of reform had greater potential to contribute to a comprehensive Chinese socialism in the future than what he termed the 'ultra-left' policies and excessive egalitarianism of the Cultural Revolution years. He reasoned that because the government was allowing certain advanced areas of the country to take the lead in becoming rich, they would set an example for backward areas to follow. The cumulative effect of wealth would also mean that different regions of the country could begin to take an independent role in, for example, local educational and medical expenses, thereby leaving a greater surplus of wealth for the state to distribute to areas that remained backward. Deng stressed that if this process could ensure an increase in the average earnings of *all* people in China, it would prove that the socialist path the CCP was following was the correct path. He insisted that his proposal was no different from the socialist path Mao had followed in the early 1950s (Deng, 1979, interview).[12] Deng reinforced this stand through the 1980s when he argued that his programme did not represent an abandonment of socialism because the state would prevent excessive gaps in incomes from occurring by redistributing the wealth over the long-term (Deng, 1987, pp. 55, 113, 163). In his speech on the role of strong central authority, given in 1988, Deng repeated this view: 'If the Central Committee and the State Council have no authority, none of this could be done.... [e]ach region would act only in its own interest without any coordination.' (Deng, 1994, p. 272) He also used this reasoning to quell fears that increased investment from abroad would lead to foreign exploitation of Chinese workers:

> At the current stage, foreign-funded enterprises in China are allowed to make some money in accordance with existing laws and policies. But the government levies taxes on those enterprises, workers get wages from them, and we learn technology and managerial skills. In addition, we can get information from them that will help us open more markets. Therefore, *subject to the constraints of China's overall political and economic conditions*, foreign-funded enterprises are useful supplements to the socialist economy, and in the final analysis they are good for socialism. (Deng, 1994, p. 361) (Emphasis added.)

For these reasons, Deng rejects the notion that his development programme will evolve toward capitalism. By emphasizing what he considers to be the two fundamental socialist principles of public ownership and common prosperity, he believes that it is possible to allow some areas to get rich ahead of others, so long as the state remains strong enough to prevent the polarization of wealth.[13] These views correspond with Sun Yatsen's objective of using capitalism, but of also restricting it through socialist principles, so as to enrich all people as equally as possible. They also mirror Sun's rejection of a laissez-faire economy in favour of what he saw as the ability of state capitalism to redistribute wealth (Chapter 5).

7.4 SUN'S INFLUENCE ON DENG'S POLITICAL REFORMS

Deng did not deny that, when compared to economic reforms, reform of the Chinese political structure must be a protracted process, and one which is largely dependent on the successes of economic reforms themselves (Deng, 1987, pp. 173, 196, and 1984, p. 241). As such, his speeches concentrate little on specific alterations to the Chinese political structure. Rather, they reflect a cautious approach, which is imbued with warnings more than it is with solutions. This section examines Deng's perceptions about political reform in China. It suggests that Deng believes what reforms to the political system should and should not include reflect the same measures that Sun Yatsen felt the Chinese political system should adapt and avoid in the 1920s.

Deng's resistance to the introduction of multiparty democracy in China is strongly influenced by the devastating consequences to China that he witnessed during the Cultural Revolution. The effects of mass movements were enough to convince Deng that an active political role for the people could not assist national objectives because mass mobilization for political purposes was unproductive and disruptive (see Gu, 1991, p. 77, and Bonavia, 1989, p. 106). Deng stated this clearly in 1980, when he said 'Historical experience has shown that no ... currently functioning systems were ever reformed or new ones established by substituting a mass movement for solid, systematic measures.' (Deng, 1984, p. 319)[14] Similarly, Deng does not accept that there is a direct connection between multiparty democracy and China's most pressing goal of rapid and efficient development. As Deng sees it, a multiparty system would divert the people's attention from development goals, hamstring the government and provoke anarchy (Deng, 1987, p. 196, and 1984, pp. 252–3). Deng's line did not soften on this issue even as China's phenomenal economic growth and corresponding stability through the 1980s and 1990s drew it further away from the widespread turmoil of the Cultural Revolution that was influencing his views. In fact, the more that pressure for democracy in China mounted from abroad, the more Deng hardened his position. He was particularly eager to convey this to American dignitaries who visited Beijing. During a talk in 1987 with former US President Jimmy Carter, for example, Deng vehemently rejected the adaptation by China of multiparty elections (Deng, 1994, p. 241). He repeated this position, though in even stronger terms, during a talk with the then serving US President George Bush in late February, 1989: 'If we conducted multiparty elections among one billion people, the country would be thrown into the chaos of all-out civil war as during the "cultural revolution" ... Democracy is our goal, but we must keep the country stable.' (Deng, 1994, pp. 277–8). It is for this reason that Deng saw the events of Tiananmen 1989 to be just as threatening to China as the mass movements of the past. Tiananmen would do nothing for 'human rights', according to Deng, but would deprive people of such dignities:

As soon as they seized power, the so-called fighters for democracy would start fighting each other. And if a civil war broke out, with blood flowing like a river, what 'human rights' would there be? If civil war broke out in China, with each faction dominating a region, production declining, transportation disrupted and not millions or tens of millions but hundreds of millions of refugees fleeing the country, it is the Asia-Pacific region, which is at present the most promising in the world, that would be the first to be affected. And that would lead to disaster on a world scale. (Deng, 1994, pp. 347–8)

Deng maintained from the beginning of his leadership that these problems could be avoided so long as China does not alter its present system, which he asserted is most conducive to successful, uninterrupted policy changes: '... when the central leadership makes a decision it is promptly implemented without interference from any other quarters....' (Deng, 1987, p. 192). He also believed that this approach would ensure a democracy of greater substance in the future than was possible under a multiparty system (Deng, 1984, pp. 267, 305). But, as was true for Sun Yatsen, Deng made it clear that a state-centred administration would be ineffective if it were not complemented by an educated elite. Even before he assumed the leadership, Deng said that China's modernization programme would not advance unless the CCP began to rely on the expertise of people from scientific and technical circles (Deng, 1984, pp. 53–4).[15] It seems that his reasons for supporting this claim can also be ascribed to Sun Yatsen's influence, especially Sun's support for a politics governed by an elite political hierarchy. Deng seemed to accept, for example, the basis of Sun's elite hierarchy, that of 'natural inequality', when he said '... we have to recognize that differences in abilities and character of different people ...' (Deng, 1984, p. 122). Deng also seemed to agree with Sun's two tier authoritarian political system based on *quan* ('authority') and *neng* ('ability'), when he says that '... learning is a must when non-professionals [those of *quan*] lead professionals [those of *neng*]' (Deng, 1984, p. 61). Once again, Deng was not expressing these ideas for the first time in the post-Mao years, but as early as 1948, when he said that they were justified by their ability to improve people's livelihood: 'In order to expand production and ... ensure the people's livelihood ... we should ... make great efforts to organize all kinds of specialized departments (engaging the services of industrialists, merchants, technicians and workers) to work out ways of restoring production rapidly' (Deng, 1992, pp. 122–3). Deng also seemed to believe that a political system that uses *quan* and *neng* can solve the problem of over-concentrated power in China: 'it is not good to have an over-concentration of power ... it is not good to have too many people holding two or more posts concurrently.... [This] leads to low efficiency and contributes to bureaucracy.... [Therefore], it is time for us to distinguish between the responsibilities of the Party and those of the government.' (Deng, 1984, p. 303)[16]

Although Deng painted a grimmer scenario than Sun Yatsen did of the consequences for China of a multiparty system, many of Deng's views are identical to Sun's. Sun also believed that in states where democracy had developed, governments had been rendered powerless. Similarly, Deng's support for a technocratic elite seems to be a recapitulation of Sun's support for a hierarchical political structure as the best way of moving society forward. In addition, Deng's views on human rights accord with Sun's condemnation of the Western position on 'natural equality', which Sun termed a 'false equality' because it did not have public welfare at heart. This is matched by Deng's statement in 1984, that 'Egalitarianism will not work' in the early stages of development (Deng, 1987, p. 45). Not only have Deng's views on multiparty democracy proved to be a repetition of Sun Yatsen's thinking, but in some cases Deng's words mirror Sun's verbatim. Like Sun, Deng said that the necessity of centralized political control would prevent China from being 'reduced to a heap of loose sand' (Deng, 1987, p. 165). Any measures to prevent this, and to maintain stability and foster economic development, even if this included the imposition of martial law (as was the case following the Tiananmen crisis of 1989), were justified, according to Deng (Deng, 1994, p. 321).

7.5   DENG'S SOCIALISM AND SUN'S *MINSHENG*

Just as Sun said that revolution would not be complete in China until the 'menace' of poverty was eliminated, Deng said that '... revolution takes place on the basis of the need for material benefit' (Deng, 1984, p. 157). For both men, good leadership should be judged by its abilities to develop productive forces, to provide high material standards, advanced methods of management, technical innovation and good incomes and collective benefits for its people (see Deng, 1987, p. 17, 1984, p. 162, and Chapter 5). Both men also believed that the nation's efforts to develop socialism would mean the development of higher levels of democracy. Deng's words that 'The more socialism develops, the more must democracy develop' (Deng, 1984, p. 176) seem to follow Sun's belief that 'the more the developing nations concentrated on "public welfare", the more equal the people would eventually become' (Chapter 5). Deng defines the nature of this democracy further: 'The constant promotion of democracy is therefore a firm, long-term Party objective. However, while propagating democracy we must strictly distinguish between socialist democracy ... and bourgeois individualist democracy.' (Deng, 1984, p. 184). Individualist democracy would cause socialism to 'retrogress', according to Deng (Deng, 1984, p. 184). On the other hand, he also said that '... ultra-Left socialism ... boils down to poverty' (Deng, 1984, p. 173). These views define the type of socialism Deng wished to see in China. This was to meet two goals: the elimination of poverty and the realization of common prosperity (Deng, 1994, pp. 256, 362, and 1987, pp. 178, 182, 118), or the identical objectives of Sun's *minsheng* principle.

7.6   SUN'S AUTHORITARIANISM IN DENG'S CHINA

Not long after Deng took power in 1978, a renewed academic interest in Sun Yatsen studies got underway in China. It could be asserted with near certainty that Deng himself was responsible for this. In 1980, Deng personally presided over a series of Central Committee meetings whose mandate was to reevaluate CCP Party history. Among the conclusions drawn in the *Resolution* of 27 June 1981 was the description of Sun Yatsen as the CCP's 'great revolutionary forerunner' (see *Major Documents*, 1991, pp. 137–8). This, and the document's prominent references to Sun's concept of 'people's livelihood' (*Major Documents*, 1991, pp. 150, 152) are evidence of the importance Deng must have placed on Sun's influences.

This conclusion would seem less important if it were not for the large number of articles on Sun that have been produced in China during and following the 1980–1 Central Committee meetings (see Zhang, 1983, pp. 78–103, and Zhang, 1980, pp. 525–31). This was the case with academic journals, such as *Economics Research (Jingji Yanjiu)* (see Godley, 1987, p. 119), as well as journals for foreign consumption, such as the *Beijing Review*.[17] Interest in Sun's ideas has also led to the publication of the 11 volume *Complete Works of Sun Yatsen* in 1986 (see Zeng, 1991, pp. 60–1).[18] No work of comparable size has been printed on any other pre-revolutionary Chinese figures.

By the early 1990s, articles on Sun no longer just referred to his important historical role, but also to the relevance of his theories to China's current modernization. The articles speak of the importance of his concept *minsheng* and his independent development path for China. They also suggest that Sun's 'open-door' approach to trade prepared favourable conditions for the growth of China's industry and commerce. One article emphasizes Sun's willingness to accept investment from Japan, even once Japan had asserted its imperialist aggressions on China in 1919. Another argues that Sun's development strategy was so well geared to Chinese circumstances that it is being utilized in China's present modernization programme. Still another argues that Sun's ideas have universal significance. The frequency with which such publications were appearing had been noted in Taiwan, where it was said that research on Sun Yatsen in mainland China had 'increased immensely' in the 1980s.[19] While publications of Sun increased in China through the 1980s and 1990s, the publication in 1980 of the *Collected Essays of Hu Shi*, a Chinese liberal who was prominent in the May Fourth Movement, was met with outrage by Party members (Ruan, 1994, pp. 76–7). No such criticism was directed at the publication of Sun's *Complete Works*. This, and Deng Xiaoping's frequent criticisms over a near 30 year period of Chen Duxiu, another central figure in the May Fourth Movement and a one-time believer in Western democracy, narrows considerably the number of important pre-revolutionary personages from whom Deng may have drawn political inspiration.[20] Considering the continual, and obviously acceptable, number of publications on Sun Yatsen in China through the 1980s and early 1990s, it also adds weight to the argument that Deng's political authority draws affinities with, and perhaps models itself on, Sun Yatsen's principles.[21]

Deng's support in 1980 for Sun Yatsen's positive role in China's revolutionary period, and the surfeit of articles on Sun that followed, may also reaffirm beliefs that Deng held as early as the 1920s. During his work-study programme[22] in France, Deng not only threw his support behind Sun Yatsen's revolutionary government, but condemned the possibility of any other government in China as intolerable.[23] When Deng left Paris for Moscow in 1926, it was to attend the Sun Yatsen University of the Working Chinese.[24] When he returned to China in January, 1927, it was to take up a position as a political instructor at the Sun Yatsen Military Academy in Xi'an (see Goodman, 1994, p. xv, and Franz, 1988, pp. 71–2). Although Deng's political views would have changed and matured in later years, the nature and intensity of these early years could not have been easily etched from his memory. And from the prominence of Sun Yatsen studies in the post-1978 period, it appears that Deng's formative political years may have set the political course he later followed.

7.7 CONCLUSION

Deng said in late 1987 that the impetus behind the current Chinese reform programme was 'never mentioned by Marx' (Deng, 1994, p. 253). This may be one reason why Western interpretations of Deng in the 1990s turned to comparisons between his politics and those of pre-revolutionary figures in China, as was noted in Section 7.1. These comparisons are indeed useful, particularly in the way they confirm the consistency of opinion that Chinese political figures have held during the course of the twentieth century. Both Deng and figures like Kang Youwei and Liang Qichao agreed that the Chinese road to development required gradual, steady and experimental steps (see Deng, 1994, p. 253, and 1987, p. 118, and Chapters 3 and 4). Each shared the conviction that only a strong state-orchestrated political system could ensure the success of this development (Deng, 1994, p. 291). All accepted that sustaining central political authority required a delegation of certain economic and political powers to local levels, and a removal of political interference from the management of enterprise and from entrepreneurial activities (see *Major Documents*, 1991, p. 12).

This chapter has demonstrated, however, that the economic and political patterns that Deng followed were similar to those of Sun Yatsen, or to Sun's policies as Mao adapted them during his New Democratic period. Deng's allegiance to the policies that were put forward during new democracy, his adherence to the importance of 'truth from facts' and his strong support for the idea that foreign capital could be used to serve Chinese socialism all draw him nearer to the theories of Sun Yatsen than to any other political figure. The unimportance of Li Dazhao's theories to post-Mao reforms was mentioned in Chapter 5. This and Deng's (and the CCP's) condemnation of Chen Duxiu and Hu Shi, as noted in this chapter, eliminate two other possible influences on Deng. But even Kang Youwei and Liang Qichao disqualify to a certain extent because they did not articulate, as Sun did, the political ideas that later became so important to Deng: strong nationalism, uneven economic growth for long-term prosperity and capitalism to serve socialism. Deng never threw his full support behind

Sun's 'Three People's Principles' but he hinted that it could be integrated with CCP policy (see Deng, 1987, pp. 65–6, 75–6).

The parallels between Sun Yatsen and Deng Xiaoping also lend support to the argument that contemporary Chinese political authority is strongly influenced by the political patterns that Xunzi established. Chapter 2 touched on the similarities between Xunzi and Deng but because of Deng's theoretical links with Sun, this argument can be strengthened further. Sun's 'knowledge for action' and Deng's 'truth from facts' unites both men with Xunzi's view that ideas and principles which should be discussed are only the ones that have specific goals in mind. For all three men, these goals were the same and were mutually inclusive: an end to disorder, the creation of wealth and the enhancement of people's welfare. This also meant that theory was subject to change if it could serve these ends. Sun urged his followers to use the 'Three People's Principles' '... not as the expression of a fixed and static ideology but rather as an evolutionary and changing set of concepts....' (see Chang and Gordon, 1991, p. 163). And Deng said that any theory that could not be integrated with actual conditions in China was useless (Deng, 1984, p. 131). This, along with Deng's belief that a legitimate state must embody 'vast material wealth', that this required a hierarchical political structure and that greater freedom and greater justice were the outcome of political authoritarianism, can all be traced to Xunzi's philosophical antecedents.

From this it is evident that, like the Confucian scholar–officials who came before them, China's most important revolutionary leaders this century would not change the basic components of political authoritarianism if this compromised the long-term focus of the people's welfare. The main difference between the revolutionaries and Kang Youwei and Liang Qichao rested in Sun Yatsen's idea, which Deng Xiaoping later used to great effect, that there need not be a conflict between a 'national socialism' and encouraging private capital from abroad. Deng saw no alternative to this after Mao's radical period delivered nothing but tragedy to China. The 1960s and 1970s were not the first time that famine ravaged considerable parts of the country, but this period brought home to Deng the consequences of a leadership that ignores the prime concerns of order, wealth and welfare that have defined legitimate authoritarian rule in China for centuries. Part III (Chapters 8 and 9) discusses the implications of this legacy on China's 'new authoritarian' debates in the late 1980s and early 1990s.

Part III:
New Authority and Welfare

8 The 'New Authoritarian' Debates

8.1 INTRODUCTION

> Putting this in historical perspective, it is clear that the debate on the nature of 'modernised values' in China today does hark back to the still unresolved debates of the last century.... That is, can China maintain a social structure based on traditional Chinese norms while adopting Western technology for practical application? (Burton, 1986, p. 273)

The origin, tenor and collapse of the debates on new authoritarianism (NA) in China in the late 1980s have been amply documented and disputed. The debates are said to have been rooted in discussions that began in 1986, to have been initiated in Shanghai, to have been halted because of the central leadership's campaign against 'bourgeois liberalization', to have emerged again because of the failure of reformers to eliminate the dual-track price system, and to have broken down completely during the student demonstrations in 1989.[1] NA's theoretical inception is said to be rooted in Zhao Ziyang's theories[2], in Deng Xiaoping's theories[3], in a combination of Zhao's and Deng's theories,[4] in the theories of Su Shaozhi,[5] and in the views of the so-called 'Princelings' *(Taizidang)*.[6]

This chapter's contribution to the existing surveys of NA[7] is to suggest that the debates should not be seen as an isolated series of meetings that signalled a change in political direction in the late 1980s, or as the exclusive creed of Zhao Ziyang or Deng Xiaoping, but as a continuation of China's unresolved political debates from the past. The chapter extracts and analyzes documented segments from the NA debates whose arguments are based on the advantages and disadvantages to the present period of authoritarian political systems from China's past. The chapter also relies on NA participants' views, which were collected in Beijing and Shanghai during interviews in 1992–3. The next section suggests that the NA debates also may have been influenced by the Chinese 'Cultural Debates' of the mid-1980s. Based on this, the remainder of the chapter examines the arguments of NA supporters and opponents from a historical perspective. It considers NA participants' definitions of NA, their comparisons of these to old authoritarianism (OA) and whether elements of one are essential to the workings of the other. Part Four concentrates on particular features of authority found in Confucianism, which are upheld as adaptable to modern Chinese politics by NA supporters but which are criticized as detrimental to Chinese politics by NA opponents. Subsequent sections follow the same pattern, that of NA supporters introducing and supporting systems of authority from China's past, and of opponents condemning and rejecting them. It should be noted that opinions expressed in the debates are divided into sub-groups. This is done simply to indicate on which issues NA participants showed consistency in their opinions rather than to suggest that there were official sub-groups debating with one another. Apart from those who align themselves with the 'Southern School' of NA, the NA debates ran for too short a period for sub-groups to establish themselves officially.

8.2 CHINA'S 'CONFUCIAN REVIVAL' IN THE 1980s

A Confucian revival spanned 1980s China. Its emergence, contents and political implications were of interest to Chinese academics and politicians alike. Its origins have been traced to a conference on 'Chinese Philosophy' convened in Hangzhou in 1980. Some time after this, in 1984, 'The China Confucius Foundation' was established. It was responsible for organizing large international conferences for specialists in Confucian studies. It gained state support and the frequent attendance of top officials. Li Xiannian, for example, the Chair of the National Committee of the People's Consultative Conference at the time, was on hand at one such gathering in Beijing which commemorated Confucius's 2540th birthday in October 1989 (just months after the Tiananmen crisis). It was at this conference that the leadership's backing for 'The China Confucius Foundation' was made official, as the first line in the prospectus that accompanied the meeting indicates: 'The China Confucius Foundation is a nationwide people-to-people academic body supported by the government' (De Bary, 1995, p. 180).[8] It was also at this conference that Chinese culture was endorsed by China's political officials when Gu Mu[9] spoke of it as the guide to economic and political development:

Culture serves both as the emblem of the level of civilization of a nation or a country and the guidance for its political and economic life. To promote prosperity and peace for a nation and for mankind in general, it is necessary to develop a compatible culture. In this regard, a proper attitude toward the traditional national culture is very important. It is inadvisable either to be complacent about the past or to discard the past and the tradition. The correct attitude is to inherit the essence and discard the dross. The Chinese people are working hard to build socialist modernization and a prosperous and strong socialist country. In order to reach this goal, we must develop and improve our new culture, which, we believe, should be national, patriotic, scientific and democratic. This calls for inheriting and reforming the traditional culture of our nation and parallel efforts to courageously and yet selectively assimilate the advanced cultures of the outside world, merging the two into an integral whole. As for the attitude toward the traditional culture and foreign cultures, there is no doubt that the traditional culture should be kept as the mainstay.... (quoted in De Bary, 1995, pp. 181–2)

The 'national', 'patriotic', 'scientific' and 'democratic' components that Gu defines as the basis of Chinese socialist modernization, as well as his view that prosperity and peace depend on the guidance of culture, are the same elements that were emphasized in the 'Cultural Debates', or 'Cultural Fever' (*Wenhua Re*), in China between 1985 and 1988. The Cultural Debates are now acknowledged to have influenced the NA debates (see Gu and Kelly, 1994, p. 222, and Xiao, 1993, interview One). A brief summary of the Cultural Debates is therefore worth noting.

The Cultural Debates were divided between what became known as the 'Positive School' and the 'Negative School' (see Zi, 1987). The Positive School favoured a modernization process that instilled new contents into the ancient system of cultural hierarchy based on the Confucian *li* ('rite', 'social order'). Members of the Positive School argued that although *li* upholds an authoritarian hierarchy and suppresses individuality, it remains *the* 'core' Confucian value because of its ability to integrate the individual with the state in a way that has maintained Chinese cohesion for over 2000 years.[10] The Negative School opposed attempts to modernize *li*. Members of the Negative School viewed *li* as the basis of absolutism, as a burden on development and as a concept that had come to a historic end. They

believed that *li* had in the past created a system of personal depend-
ence not between subject and ruler but between slave and master. To
end this pattern, the Negative School argued that modernization
should draw on the ideas of the 'New Culture Movement' advocated
by the May Fourth generation of 1919-21, a period known for its
steadfast rejection of Confucianism (Zi, 1987, pp. 444, 448, 450–1,
456).

The similarity between Gu Mu's statement and the contents of the
Cultural Debates also underscores a prominent theme in the NA
debates, that of not whether but in what way the Chinese past can be
used to serve the present. Even more striking are the similarities in
the arguments that encompass the two sets of debates. The Positive
School's emphasis on tradition, on the integration of the individual
with the state and on stability are as much a part of the NA defence
of authority as a disavowal of tradition, of Chinese absolutism and of
the system of dependency these are seen to create, underline its rejection by NA opponents. It was in this environment that the discussions
on NA emerged.[11] If the argument that favours a link between the
Cultural Debates and NA is accepted, it accentuates the consistency
of Chinese intellectuals' opinions on modernization in the 1980s, and
provides compelling evidence for the argument that the debates on
NA were informed by traditional and modern historical periods that
defined Chinese authoritarianism and democracy in the past. The
questions that will be addressed in the sections that follow are how
much of the contents of the Chinese debate on NA is 'new' and to
what extent were they influenced by OA?

8.3 OLD AUTHORITARIANISM AND NEW AUTHORITARIANISM

Virtually every Chinese scholar who participated in the NA debates
makes his case for or against NA by comparing it positively or negatively to elements from OA. One group, which referred to itself as the
'Southern School' of NA supporters, believed that NA's evolution
from OA should be seen as positive. Xiao Gongqin is of the strongest
conviction among members of this group that NA must incorporate
elements from OA.[12] He believes that it is the Chinese traditional
values found in OA that best legitimate the authority of the present
regime because each embraces the central guideline that stability is
the only means to strengthening the nation. The difference between

the two, he suggests, is that while the traditional centralism of Chinese emperors was revered as a fundamental and exemplary model of virtue to be followed for all time, contemporary centralism under NA opposes any doctrine that does not change with the economic and political needs of the nation (Xiao, 1993, interview One, and Xiao and Zhu, 1989, pp. 55–6). Others in the Southern School generally adhere to this line, but with some variations for its justification. There is the justification of historical continuity, which says that present reforms *do* rely for their dynamism on the patriarchal, sage-like wisdom of Deng Xiaoping, rather than on a newer and possibly more rational, form of authority (Lin, 1993, interview).[13] There is the pragmatic justification, which says that leaders attain their power in China because they understand that any new system of authority they introduce is obligated to include elements of OA (Luo, 1993, interview).[14] And finally, there is the politico-cultural justification, which says that OA's influence on NA is the rational outcome of the failings of Marxism–Leninism, particularly when the shared Confucian cultures of the Asian newly industrializing countries (NICs) have proved the worth of traditional values in accelerating economic development (Ren, 1993, interview).[15]

Among those who take the view that inheriting elements of OA is disadvantageous to modernization, some say that the proof for their argument is in the failure of the traditionally-inspired enlightened despotism *(kaiming zhuanzhi)* of the post-1898 reform period.[16] The collapse of *kaiming zhuanzhi* is held as evidence of NA's deficiencies, of its 'retreat' to the past and of its incapacity to redefine itself except along 'autocratic' lines.[17] Criticism is also directed at NA supporters' definition of authority, which is said to leave it indistinguishable from the concept of 'power'. One NA opponent defines 'power' as a situation in which 'subjects are subordinated to objects by forceful means', and 'authority' as a concept in which 'subjects submitted themselves voluntarily to the objects'. He concludes that the appropriate definition for NA is 'power', not 'authority' (Li, 1989, p. 7). Another criticizes the rationale on which NA proponents base their theory of transformative authority. He maintains that there is no social basis in China's history for the argument that strong authority will transform itself from authoritarian to democratic politics. He suggests that the only way this can come about is once rational-legal authority has replaced charismatic authority (Guo, 1989, pp. 207, 209–10).

Others say that NA and OA are not alike, and that it is the difference between the two that makes NA advantageous to modernization. NA's departure from OA is described as a departure from both 'traditionalism' and 'totalitarianism' as well as from the impediments these have had on development (Hua, 1992, interview). NA is also seen by some members of this group to circumscribe new boundaries which prohibit the OA–NA synthesis from recurring in practice. Unlike OA, this group believes that NA will exercise democratic pressures, both in the National People's Congress and in the Chinese People's Political Consultative Conference. It will also emphasize a vigorous market, which will ensure the enhancement of individual liberties that were never possible under traditional centralism. This process will assist NA's main purpose: the dismantling and redistribution of the old system of power into a modern system of rational authority.[18]

A fourth group argues that there is indeed a difference between OA and NA but that NA still remains disadvantageous to modernization. Like the previous group, this group disputes the assumption that Chinese political authority today is derived from OA. But unlike the foregoing argument, this one does not accept as sound the idea that the separation of NA from OA is reason enough to continue supporting NA. Another distinguishing feature here is in definition, which, unlike all other groups' definitions, relies on modern political references and on modern Chinese political figures who represent these. Old authoritarianism is defined synonymously as 'totalitarianism', 'Maoism' and 'irrationalism'; new authoritarianism as 'authoritarianism', 'Dengism' and 'rationalism'. Evidence for this claim is drawn from Deng Xiaoping's talk with martial law officials after 4 June 1989. Deng's words that 'the reform and open door policy should not be changed at all, and the report of the Thirteenth Party Congress [1987] should not change even a word', are seen to stand in conspicuous opposition to Mao's frequent and varied abuse of authority when similar crises had befallen China during his political tenure. That Deng adhered to policies as they were laid down is cited as a key difference between old authoritarians and new authoritarians (Jiang, 1993 interview, Ai, 1989, p. 12).[19]

Although it may be inferred from this a belief in a system of authority that is sustained by NA, this is not the actual conclusion that this group draws. For them, it is democratic principles (defined by one critic as 'Chinese' in substance) (Jiang, 1993, interview) that reduced the concentration of power in China in the post-Mao years, and it is also democracy that will continue to sustain centralized political power and the role that it plays in modernization. Although NA marks an improvement over OA, and though it is considered to be more rational than its forerunner in times of crisis, there is a fear among certain members of the group that NA is not entirely above exploitation by ultra-leftists who may attempt to suppress moves toward democracy (Ai, 1989, p. 12).

8.4 THE DEBATE ON INSTITUTIONALIZED CONFUCIANISM

The most substantial portion of the NA dialogue with the past centres on Confucianism, its benefits, its obstacles and its adaptability to modernization. One group argues that the persistence of Confucian political institutions in China should be viewed positively. Members of this group suggest that the resilience of Confucianism in post-Mao China is based on two factors. One is that the system which Confucianism created, despite opposing philosophies and political ideologies, has not been abandoned, and is therefore familiar and practicable. The second is that the collective mentality that Confucianism advocates provides the best framework for mass industrialization.

The rationale for the first factor relies on historical example, which dates to the ethical standards established in China's Zhou dynasty. Confucian ethics are described as having influenced a system of imperial 'virtuocracy'. But ethics became ritualized to the point that they no longer represented moral instruction but rather a fortification of the emperor's omnipotence. This is argued to have had a powerful influence on Chinese culture and politics, one which may have distorted the purpose of Chinese ethics but which nonetheless remained intransigent to change, and which towered over Western liberalism, Marxism–Leninism and Stalinism as they were introduced and failed in twentieth-century China. It is also viewed as the system to which Chinese people have grown accustomed, and therefore the one that is best able to define the methodology and social designs of the present Chinese modernization (Kong, 1992, interview, and Miao, 1992, interview).[20]

The second factor suggests that a rapid, successful and comprehensive development programme has proved to be the culmination of a modernized Confucianism in regions where it has been applied. The Confucian beliefs in social stability, the need to submit to the organization, confidence in an education for the purposes of developing social conduct and good morals, and the tradition of a civil official system are all deemed to be relevant to successful development models in East Asia. The conclusion is that while individualism may have had its day in the pioneering period of Western industrialization, the 'collectivism' of the latter-day Confucianism may prove itself to be better suited to periods of mass industrialization (Ding, 1990, p. 31).

The rebuttal to the positive view about Confucian institutions sees them as something whose 'unquestionable standards' were built on two related objectives: survival and the institutionalization of a patri-monial state. Therefore, to employ past conventions in the present period would also mean perpetrating the worst abuses of these objectives. One critic in this group says that a concern with survival has engendered the view that to be 'democratic' requires selflessness or 'submerging oneself for others', a view he says was wrongly embraced by the Chinese for thousands of years. Similarly, an emphasis on a patrimonial state, on the notion that the emperor and his bureaucrats protect, clothe and feed the people, has impinged on political reform because it clings to a politics of patriarchal hierarchy rather than one that modernizes and redefines state-society relations. For this reason too, it is considered wrong to equate patrimony with benevolent authoritarianism because whenever a patrimonial state has been extolled as an objective worth defending in China, anything that stands in its way has been condemned as an enemy of the state, and a source of evil (Qin, 1989, pp. 20–2).

Another critic, Rong Jian, challenges two other NA arguments that favour a Confucian role in modernization. He questions the causal relationship that NA proponents say exists between Confucian authority and the successful liberalization of the Chinese economy. He also disputes the NA assumption that the connection between strong authority and the successful growth of individual economies originated in, and can be proved by, the example of feudal Europe. Rong says that European economic liberalization did not depend on a powerful monarchy but on the relative weakening of the monarchy that was a result of the separation between church and state. This, along with the enforcement of the feudal land system and the growing independence of the aristocracy, he says, was influential on the ascendency of the bourgeoisie, the increased independence of cities, the proliferation of commodity production and the emergence of autonomous spheres of politics and economics. In short, European economic power arose because of the decline of monarchical authority, not because of its preponderance, according to Rong (Rong, 1991, pp. 48–50 and 1989, pp. 116–18, 123).[21] He adds that the problematic nature of authoritarianism is even more pronounced in China because church and state have never been separated from the time that the country was unified in 221 BC. Not only had Confucianism remained a state-endorsed philosophy but the Chinese nobility, unlike its European counterparts, continued to show allegiance and obedience to this philosophy, regardless of the autocratic excesses that it represented. This high concentration of state power constrained what Rong believes to be the end product of weakened central authority: the independence and economic dynamism of cities. On this basis, he suggests that the NA proponents' choice of a European example to support their view misrepresents the true basis of economic liberalization, historically, politically and culturally (Rong, 1991, p. 50).

Following the NA argument that Confucianism is 'familiar', 'collective' and best suited to mass industrialization in today's China, Xiao Gongqin goes a step further, arguing that these customs and organizational standards are not based on Confucius's teachings but on Xunzi's teachings. Xiao speaks of Xunzi's concept of *fen* ('status' or 'social role'), which he claims is Chinese antiquity's solution to maintaining social order. He also suggests that *fen* is China's means of cultivating a traditional institutional culture whose dynamics depend on uniting 'homogeneous individualities'. Attempts in China's modern history to implement Western institutional culture have clashed with, and destroyed, Chinese reform measures, according to Xiao, because they have come up against this social structure of homogeneous society.[22] Therefore, current Chinese reforms and what has ensued in their wake, the increased autonomy of the people, the proliferation of private enterprise and a greater awareness of 'individualism', should not be embraced as the dawning of heterogeneous society in China, according to Xiao. Rather, he says that reforms have been generated from within an authoritative administration based on *fen*. For this reason too, he believes that if Western social institutional culture is transferred and accepted to resolve economic and political problems in China, it will result in *anomie* (Xiao, 1992, pp. 13–15).[23] This does not mean that *fen* will block the implementation of democratic institutions in the future. Xiao believes that democracy should be built on the customary and eventually modernized authority of *fen*. This, combined with the successes of a market economy, would gradually permit the idea of 'heterogeneous individualities' to mature in Chinese society.[24]

One of Xiao's critics, Yang Xinyu[25], agrees that Chinese people have always believed that enlightened politics emanated from the wise words of a strong man, and that to change this would be to break a familiar pattern (Yang, 1993, interview). But he questions whether Chinese academics should support old ways when their prevalence in the past was more likely upheld because of fear than because of familiarity. He says that acceptance of such patterns could contribute to the problems that manifested themselves after 1949, when Mao's 'wise' words triggered disaster. For this reason too, Yang disagrees with Xiao that economic reform in China under NA will eventually make people more autonomous, economically and politically. According to Yang, this goal could only be fulfilled under Xiao's scheme if elements of strong man politics were modified in the short-term rather than in the long-term.

A second critic, Hu Shaojun[26], says that instead of placing high expectations on a strong man's ability to rule, they should be placed on the 'authority of the masses' *(minben zhuyi)*. By devolving more authority to the masses, Hu does not mean that there should not be strong centralization at the upper levels but that there should be a more balanced or 'moderate' authority of the type that Mencius described. This would also emphasize educating the people that the attainment of democracy depends more on them than it does on the transformative abilities of a strong man. Hu defines the difference between the authority Xiao Gongqin advocates and the one he supports as one of 'monolithic' versus 'multiple' authority (Hu, 1993, Interview).

8.5   THE LESSONS OF THE LATE QING

Scholars also discussed the authoritarian political models that were proposed by Confucian scholar–officials of the late Qing. Many agreed that important political precedents were set as a result of the failure of late Qing reforms. Some NA supporters claimed that the reason for this failure was the haste with which reformers' theories were embraced and implemented (Dai, 1989, pp. 87–8; Luo, 1993, interview). For example, Kang Youwei's 1898 reforms are considered innovative and relevant to current modernization. Their failure to provide lasting benefits is blamed on the way they were executed by the Emperor Guangxu, who was impatient to see the fruits of Kang's reforms in practice. The journalist Dai Qing[27], for instance, suggests that had Guangxu waited to push reforms ahead until after he had built up a cooperative power base that included the 'Self-strengtheners' and the military, the reforms may have been successful (Dai, 1989, pp. 87–8). Wu Jiaxiang argues more emphatically that the desire to dispatch reforms quickly in the late Qing '… plunged China into a protracted stage of chaos where there was no clear idea of authority….' (Wu, 1989c, p. 51). The historical lesson is clear for Wu: haste is to be avoided and gradualism to be enforced. Wu also believes that the downfall of Qing reforms proves that authoritarianism must not be based on a fixed political theory, but on an organic process from OA to NA to liberal democracy, which develops in accordance with political and economic circumstances. This is corroborated by another NA supporter, who says that the tendency after 1898 to push aside the old, simply because it was Chinese, and to grasp hold of the new, solely because it was Western, led to a prolonged stage of instability that lasted until the early 1920s. The brief appearance of a parliament following China's 1911 Revolution and the rejection of Confucianism during the May Fourth period (1919–21) are cited in particular as events that exasperated this instability (Wu and Zhang, 1989, p. 10, and Chen *et. al*, 1989, pp. 55–6).[28]

Xiao Gongqin also includes his view that elements of Xunzi's philosophy have a modern application in the debate about the Qing reforms. Xiao's purpose is to point out that against Western scholars' perceptions, no major political figure from the late Qing was a democrat. He directs his attack at Benjamin Schwartz's analysis of Yan Fu. Xiao claims that Yan was not a liberal, as Schwartz suggests[29], but an authoritarian, or more accurately a 'new conservative'.[30] Nothing confirms this more clearly for Xiao than what he terms Yan Fu's quintessential statement about strong man politics, that, in order for reform to succeed, China needed a 'Napoleon' not a 'Washington'. This, and Xiao's survey of Yan's *Collected Works*, lead him to conclude that Yan's ideas draw much nearer to Edmund Burke's conservatism than they do to John Stuart Mill's liberalism. Xiao concedes that there were equivocations in Yan's conservatism. But he says this was common among Chinese scholars of the day because of the pace and magnitude of historical events that confronted and often contradicted any theoretical certainty. In Yan's case, this amounted to a rejection of China's authoritarian traditions after Japan's victory in the Sino-Japanese war of 1895. Not long after this, though, Yan aligned his views with Liang Qichao's shift from liberalism to enlightened despotism, according to Xiao. Xiao concludes that a low economic base, low levels of education and a mass population that had no understanding of liberal democracy steered both men toward the belief that political strength must remain with an enlightened monarchy in China. Yan adhered to this view more tenaciously after the 1911 Revolution, when it became clear to him that steps toward constitutional democracy were failing (Xiao, 1993, interview One).

Xiao also claims that the views of Yan and Liang were adopted by Yuan Shikai, whom Xiao sees as China's first modern strong man, during his short period as president of the republic (1912–16). That Yuan's presidency was short-lived is not ample proof for the deficiencies of strong man politics at the time, or in the present, according to Xiao. He says that the desire for strong authority by some in the China of the early 1900s was displaced by those who defended democracy, and that the views of the democrats amassed so much blind support that they could not help but gain the high ground over any other political theory at the time. But Xiao says that it has become patently clear that this was not the correct response to the political uncertainties of the day, and that any criticisms of Yuan Shikai's dictatorial ways must be set against the disintegration and rampant warlordism that followed his death in 1916 (Xiao, 1993, interview One, and Gu and Kelly, 1994, p. 222).[31] In another article, Xiao argues that the same disorderly circumstances occurred when a Western-style parliamentary democracy was introduced in China at the beginning of the republican period. They were bound to, he argues, because parliamentary democracy was a product of the historical, social and economic evolution of Western societies that was completely foreign to China (Xiao, 1993, p. 86).

Xiao's critics do not deny the existence of a conceptual thread between ancient and modern Chinese authoritarianism. Nor do they dispute his assertion that contemporary NA has its antecedent in Liang Qichao's enlightened despotism. What they object to is Xiao's certainty that strong political centralization is inherently capable of attaining goals that benefit the entire nation, especially when modern Chinese history has proved otherwise. Jiang Yihua argues, for example, that in each regime that has been established on an authoritarian basis in the post-Qing years, the very ends toward which authority was justified – stability, order and efficiency – were distorted or completely destroyed. Yuan Shikai's monarchical revival led to warlordism, Chiang Kaishek's autocracy led to civil war and Mao Zedong's totalitarianism led to the Cultural Revolution. Further to this, Jiang sees as flawed Xiao's argument that the 1895 war returned scholars to the belief that strong man politics was the only way to shore up economic growth. Jiang claims that it was not because of a strong man but the May Fourth Movement that the post-war period led to what he describes as an economic boom and the emergence of a middle class. He adds that this period also nurtured a democratic conscience and a better perception of what it meant to be a citizen in China, but that this was quelled by successive Chinese autocrats in the decades that followed May Fourth (Jiang, 1993, interview). For Jiang, and other democrats, the argument that favours strong authority has been tarnished without exception from the late Qing onward. For this reason also, the problems of the post-Qing years provide further evidence for them that reforms in the present must be prompted by democracy not authority (Hu, 1989, p. 32, and Fan, 1989, p. 5).[32]

8.6   THE DEBATE ON SUN YATSEN'S AUTHORITARIAN POLITICS

Sun Yatsen's doctrines have had considerable influence on the NA debates.[33] Sun's refusal to ally himself with the Manchu regime at the beginning of the twentieth century, his introduction of independent and patriotic political views, which have proved themselves successful in Taiwan, and his moderate political outlook (described by one scholar as a compromise between the excesses of Stalinism and Western capitalism) (Yin, 1993, interview)[34] give his beliefs and personality a far-reaching appeal (Luo, 1993, interview, and Dong, 1993, interview Two).[35] Added to this – the greatest boost to Sun's status – is Yin Xuyi's argument that the problems which have descended on China the past several decades are due to the fact that the 1911 Revolution was left unfinished and that Sun died too early. The CCP's opposition to the full fruition of Sun's 'Three People's Principles' was a tragedy, according to Yin, because Sun's hopes for land reform and the regulation of capital had the potential to begin building the Chinese economy and reforming Chinese politics at a much earlier stage in the twentieth century (Yin, 1993, interview).

Yang Baikui[36] also advocates Sun Yatsen's political theories. In particular, Yang upholds as worthy of emulation by all developing countries Sun's 'Three Stages of Government' (military, tutelary, constitutional). He also believes that what Sun proposed in the 'Three Stages' does, in fact, mirror the development patterns that Western nations have followed in the past (Yang, 1989, p. 92). Britain and France are cited as proof for this claim. Yang argues that from the mid-seventeenth century until the end of the Glorious Revolution, and particularly during Cromwell's era, a military dictatorship reigned in Britain and pushed British society forward. Tutelary government followed, with executive and judicial powers remaining in the hands of the monarch and the nobility, which, according to Yang's argument, guided and established the democratic constitutional system that exists in Britain today. But this did not grant the franchise to all people. Even in 1882 the number of the enfranchised in Britain, by Yang's estimation, was only five per cent of the total adult population. Yang claims that similar political boundaries defined post-revolutionary France. He says that constitutional government did not appear in France until the last two decades of the nineteenth century, following almost a century of military and tutelary government under the Napoleonic imperialist system and the restored Bourbon monarchy (Yang, 1989, p. 92).

Sun's equation also applies to the Japanese and German patterns of development, according to Yang, as it does to the successful patterns of development in post-war Asia, Africa and Latin America. In fact, Yang concludes that without following the sort of blueprint Sun put forward, countries that are attempting to transform themselves from traditional to modern societies are bound to fail, and that this is especially true if they introduce constitutionalism prematurely. Yang lists Brazil, Chile and the Asian Dragons as post-war success stories, which employed models comparable to Sun's strategy, and which experienced extremely rapid economic growth. Yang attributes this outcome to a common understanding that there is a connection between successful indices of economic development and the ascendency or termination of compatible stages of government. But more than just the hard evidence of economic successes and failures, he claims that political theory generally agrees with the institutional and social bases of development as Sun has described them (Yang, 1989, pp. 93, 95, 101).

Huang Wansheng criticizes Sun's belief that democracy must be an *a priori* process (Huang, 1989, p. 79). Qin Xiaoying agrees with Huang, saying that tutelary government, combined with Sun's 'loose-grains-of-sand' argument (Chapter 5), encourages autocratic politics. To comply with Sun's rejection of basic liberties, to accept that China's 'loose grains of sand' must be cemented together for a common purpose, only serves to return China to the Confucian ideal of 'submerging oneself' for the common good, according to Qin. He admits that this attitude has gained currency in successive Chinese administrations, but he says that it has done so in a cynical manner, which leaves the people acquiescent to a government that remains untouched. The basic freedoms and inviolable rights of the individual, normally protected by law in democratic regimes, would be ground-less, and could collapse under the inevitable impulses of the arbitrary authority that Qin believes Sun's tutelary government and criticism of liberty would perpetrate. Qin's solution is a combination of 'state democracy', which '... takes effective control over the power of the state', and 'non-state democracy', which accounts for '... the legal definitions and parameters of the personal freedoms of all members of society' (Qin, 1989, pp. 20–2).

Qin also challenges Sun's argument that the 'Three Principles' are inherently capable of transforming themselves as economic and polit-ical conditions demand. He mainly criticizes Sun's followers, whom he believes made posthumous use of Sun's prestige to further their own support for an autocratic state. At least part of this prestige was built on their belief that there existed an 'unbroken line of orthodoxy' between Confucianism and Sun Yatsen's theories. Qin thinks this belief sufficiently vague to alter and distort Sun's original intentions. In the early post-Sun years, this was what happened, according to Qin, as Sun's principles became more oppressive, and the prospect of popular participation under the GMD was hurled into an even more uncertain and distant future. For Qin the 'Three People's Principles' became a 'One Person Principle', and this underscores the weak-nesses of any transitional theory whose basis, justification and thrust rely on authoritarian prerequisites (Qin, 1989, pp. 22–3).

8.7   THE DEBATE ON MAO ZEDONG'S AUTHORITARIAN POLITICS

The NA debate on Maoist authoritarian politics considered one major question: whether Mao's period of New Democracy (ND) depicted him as a 'democrat' or an 'authoritarian'. Proving one or the other hypothesis would obviously add weight to either side's argu-ment. Yet there are fewer in the way of agreed conclusions in each group than there is an overall consensus that ND's early demise had unfortunate consequences for China.

Xiao Gongqin, Yin Xuyi and Luo Rongqu agree that Mao's New Democracy represents the last time that a system similar to NA was introduced in China. They believe that, like NA, ND defended strong authority, that it depended on the vitality and successes of capitalism to legitimate this authority and that it was not a political end in itself but a means to this end. However each scholar diverges in his specific reasoning for and placing of the decline of ND. Yin points to a hastened drive toward socialism, a heightened ideological posturing and the collapse of the Lenin-inspired New Economic Policy in the post-1949 years (Yin, 1993, interview). Xiao underlines the conflict at the Eighth Party Congress in 1956 between Liu Shaoqi 'red capitalism' and Mao's rejection of policies that did not encompass 'class struggle' as their primary objective (Xiao, 1993, interview Two). Luo's evaluation uniquely places the breakdown of ND in the pre-1949 period, in 1945, and suggests its expiration was provoked exogenously.

He also adds a third component to his argument, one of definition, which identifies ND with 'Maoist realism' and 'Confucianised Marxism'. Luo suggests that Mao combined the best of Confucianism, Marxism and capitalism into the realistic development model that was at the heart of ND.[37] As proof of this, he points to the period between 1935 and 1945, which he says showed Mao's willingness to cooperate with, be advised by and invite investment from the United States on the condition that the US recognized a CCP–GMD coalition (Luo, 1993, interview). The continued loyalty of the US to the GMD signalled the death knell of ND, according to Luo, as Mao became increasingly embittered and more determined to follow an autarkic course of development (see Chapter 6). This conclusion is given added weight by a fourth supporter in the group, who says that what ND represented, and what its termination halted, the contract responsibility system in the countryside, the system of stockholding enterprises, a defined system of property rights and a freer economy, did not appear again until after Mao's death (Dai, 1989, pp. 88–9).

Qin Xiaoying argues that Mao's New Democracy was based on democratic principles, that initially ND represented Mao's sincere wish to 'break with thousands of years of Chinese feudalism', but that the 'pull' of tradition caused him to fall back into the patterns of previous Chinese autocrats (Qin, 1989, pp. 18–19). Yu Haocheng argues that the relation between ND and Maoist democracy can be viewed in Mao's essays, *On New Democracy* and *On Coalition Government*, written during the new democratic period. He says that the essays clearly illustrate Mao's adherence to the view that development required a democratic basis. This is reinforced, for Yu, in Mao's 1957 essay *On the Correct Handling of Contradictions among the People*, in which Mao said, 'This thing we call democracy; sometimes it appears to be a goal, but in reality it is ... a means [to socialism].... That is, in the final analysis, it serves the economic base; the same is true of freedom' (Yu, 1989, pp. 52–3). On this basis, Yu argues that if comparisons are to be made between ND and the present period, it is best to root them in ND's democratic imperatives. After all, he adds, China's Twelfth and Thirteenth Party Congresses (1982, 1987) spoke not of an authoritarian but of a 'democratic socialist political system'. He concludes that this is one further reason to consider as faulty arguments that seek parallels between NA and ND (Yu, 1989, pp. 53–4).

8.8 CONCLUSION

Both ancient and modern Chinese political discourse influenced the NA debates. This is evident in the connections that were drawn by NA scholars and Western commentators between the Cultural Debates and the NA debates. The divisions in the Cultural debates between members of the Positive School, which upheld the value of the traditional concept *li* to Chinese modernization, and members of the Negative School, which opposed attempts to modernize *li* because they believed it a burden on development, is evidence of *li's* continued influence on mainland China's political discussions. NA proponents supported the preservation of authoritarian elements from the past for five main reasons:

1. that these elements provided the central guideline for the idea that stability is the only means to strengthening the nation;
2. that they were familiar to the Chinese people and therefore practicable;
3. that they provided the best framework for mass industrialization;
4. that they have proved themselves intransigent to outside political influences in the twentieth century such as Western liberalism, Marxism-Leninism and Stalinism;
5. that the traditional elements in NA were best suited to the transition from authoritarianism to democracy.

With the exception of Xiao Gongqin, none of the NA proponents spoke of Xunzi's influence on traditional political authority in China, and Xiao referred not to Xunzi's use of *li* but of *fen*.[38] But if a connection exists between the Cultural Debate's 'Positive School', which supported *li* as the core Confucian value, and NA supporters' defence of a Chinese political authority that is influenced by traditional and post-Qing antecedents, then, as Chapter 3 to Chapter 7 demonstrated, much of this seemed to reflect patterns of authority that Xunzi had introduced.

NA opponents rejected the preservation of authoritarian elements from the past for two main reasons: (1) that there is no guarantee that NA would depart from the old hierarchical system that was defined by OA; (2) that events in the twentieth century, such as the failure of late Qing reforms, of republicanism and of Maoism in the 1960s and early 70s, prove that NA is unable to redefine state-society relations except along autocratic lines. Yet the democracy that NA opponents describe also seems to be influenced by past Chinese systems of authority. Jiang Yihua's democracy is 'Chinese' in substance and is to 'continue to sustain centralized political power and the role that it plays in modernization'. Qin Xiaoying speaks of a democratization that includes a role for 'state democracy'. Hu Shaujun does not wish to replace authoritarianism with democracy but to transform 'monolithic authority' to 'multiple authority'. This does not suggest that the democrats were themselves authoritarians. But it does indicate a greater similarity in the view on political authority between opposing sides in the NA debates than previous analyses of the debates suggest. The next chapter will investigate whether the Tiananmen crisis inspired a greater demand for democracy among NA debaters in the post-Tiananmen period.

9 The Impact of Tiananmen

9.1 INTRODUCTION

'It's peculiar,' said a young lecturer in philosophy, discussing the means and ends of reform. 'It's like looking through a glass wall. We can see where we want to go, but know we can't go straight there without triggering disaster. If we try to go straight to democracy and a market economy, there will be chaos, and from chaos will certainly grow authoritarianism – not the new kind, but the *old*, feudal authoritarianism. Feudal authoritarianism is what sprouted from the chaos of the Cultural Revolution, and it happened in countless large and small localities all across China. It is what grows naturally in China, and it will sprout again if chaos reigns again.' (quoted in Link, 1992, p. 286)

This chapter concludes Part Three of the book. It analyzes the political arguments of the NA debates following the Tiananmen crisis of 1989. The next section first summarizes the political arguments of the three groups involved in the debates of 1988–9: NA supporters, elite democrats and democrats. It suggests that the debaters of all distinctions were not so concerned about whether democracy or a new form of authoritarianism should replace CCP rule, but whether the CCP should exercise greater use of the Chinese legal system to sustain its authority. Section 9.3 surveys the post-Tiananmen debates. It indicates that events during the Tiananmen crisis may not have altered significantly the intellectual stand of democrats and authoritarians who contributed to the pre-Tiananmen debates. It also shows that in some cases there was greater acceptance of strong authority if it could continue to assist economic growth and prevent disorder. Section 9.4 examines Tiananmen's impact on the Chinese people. It attempts to determine whether they held views that were similar to those of democrats or authoritarians in the NA debates. Under the assumption that a political system approximating NA may be at work in contemporary China, the chapter concludes by demonstrating how the NA proponents' theory of 'transitional authoritarianism' is working in practice.

9.2   THE FIRST PHASE OF THE DEBATES, 1988–9

The New Authoritarians' Argument

NA supporters in the pre-Tiananmen period argued that a strong modernization-oriented leadership is the best way to deal with the plethora of complex political and economic problems of reform. They also claimed that strong authority is the only way of safeguarding the overthrow of the CCP in a world where democracy is so urgently demanded.[1] They believed that state-orchestrated reforms provide the best foundation for rapid democratization because such reforms enable the leadership to guide to maximum economic effect the development of a market economy (Xiu, 1990, p. 38). They said that these goals are best met not by the existing political structure but by a political elite which is advised by a technocratic elite. Although such a regime would remain relatively centralized for some years to come, NA supporters also accepted the necessity of the gradual devolution of powers to regional and local levels of government if this proved conducive to the market's vitality and efficiency. If it proved otherwise, they said that devolution must be curbed, or in some cases halted.[2] The goal of devolved economic powers is to reduce the state's role in the management of economic affairs, especially as private ownership and the affirmation of property ownership rights increased. Economically, NA supporters maintained that the expanding market would rationalize the economy. Politically, they said that NA would determine the degree to which economic and political spheres could be separated in the future.[3]

New Authoritarians did not exclude elements of democracy from their theory. They argued that the market itself provides democratic freedoms because increased property ownership rights and the encouragement of individual entrepreneurs gives greater scope to personal decision-making. As people become more independent, the NA argument followed, government bureaucracies would be made more rational through a legal system that develops in response to people's economic needs. NA proponents argued that the legal system's responsiveness to the demands of a growing middle class will determine the government's legitimacy, and ultimately its existence.[4] They defined this process as 'stable democracy' or 'moderate democracy' (Wu and Zhang, 1989, pp. 7–15). They also described it as a political system of 'hard government, soft economy' (Chen *et. al*, 1989, pp. 47–8),[5] 'semi-authoritarianism' (Zhang, 1989, pp. 13–14) and as a balance between the 'extremes of parliamentary democracy and totalitarianism' (Xiao and Zhu, 1989, pp. 56–7, and Waterman, 1990, p. 16). They believed that as the market guides development toward a greater pluralization of society's economic interests, political legitimacy would eventually rely on a system of voting by the populace, on the possibility of two or more political parties and on an enhanced role for the constitution. They also believed that the success of the market on its own would create the necessary legislation to protect the new citizenry (Wu, 1989c, pp. 48–9).[6]

NA supporters did not consider NA to be the best form of governance, but a 'necessary evil' at the beginning of development. NA was also thought to be the best way to accommodate new horizontal and vertical divisions of power when they occur, and to avert crises in the process (Xiao and Zhu, 1989b, p. 58, and Xiao, 1993, interview One). Ma has noted that NA descriptions of political authoritarianism seemed more concerned with a political system that was 'rational' and 'orderly' than with what would be described as 'authoritarianism' in a Western political sense (Ma, 1990, p. 8).

The Elite Democrats' Arguments

Elite democrats did not neglect the important role of strong leadership in the process of modernization, but believed that the authority of institutions should play a more important role.[7] They also disputed the NA view that democratic institutions naturally evolve out of successful economic development. They claimed that there exists no direct connection between the two, and still less between economic growth and the prevention of arbitrary authority (Gao, 1989, p. 1). Elite democrats suggested that NA proponents' support for the combination of strong leadership and a vigorous market be supplemented with a legal system which they felt could alleviate the hazards of random authority. They believed that this would speed up the reform process once administrative and ideological control was subordinated to the constitution and the law. This would also assure the nation that its new-found economic and political privileges were not relinquished overnight. In addition, elite democrats endorsed a system of greater openness between government and society, one which made the leadership more accountable by gradually extending to the people the opportunity to participate in politics (Yue and Zheng, 1989, pp. 200–2).[8] Unlike NA, which elite democrats said remains closed to society in practice, elite democracy proposed the development of an open mechanism of mobility and circulation that draws its talent from those in society deemed worthy of contributing to the development process.

Elite democrats also supported the restructuring of the National People's Congress (NPC). They suggested that more extensive powers be granted to local congresses, to the People's Political Consultative Conference and to an independent judiciary (Waterman, 1990, p. 22). They argued that government would then be placed more effectively under the supervision of the people than if NA methods were employed. But 'people' is specifically defined here, and by no means includes the entire populace. Those designated to play a supervisory function would be recruited from 'intellectual', 'technocratic' and 'entrepreneurial' circles only (Huang, 1989, p. 91). Therefore, insofar as elite democrats wished to make government more accountable to the people than NA supporters had intended, the openness that they described was in itself limited to specific sectors of society. Further to this, while NA supporters did not support 'openness' to the degree that elite democrats did, they also did not oppose the idea that the ranks of government should in time be filled by the sectors that elite democrats identified.

In some cases, elite democrats were willing to accept even stronger state authority than their counterparts – even a military dictatorship, if it were capable of stabilizing politics and social order. But they said that this would only be acceptable if a military dictatorship also functioned according to legal restrictions that were placed on it. Some elite democrats believed that the combination of a military regime and a comprehensive legal system would be capable of pushing development ahead faster than strong political authority on its own (Cao, 1991, pp. 24, 27, 30–1).[9] They suggested that stronger authority can survive, and can be prevented from returning to autocracy, so long as it works within the parameters of a legal system that preserves a degree of openness with society. However, this openness is not only limited, as has been suggested, but resistant to challenges from the general public. Elite democrats said that a technocratic elite was not to be challenged by the general public until economic and political developments were able to sustain a system of checks and balances in the future (Chen, 1989, p. 3).

The Democrats' Argument

The democrats' views during this phase of the debate may be best summarized by Huang Wansheng, who said that 'Democracy does not reject or exclude authority; authority can be generated on the foundations of democracy just as well. What democracy does reject is despotic authority.' (Huang, 1989, pp. 148–9). Almost without exception, those who referred to themselves as 'democrats' in 1988–9 could as easily be termed 'moderate authoritarians' or 'elite democrats'. Like the elite democrats, democrats were critical of the continuation of 'personal rule' *(ren zhi)*, or 'enlightened rule' *(kaiming zhuanzhi)* (Wang, 1989, pp. 189–90). Democrats also favoured a political system that functioned on a legal basis, and which was more open to society. When democrats spoke of 'democratic freedoms', they did not generally refer to the political freedoms of the individual but to a system that allows the state greater flexibility to deal with the shifting roles of different power structures. When democratic freedoms were discussed in relation to the 'individual', their reference was not usually political but economic. It referred to the ways in which such freedoms could unharness the potential of the individual to contribute to the expansion of the market (Qin, 1991, pp. 24, 26–8).

The difference between democrats and elite democrats was in the extent to which the former wished not only to reform but to strengthen the NPC's role. Members from both groups expected NPC representatives to be more accountable to the people. Both believed that this was best achieved through a nomination system in which NPC representatives are directly elected. This differs from the current system in which representatives are effectively pre-selected by the Party. Where democrats differed from elite democrats was in their desire to strengthen the financial power of the NPC by, for example, placing the State Statistical Bureau and Auditing Administration, now under the State Council, under the leadership of the NPC's Standing Committee. In addition to this, democrats spoke of the need for an appeals and control system, monthly meetings of the Standing Committee, increased lobbying and the publication of an NPC newspaper, which would provide daily accounts of NPC activities. Waterman terms this approach an NPC-centred democratization, which would include a gradual modification of the constitution and the future possibility of replacing the government through the legislature (Waterman, 1990, pp. 24–5).

Not all democrats accepted democratic reforms along these lines. But those democrats who wished to go beyond the generally accepted top-down strategy that combined legality with openness and a revitalized NPC, did so in a way that seemed to contradict itself. For example, the 'societal pressurists', a sub-group of the democrats, spoke both of the need for an autonomous struggle for democracy among the people that would remain uninfluenced by the struggle within the Party, and at the same time a higher level of dialogue between the government, the students and the people. Another contradiction was that while the societal pressurists spoke of a grass-roots struggle, they did not intend it to topple the government; they did not even oppose the CCP. Moreover, they believed that only the CCP was capable of leading China. Their intention appeared to be to criticize the Chinese leadership, but without offering alternatives that had not been suggested by the democrats themselves. In the end, the societal pressurists were considered to have an idealized and over-simplified view of democracy (Waterman, 1990, pp. 27–31).[10]

Summary of the First Phase of the Debates

The NA debates in 1988–9 did not expose huge differences of opinion between authoritarians, elite democrats and democrats. Rather, the debates seemed more concerned with the potential for varying degrees of authority to govern China at different institutional levels. The debates also illuminated many points of agreement among the three groups. Each group, even the democrats, wished for an incremental approach to democracy that would be built on the principle of harmonious relations between government and people (He, 1991, pp. 25–6). Each believed in the guiding role that a strong state would play in both economic and political reform. Each treated as essential a coalition between a political and intellectual, and in some cases entrepreneurial, elite. All three groups were concerned about the leadership's ability to build consensus, to direct economic and political reforms in a sound manner and to improve people's standard of living.

Where NA supporters differed from the elite democrats and democrats was in their belief that the combination of strong leadership and the success of the market would on its own determine the division and redistribution of authority as development proceeded (best described in Zhang Bingjiu's 'semi-authoritarian' and 'division-of-power' models) (Zhang, 1989, pp. 13–18). The democrats of both distinctions, on the other hand, seemed to believe that a divided and redistributed authority that was channelled through an improved legal system and a more efficient NPC would assist the expansion of the market and improve the regime's legitimacy. But they did not support the idea that democratic participation could extend to every sector of society, or that it should include wide-ranging political freedoms. The main difference between the three groups was in the pace of restructuring. In this respect, the NA supporters followed the most incremental strategy and the democrats the least. One scholar who participated in the debates said that they were not so much a question for him of conservative versus radical views, but of a political outlook that came between the two, one which combined strong authority with top-to-bottom reforms, and which included 'certain democratic elements' (Hao, 1993, correspondence). Some democrats even conceded that NA objectives were more pragmatic than their own because they require less in the way of major reforms (Wang, 1991, p. 65). Others said that they were less concerned about defining appropriate conditions for democracy than they were about adapting a political system that would prevent such calamities as the Cultural Revolution occurring again (Waterman, 1990, p. 24).

9.3 THE POST-TIANANMEN DEBATES

A little documented fact is that the NA debates continued outside of China after the Tiananmen crisis of 1989. These debates took place in Britain, the United States and Canada between 1990 and 1992. They included mainland Chinese scholars who were studying in the West at the time, as well as Western scholars who were invited to take part. This section attempts to determine how the events surrounding Tiananmen affected the views of participants in the debates of the early 1990s.

The Democrats' Argument

As one might expect in the post-Tiananmen period, NA opponents prefaced their solutions to the Chinese situation with the words 'freedom', 'democracy' and 'rights'. But, in almost every case, they did not propose changes to Chinese politics that reflected Western institutional manifestations of these words. In addition, criticisms were not always directed at authoritarianism, but at the likelihood that centralized authority would be less capable of dealing with social or economic disorder than a redistributed authority (Rong, 1991, pp. 57–64). Eastern Europe was hailed as a successful example of political democratization not because of the freedoms it offered, but because it shifted and broadened authority in a way that led to a

greater division of responsibilities and because it oriented a greater
number of economic reforms toward the establishment of a market.
Mikhail Gorbachev was applauded as a model leader not because he
was a 'democrat' but because his willingness to reform the power
structure within the CPSU, his enshrining in law a system of private
land and enterprise ownership and his demand to ratify major decisions through the Central Committee of the CPSU (rather than
through the old rubber stamp method of the Party), made him a 'true
example of a new authoritarian' (Hu, 1989, pp. 33–4, 44–6).[11] The
Chinese leadership was described as alienated from the people not
because the people were denied democracy but because the CCP's
attempt at price reform in 1988 had failed, and because the CCP was
not relying to a significant enough degree on a politics that combined
leadership with merit, and that was restricted by a system of checks
and balances (Ruan, 1990, pp. 102–3).[12] The absence of these
constraints, and their consequences (specified as 'corruption' and
'nepotism'), and not a profound concern with individual rights, led a
number of scholars to repeat the democrats' pre-Tiananmen demand
for a more vigorous legal system, rather than the extension of a
complete democratic franchise. Democrats believed that without an
improved legal system, even the NA proposal for economic decentralization and greater devolution of political powers to local
government was bound to have problems because local governments
would consider themselves above the law, and would become corrupt
and more dictatorial (Su, 1990, pp. 109–12).

Democrats' solutions in the post-Tiananmen period seemed to be
more economic than political in nature. They wished for a reform of
state ownership, which included an increased (but gradual) separation
between government and enterprises, the formation of an independent management mechanism in enterprises and the growth of an
entrepreneurial stratum in society. They believed that only through
this process could the individual exercise restraint over the state's
political power. Rights were indeed mentioned, including 'citizen's
social rights', but behind an emphasis on rights that were seen to be
more immediately linked with expanded marketization, including
'property rights', the 'right to work', the 'right to housing' and the
'right to relocate'. Similarly, as in the pre-Tiananmen debates, these
rights were subordinated to the desire for procedural correctness of
the government's powers and its policymaking behaviour, for the
supervision of the People's Congress over the government and its
power of restraint and query, and for the establishment of a legal

system. One democrat said that the establishment of a legal system was 'one and the same process' as democratization (Rong, 1991, pp. 61–4). Moreover, the democrats also conceded that at its current stage of development, China did not have '... the conditions for realizing on a large scale the forms of democracy, such as the system of representative government and the system of general elections, that are already prevalent in the West' (Rong, 1991, p. 63). One new solution that the democrats offered in the post-Tiananmen period was the suggestion that a federal system replace China's current political system. They proposed a federalism which would consist of two sets of Member States, mainland China and the combination of Hong Kong, Taiwan and Macau. Each of these would have its own constitution, its own currency and its own judiciary. Each could limit the activities of the federal government. Some democrats saw this as the best way toward freedom, democracy, unity and wealth in the future (Yan, 1992, pp. 79–85).[13]

From this, it is evident that the democrats did not accept Western liberal democratic models even in the post-Tiananmen period. One democrat supported what he termed an East Asian model of democracy. He said that compared to Western democracy, East Asian democracy is a 'rationalized' democracy that is more capable of attaining economic modernization (Ding, 1990, p. 35). Some Western democrats in the post-Tiananmen debates, on the other hand, believed that in light of 4 June, Chinese stability depended on taking the road to democracy immediately and on involving the masses directly in the process. They maintained that this would prevent a second Tiananmen (see Riskin, 1990, pp. 98–101). But even in the absence of these measures, Western democrats admitted that their prediction that another democratic reaction would shortly take place after Tiananmen had been proved wrong (Gittings, 1992, pp. 67–8). Not even representatives for the Chinese Alliance for Democracy (CAD), either before or after Tiananmen, or inside or outside of China, wished to overthrow the Chinese government. Rather, they called for peaceful and rational dialogue with the CCP, and only the possibility of discontinuing the CCP's monopoly of power in the future (He, 1991, p. 33). Only one Chinese democrat in these discussions demanded an immediate turn to democracy. But his reasons for supporting this stand seem weak. For one, he believed that the Chinese people were 'intrinsically democratic' and that they had exhibited their 'democratic spirit' not only in the Tiananmen protest of 1989, but also during the Tiananmen Event of 1976 and the Xidan

Democracy Wall movement of 1978–9. Another reason that he gave was that protest in the post-Tiananmen months had become necessary because of the widespread spiritual malaise among the Chinese people and the inability of the CCP to control society (Liu, 1990, pp. 114–15).[14] As Section 9.4 illustrates, however, these conditions and demands may not have existed (before or after Tiananmen) to the extent that Liu has suggested.

The Authoritarians' Response

Those who supported Chinese NA during this period acknowledged that their view was unpopular and untimely when historically it was so near to the events of Tiananmen. But, as they said, their solutions were based on pragmatic considerations. Zhang argued that any development model that was embraced in China should be the least costly model and the most beneficial to the nation as a whole. He said that only a combination of economic liberalism and continued interventionist party rule could continue to ensure this (Zhang, 1991, pp. 67–9). His evidence was the economic success in China under such a system during the first ten years of reform. Zhang said that this transformed for the better the livelihood and mode of production of the entire peasantry as well as the livelihood of considerable numbers of urban citizens. He concluded that it simply did not make sense to overturn the familiar and workable in favour of the unknown and possibly impracticable (Zhang, 1991, pp. 70–6).

NA supporters acknowledged that communist parties had not generally been able to lead their countries from Stalinism to a market economy. Nolan, for example, agreed that this was also the case because a one-party communist state cannot, or will not, construct a legal system that includes clearly defined property rights (Nolan, 1990, pp. 5–8).[15] But he suggested that these assumptions turn a blind eye to the actual demands put forward during the Tiananmen demonstrations as well as to the outcome of hastened democratization in Russia and Eastern Europe. Nolan took issue with the view that Tiananmen was provoked by the Chinese leadership's resistance to people's demands for a changed political system. He suggested that the people were more concerned about the retirement of elder leaders and the sacking of those involved in corrupt activities. Similarly, he did not accept that the Chinese leadership wished to retain power for its own sake, as so many analysts claimed, but because leaders sincerely believed that the interests of the Chinese people were not likely to be served best by a rapid transition to democratic institutions. Nolan added that the Chinese leadership's view is not an uncommon one to hold in the early stages of development. He said that historically it rarely has been the case that a universal franchise and a multiparty system were achieved in parallel with economic development (Nolan, 1990, pp. 9–11).[16] He claimed that nothing proved this more convincingly than the rapid democratization in Eastern Europe and in Russia, where people have gained rights but have not been meaningfully empowered by the new political process (Nolan, 1992, p. 141).

Hua argued that Russian citizens did not feel that the end of communist rule brought democracy to Russia. He said that despite the introduction of a multiparty system, many Russians were unclear about which party they should join. Their new-found freedoms had paradoxically put them in less control of the political situation than they had been in the years before such dramatic changes took place (Hua, 1992, p. 141). He also challenged the NA democrats' argument that supported a federal government for China. He said that federalism assumes that everyone wants to join a federation. From discussions he had had while travelling in Russia and Eastern Europe, he found that the desire for a federalist system was rare. Nations that had been part of the Soviet Union, including those which had never been independent before, wished for continued independence. Hua believed that a similar outcome would be imminent in China should the leadership consider a Chinese federation (Hua, 1992, p. 134).

NA supporters' main argument in the post-Tiananmen years was that it was politically dangerous for China to leap from totalitarianism to democracy without first going through an intermediate authoritarian period. They believed that China should not abandon planning, but abandon Stalinist planning by relying on a system of 'transitional rational authoritarianism'. This would include a strong concept of state action to overcome market failure, and which would guarantee basic needs for all of China's citizens. Nolan argued that this position had already gained acceptance by some Russian critics in early 1990 (Nolan, 1990, pp. 26–7).[17] Zhang also believed that Tiananmen taught the Chinese leadership the value of greater compromise. He suggested that even though the conservatives may continue to represent the existing order in the Party, they can no longer act independently, and must cooperate with reformers in order to solve the economic dilemmas that led to Tiananmen in the first place (Zhang, 1991, pp. 79–80).

Summary of the Post-Tiananmen Phase of the Debates

One scholar in the post-Tiananmen debate supported neither NA nor democracy because he could not see a fundamental difference between the two (Wu, 1990, pp. 75–9). Another criticized the NA argument that democrats proposed radical reform measures. He said that when compared to the support for economic 'shock therapy' that was evident in Russia, no radical theories emerged in the NA debates (Gu, 1995, interview). Although other democrats did not fully accept the NA line, some conceded that even in the wake of Tiananmen the people of China may tolerate an authoritarian government if it means stability, economic progress and gradual steps toward democracy (Gittings, 1992, pp. 70–1). There was also a greater acceptance than in the pre-Tiananmen period that the increased recognition of individual property rights could over time affect civil rights in a positive manner.[18]

One NA participant who claimed he stood somewhere in between NA supporters and democrats argued that it was unhealthy for NA supporters to see the market as the answer to everything. He said that they must understand that Western economies for the most part are Keynesian in nature, and represent a 'convergence of capitalist and socialist forms' that put constraints and regulations on economic growth (Dong, interview One, 1993).[19] He also argued that both NA supporters and democrats should be aware that at this stage in China's history there is no single theory for development. Instead, theory must be flexible and adjusted as historical circumstances dictate (Dong, 1993, interview Two). Another participant suggested that reforms neither need to represent a major overhaul of Deng Xiaoping's reforms nor a change of the party structure at the grassroots level. What are needed instead are intermediate level reforms in institutions (universities, work units) that do not affect the rest of the country but which over time will yield a positive result (Gu, 1995, interview).

9.4   TIANANMEN'S IMPACT ON THE PEOPLE

There is no way of knowing whether NA proponents' or opponents' views were representative of Chinese people's views at the time of the Tiananmen crisis. The vast numbers that turned out to support the 1989 demonstrations in Beijing and other major cities in China may suggest that had the Chinese people been given the opportunity to choose sides in the debate, they would have supported NA opponents. During Tiananmen, one Western commentator on the scene claimed that China's leaders were avoiding democracy because they knew that its inception would signal their own demise and the rapid decline of the CCP's monopoly of power (Salisbury, 1989, p. 56). But it should be made clear that the student leaders in Tiananmen Square did not wish to overthrow the CCP. They said that they opposed certain practices of the Party but they did not wish to destroy it (Ren, 1989a, p. 50).[20] Similarly, students demanded dialogue with leaders, but they did not believe that the absence of dialogue foreshadowed the collapse of the Chinese political system, as another commentator outside China suggested (Tang, 1991, p. 321). The demands the people placed on the Chinese government during the 1989 crisis did not in all cases reflect a desire for the implementation of Western democratic institutions. The surveys that follow, of course, can in no way be seen as representative of all people in China. But they do suggest alternative views to the ones that commentators believed were most widely accepted in 1989.

The Students as 'Authoritarians'?

Like the democrats in the NA debates, student essays, placards and wall posters derided authoritarianism, and new authoritarianism during the student demonstrations. Many students also believed that only democracy could stabilize China (Ren, 1989a, p. 53). Similarly, the students argued that unless China followed the political developments of countries like Poland, Hungary and Czechoslovakia, Chinese democracy would not exist in the future (Wang, 1989b, p. 38).[21] But, also like the democratic scholars in the NA debates, the students did not build their mandate on demands for multiparty politics. In fact, they objected to excessive freedoms and what they termed 'total freedom of speech' if subscribing to these sacrificed order. Even during Tiananmen itself, student leaders called on demonstrators to organize themselves according to what was legally permissible (Wang, 1989a, p. 41, and Ren, 1989b, p. 47).

Some demonstrators in the square even called on the students to recognize the gradual nature of democratic development, implored them to avoid conflict that could undermine the cause of reform and democratization, and asked them to leave the square during the Sino-Soviet summit (Han, 1990, p. 208).[22] In addition to this, not all students felt that change in China depended on liberal leaders. Student leader Wuer Kaixi[23] made this clear in an interview on 2 June:

> Let me emphasise that whether Li Peng steps down or not is unimportant compared with the broad acceptance of our slogans, which will mean social pressure to place constraints upon government. If Li Peng were to step down, to be replaced by some other party figure, it would mean nothing. Even if Zhao Ziyang retains power, and is a good secretary, restraints should also be placed on him. (interview with Wuer Kaixi, 1989, p. 150)

It is also questionable whether the students in the square were interested in leading a populist movement. Commentators have suggested that the democracy movement was not carried out on behalf of the Chinese people, but rather that it was notable for its reluctance on the part of the student activists to welcome the full participation of other urbanites in the demonstrations.[24] Wuer Kaixi as much as confirmed this when he lamented shortly before 4 June, and two weeks afterwards during an interview in Hong Kong, that the Chinese people lacked an understanding of democracy (interview with Wuer Kaixi, 1989, p. 153).

Many students also seemed to accept, as NA participants did, an elite consultative process because they believed that involvement of the common people in Chinese politics hindered the fulfilment of national objectives (Perry, 1992, pp. 151–2). Where these students differed from NA participants was in their adoption of 'mass mobilization without Party authorization' (see Ma, 1990, p. 1). But even in this respect, many students did not wish to overturn the government, but maintained that large-scale mobilization was the best way to make their opposition to the government known. Some accounts suggest that students' concerns focused mostly on the leadership's arbitrary use of power, on government ineffectiveness in fighting corruption, on bureaucratism and on servility among ministers of party chiefs, as well as on the Central Committee's unsuccessful proposals to control prices, curb inflation and improve people's living standards (see Han, 1990, pp. 26–7, 31–2, 42, 77, 119). Certain Western scholars now believe that Tiananmen did not represent a rebellion but an expression of patriotism (the movement, after all, referred to itself as a '*patriotic* democratic movement') (Friedman, 1989a, p. 30). They claim that this drew on the traditional role of intellectual remonstrance against the leadership, which said that unless the ruler returned to sound policies and ethical principles, he would not retain the loyalty and obedience of his subjects, and *da luan* ('great chaos') would result (Cheek, 1992, p. 129, and Cherrington, 1991, p. 12). According to Bergère, this manifested itself most clearly in the students' hunger strike, which was not only patriotic but Confucian in the way that it attempted to set those of virtue against a corrupt regime (Bergère, 1992, p. 137).

In addition to this, the Tiananmen demonstration, despite its large numbers, was not representative of all student views. A survey of students at Fudan University (Shanghai) in December 1989 gives evidence of this. To the statement 'Nowadays university students are indifferent to politics', 22.4 per cent of students 'strongly agreed'; 21.8 per cent 'generally agreed'; 25.9 per cent 'agreed somewhat', while only 21.1 per cent 'disagreed' and only 5.4 per cent 'firmly opposed' it (Rosen, 1990, p. 221). To the question 'From what you've seen and heard [of recent events in China], what is your understanding of the concern university students now have toward current events (reform and the open policy)?', 40.4 per cent responded 'not too concerned', while only 11.3 per cent said 'very concerned' (Rosen, 1990, p. 221). To the question 'Do you have confidence in the future of reform?', 37.4 per cent responded that they were 'confident', while only 14.9 per cent said they had 'no confidence' (Rosen, 1990, p. 222).[25] A survey of students in Guangzhou in late 1989 bears similar results. To the question '[What are the] criteria that make a country successful', 88.7 per cent ranked 'a high standard of living' number one; 'social stability' (66.7 per cent) number two; 'power' (42 per cent) number three; and 'high international status' (38.5 per cent) number four. 'Fully guaranteed individual rights and freedoms' was ranked number five at 34.8 per cent (Rosen, 1992, p. 172). In other words, the very justification on which Chinese leaders base, and have based authoritarian rule in the past, improved wealth, welfare and a stronger international role for China, are the same criteria that comprise some student views.

Did the People Want Democracy?

Assessments of some peoples' attitudes before, during and after Tiananmen suggest that democracy was not always a chief concern. Many worried more about the problems of inflation, which by 1988 had run to its highest level since 1949. The problem was exacerbated for some peasants, who were not being paid for their crops but were instead given IOUs (see Fathers and Higgens, 1989, pp. 9–10). These factors, along with a widening gap in incomes and resentment toward the new monied elite, led to tensions and confusion, but not to the extent that all peasants and workers believed that a rapid transition to democracy was the solution (Chan, 1991, pp. 105–7).

Some people's opinions on what Chinese reforms required did not differ significantly from those of certain NA participants or of the results from the student surveys noted. In a random survey conducted in 1987, Beijing residents believed that the major preconditions of political reform were the following: 'separating the Party's function from the government's', 'simplifying official institutions and improving [their] efficiency' and 'eliminating various bureaucracies'. This survey also shows that most people interviewed either supported the party line or were indifferent to it, and that they were optimistic about the future. Those who sought radical change only comprised seven per cent in the survey (Zhu, *et. al*, 1990, pp. 993, 996).[26] In another study, 58 per cent of the people surveyed agreed with the statement that 'China has, to some degree, democracy at present but this should be improved upon', while only 17 per cent agreed that 'China is deficient in democracy and freedom at present, which are the necessary conditions for modernization' (He, 1992, p. 125).[27] These results, and the results of the first survey, indicate that a significant number of people believed that a transition to democracy should rely not on dramatic changes in the political system but on a rationalization of existing Party and government bodies.

Even in the politically-charged environment of the post-Tiananmen period, a survey conducted in 1990 suggests that the majority of people neither understood the role of local or national government nor believed that either had a significant influence on their lives. Only 5.4 per cent of the people surveyed agreed that local government had a great effect on their daily lives; only 9.7 per cent per cent felt the same was true of national government. These figures reflect a much lower score than those of respondents surveyed in other countries (see Nathan and Shi, 1994, pp. 99–100).[28] Similarly, to the question of whether they 'understand very well' local or national affairs, the people surveyed in China scored the lowest of all countries surveyed (1.9 per cent and 0.9 per cent).[29]

Regardless of the millions who did not participate in the Beijing demonstrations, the sheer numbers of those who did, let alone the numbers that comprised similar demonstrations in other major cities in China at the time[30], made for a veritable tinderbox of political dissent, and possibly nationwide chaos. As this section suggests, however, the demands placed on the Chinese government did not all have to do with democracy. One critic who analyzed the demonstrations has suggested that the words 'freedom' and 'democracy' must now be seen merely as 'fetish words' (Bergère, 1992, p. 140). Stability, order, less corruption, lower inflation and a greater division of governmental powers may describe what the majority of the people in China want. Baum's view that in the post-Tiananmen period China's age-old fear of chaos *(luan)* is more on the minds of the Chinese people than demands for freedom and democracy seems to confirm this:

> ... large numbers of Chinese citizens – including many erstwhile liberal supporters of the 1989 student demonstrations – cite 'fear of chaos' as a primary reason for their lack of enthusiasm for renewed political protest. (Baum, 1992, p. 493)

Some Chinese scholars also reject that Tiananmen reversed the reform process. They say that although the Chinese people are now aware that modernization entails political modernization and democracy, they are less inclined to be of the illusion that these must come quickly. Others add that the people may accept that the overall success of modernization depends on the stability that strong authority provides. They support a revised authoritarian system, one that is more earnest in its desire for adjustments, for a new working relationship between central and local governments and for a decision-making process that has become more rational. They also suggest that intermediate and top-level leaders are more willing to listen to experts than they used to be, and more than Western critics may be aware (Ren, 1995, correspondence, and Lin, 1993, interview).[31] Much of this may have been influenced by Chinese scholars' awareness of the failed 'shock therapies' for economic growth that were employed in Russia and Eastern Europe at the time, as well as the chaos surrounding the failed coup in Russia in August, 1991 (see Kelly, 1996, and Gu and Kelly, 1994, p. 220).

9.5 TRANSITIONAL NEW AUTHORITARIANISM?

Perry has argued that China's Party General-Secretary Jiang Zemin's keynote political report to the Fourteenth Party Congress in 1992 showed tacit support for new authoritarianism (Perry, 1993, pp. 13–14).[32] There is of course no way of knowing whether there was support in China for either the democratic or the authoritarian line in the NA debate (the vast majority of the population would not have been aware of the debates). However, if some form of NA is at work in China, its success can to a certain degree be tested in practice. A major argument of NA proponents was that the difference between OA and NA rested in NA's transitional capabilities (Chapter 8). In a number of areas, transitions in the form of decreased and rechannelled levels of authority do seem to be taking place.

Bachman argues that it is already apparent that China's third generation of leaders, Jiang Zemin, Li Peng, Li Ruihuan, Qiao Shi, Yang Baibang, Zhu Rongji, Zou Jiahua and Ye Xuanping, have significantly less power and fewer political resources at their disposal than Deng Xiaoping had (Bachman, 1992, p. 1047). Yin points out that the middle class was represented for the first time in China's history at the first session of the Eighth People's Congress in the Spring of 1992 (Yin, 1993, interview). Howell suggests that new semi-official social organizations in China enjoy greater autonomy than the old social organizations, and that these organizations are likely to become more independent of the state in the future (Howell, 1995, pp. 78, 82). White also speaks positively of China's incremental steps toward the organization of 'group interests' in 'civil society' (White, 1994, p. 89). Lawrence's study of grass-roots democracy in a Hebei village indicates that local leaders are becoming more accountable, that this is having a positive influence on leaders at the next level of government, and that it is reducing corruption and leading to greater openness in the decision-making process:

> Despite the shortcomings of Beiwang's election process, institutional reforms in the village have clearly made local cadres more accountable than in the past ... the principles of accountability and public disclosure [extend] all the way into the Party branch ... by promptly disciplining Party officials who slip into corrupt behaviour and by opening up some of the Party's decision-making processes.... (Lawrence, 1994, pp. 66–7)

This point not only lends strength to the NA argument, but shows the effectiveness of an educative democracy that starts at the village level and grows in significance as people become familiar with democratic institutions. This was the same type of incremental democracy that

Kang Youwei and Sun Yatsen advocated at the beginning of the century (Chapters 3 and 5).

9.6 CONCLUSION

In the post-Tiananmen period, democrats did not seem to show a deep interest in individual rights. They were more concerned about the procedural correctness of the government's powers and its policy-making behaviour. In this sense, they believed that the individual could exercise greater restraint over the state's political power through economic reforms that included the reform of state owner-ship and a greater separation between government and enterprises. None of the democrats supported a system of representative democ-racy, and one democrat suggested that China's current stage of development did not provide the conditions for a representative system. Some also supported the idea that China adopt a system of federalism, which was not discussed by democrats in the pre-Tiananmen debates. The main argument of NA supporters in the post-Tiananmen period was that China must not leap from totali-tarianism to democracy without first going through an intermediary authoritarian period. They said that the NA model was the most pragmatic, least costly model, and that the success of economic reforms over the past ten years had proved this. They also challenged the assumption that Tiananmen was provoked by Chinese leaders' resistance to a demand for a changed political system. They argued that Chinese leaders may have genuinely believed that people's inter-ests would not be served by a rapid transition to democratic institutions. NA proponents cited the problems that have occurred because of rapid transition in Russia and Eastern Europe in defence of their view.

The chapter also has shown that China's students may have objected to excessive freedoms and a hastened reform process if these led to civil unrest. It demonstrated that students did not seek more liberal-minded leaders as much as they sought to constrain leaders. The surveys that were used suggest that some students sought a high standard of living and social stability ahead of individual rights and freedoms. These conclusions were also evident in the views of workers. Some people who were interviewed believed that Chinese democracy had already progressed well beyond what it once was. Of course, these views represent only a very small sample of the Chinese population. But they do suggest that a certain accord in political outlook exists between different sectors of society. It would be wrong to argue that all accept a 'new authoritarianism', as it was described by NA proponents. But if following NA meant security and continued economic growth, it may be a political model that Chinese people would accept ahead of a democratic model for some years to come. In the 1990s, there seems to be more consistent agreement among Chinese scholars that China's evolutionary authoritarian route will lend itself to a more enduring democratic system with fewer political and economic traumas on the way to that goal. Increasingly, these analyses reject comparisons with the development programmes of Russia and Eastern Europe.[33]

10 Conclusion

10.1 SUMMARY

The current period of China's system reform, from command economy communism to a greater reliance on market forces, was set in motion in the late 1970s. By the late 1980s it was apparent that China's development strategy had broken with orthodox opinion at the time that said communist regimes must be overthrown to facilitate economic reform. Despite the collapse of the Soviet state and despite pressure for political change from its own people during the Tiananmen crisis in 1989 and from Western nations, the Chinese leadership rejected the idea that authoritarian rule should be abandoned immediately. Top officials in China argued that reform of the country's political structure must be a protracted process that relied on the state to direct gradual, steady and experimental steps. These would rely on a capitalism that was restricted by the state for the sake of preserving the fundamental socialist principles of public ownership and common prosperity. The leaders did not believe that a more active political role for the people through multiparty elections could assist this process, or that their view about democracy was inhumane or showed indifference to the people. They argued that in China's present stage of development, enriching the nation was more important than empowering the people politically, if the former could deliver better incomes and benefits to everyone. They claimed that authoritarian rule in China should not be set against what the West sees as the virtues of democratic rule but according to the high material standards, advanced methods of management and technical innovations that economic reforms have created in China since 1978. These views are consistent with the views of major theorists and political figures in twentieth-century China. All believed that the basic components of authoritarian rule should not be altered if this compromised the long-term goal of improving people's welfare. This book has attempted to show that the relationship between political authoritarianism and people's welfare is at the heart of what theorists and politicians in China believe to be legitimate authoritarian rule. The book also has suggested that to characterize China's current system of authoritarian rule according to Western political concepts ignores the long-term political traditions that inspired the Chinese

151

position on legitimate rule. Based on these traditions, the book has demonstrated why important political figures in China this century have rejected democratic institutions and development strategies from the West.

The second chapter examined what it was in the political traditions of China that inspired the authority-welfare nexus. The importance that Confucianism places on people's welfare and the priority that this was given ahead of 'individual rights' by reformers in modern China has been touched on before. But such studies usually suggest that the connection between ancient and modern welfare was borrowed from Mencian philosophical traditions.[1] This seems doubtful when one considers the frequency with which political discourse in modern China returned to the practical and focused considerations that Xunzi articulated. To a much greater extent than Confucius or Mencius, Xunzi believed that there could be little flexibility if a ruler was earnest about restoring order in conditions of scarcity. To this end, Xunzi challenged long-held beliefs in the philosophical traditions that preceded him. He could not accept the Mencian belief that man is inherently good or the Mohist beliefs in egalitarianism and frugality because he felt that these defeated the primary goals of authority and welfare by provoking chaos and aggravating poverty. Xunzi questioned how chaos and indigence could be seen as the work of a benevolent government *(renzheng)*, as Mencius had described it, when starvation and premature death abounded in every state. Xunzi claimed that such an outcome was unacceptable under humane government and that humane government must be based on the regulation and order that he believed were an intrinsic part of the traditional virtue *li*.

The rest of the book showed how this way of thinking, whether directly from Xunzi or otherwise, seemed to map the authoritarian course that twentieth-century China has followed. Reformers believed, and still seem to believe, that in an early development period humane government is a government that liberates people from poverty rather than one that promises 'individual rights'. It is a view that is essential to the post-Mao reforms, as Deng Xiaoping's words in 1983 indicate: '... discussion of the value of the human being or of humanism isn't going to raise [China's standard of living]. Only active efforts to achieve material, ideological, and cultural progress can do that.' (See Chapter 2.) The millennial gap between Deng Xiaoping and Xunzi may have meant that no association between modern reforms and ancient authoritarian antecedents could have been made had it not been for the writings of Chinese reformers like Kang Youwei. Kang felt that China did not need to look elsewhere to solve its problem of late development. In Chapter 3, it was suggested that Kang was the first modern reformer in China to defend a system of authoritarian rule that drew on ancient indigenous sources. The chapter demonstrated how the conceptual basis of Kang's development strategy was similar to Xunzi's defence of a strong state. Like Xunzi, Kang argued that man's 'goodness' is acquired as society grows more wealthy. Kang also claimed that the origins of a wealthy society depended on a state-orchestrated system that fostered economic regulation by upholding *li* as the prime symbol of constraint and order in the apportioning of wealth and goods. But Kang's authoritarianism was a transitional authoritarianism, which was to be extended to a democratic franchise once the state had grown wealthy. Kang's view that wealth was the only route to democracy is reminiscent of Xunzi's view that only when resources are abundant do people behave humanely towards one another.

Liang Qichao pushed the debates on Chinese authoritarianism ahead considerably. It is little wonder that Liang has been seen as a Confucian liberal and a democrat because so many of his writings focus on the theme of Western democracy. Discussions of the liberal state, constitutionalism, the 'general will', utilitarianism, freedom, equality and laissez-faire economics all fill the pages of Liang's writings. But they do so only as a study in what he believed to be the futility of democratic institutions at that time in China's history. Liang said that China did not lack freedom and equality. What it lacked was food to feed the people and wealth to support them. Even before the Chinese monarchy made an attempt at reform in 1898, Liang asserted that poverty alone in China, not Western wealth and power, not the democratic institutions that propelled Western nations towards their positions of dominance should be the driving force behind change (Liang, 1896, p. 12). For this, liberty and democracy would have to be put on hold, would have to wait not until China had established democratic institutions but until the Chinese state had created enough wealth *to* establish these institutions. Chapter 4 of this book, examined Liang's reasons for choosing this position. It was suggested that Liang's reforms also were influenced by Xunzi's philosophy and in particular the concepts *qun* ('grouping') and *gong* ('public-mindedness'). Liang differed from Kang Youwei in his view that the people themselves must be taught why authoritarian rule remained essential to China when the ever-present talk of revolution at the time suggested that centralized authority would come to an end. Only through an understanding of the economic value of *qun* and the idea that *gong* could bring benefits to everyone did Liang believe that a harmonization of interests between the individual and the state could be understood, accepted and established under the authoritarian system of rule that Kang had described.

Although not usually recognized as a supporter of Confucianism, Sun Yatsen's 'Three People's Principles' seems as much a modernized Confucian treatise as it is the work of China's first modern revolutionary. One is struck by the increasing number of Confucian concepts that are to be found in Chinese intellectual discourse by the time Sun wrote his 'Three Principles' in 1924. *Li, qun* and *gong* were all discussed by Sun, but he also pondered the usefulness in the modern era of the ancient concept *wang dao* ('way of kings') and the idea that knowledge must be a guide to action, each of which was of great importance to Xunzi. As was noted in Chapter 5, Sun asked how the traditional Confucian virtues could be used to serve the demands of a modern state, the demands of nationalism *(minzu)*, of democracy *(minquan)* and of socialism (or Sun's *minsheng*). He believed that if a unified nation could generate wealth and prospective benefits for the people, it would also foster the legitimacy of authoritarian rule. Sun likewise argued that people must be made to understand that wealth, not liberty, was the main goal of democracy when a nation was developing. Wealth would not be realized through a democratic franchise that empowered the people with natural rights and natural equality in Sun's political system, but through a hierarchical authoritarianism that demanded the 'natural obligations' of the people toward the material and cultural development of the state. Sun claimed that it could not be otherwise for a nation that sustained itself on the principle of welfare. Natural equality must be seen as a 'false equality' because it did not have public welfare at heart. And natural rights were meaningless if they could not deliver to China what Sun termed the 'complete democratic rights' of food, security, wealth, higher standards of living and greater equalization of incomes, or the goals of the *minsheng* principle. At times compared to Lenin's theory of an 'elite vanguard', Sun said that *minsheng* was never to be prompted by the political mobilization of the people, as was true of Lenin's theory, but by an economic mobilization that was underwritten by a state capitalism. In this respect, Sun did not see a conflict between a 'national socialism' and encouraging private capital from abroad. This outlook was most influential on Mao Zedong in his early years as well as Deng Xiaoping, who despite their nominally different political inspiration, did not change the basic nature of Sun's political authoritarianism even though their leadership functioned within an officially Marxist–Leninist framework.

To this end, one also has to question whether Mao Zedong was ever a devout Marxist–Leninist or whether he was a benefactor of the theories inherent in Sun's 'Three People's Principles' to which Mao often referred in his early writings. The task of Chapter 6 was to ask this question, and more generally to determine whether there was a uniformity of political conviction among the three revolutionaries the book discussed. The chapter demonstrated that Mao's development strategy during his period of New Democracy had the same goals as Sun Yatsen's plans for national reconstruction. This is evident in Mao's view that the eventual socialization of agriculture would be coordinated with the development of a powerful industry having state enterprise as its backbone to establish a complete consolidated socialism in the future. The chapter suggested that from the early 1940s to the late 1950s, Mao did not in practice show a definite political orientation toward the Soviet Union, and that he did not treat trade relations with other countries according to Marxist ideology but according to their willingness to do business with China. This seemed to be because Mao adhered to Sun's argument that foreign capital and investment were essential to building Chinese socialism. When Mao diverted from the gradual development path that Sun had advocated by insisting that socialist transformation be completed ahead of schedule, he broke with what was considered by his forerunner to be the only path to development in China.

It has only been in the post-Mao years that Mao's connection with Sun's principles has become more apparent. Scholars like Esherick, and more recently Sheng and He, have uncovered the contents of interviews with Mao and formerly classified CCP documents that reveal Mao's desire for a national socialism that was built on capitalist foundations similar to Sun Yatsen's policies. These documents also reveal that Mao's radical posturing in the late 1950s may have been because the United States and the Soviet Union would not honour or enable him to fulfill this desire. This book has suggested that we can learn more about the relationship between Mao's politics and the politics of Sun Yatsen through Deng Xiaoping's selective interpretation of Maoism in the post-1978 years. As Chapter 7 indicated, a wealth of literature has been produced in an attempt to pin down the nature of Deng Xiaoping's authoritarianism. Deng has been described as a 'rational Maoist' by some, a 'rational–legalist' by others and a latter-day 'reformer' in the mould of Liang Qichao and other pre-revolutionary figures by many. But Chapter 7 argued that Deng's reforms restored the pattern that Sun Yatsen established in his 'Three Principles', and which Mao adopted during New Democracy. Mao's departure from New Democracy and his leap toward socialism proved to Deng that poverty could not be eliminated in China without the incremental economic strategy that Sun Yatsen advocated. Deng did not oppose democracy in the long-term but he argued that political change in China must be a protracted process that was built on long-term stability. The best way to do this initially was not for the state to grant sovereignty to the people through multiparty democracy but through a political elite's assurance about the well-being of the people. The wealth of publications in China on Sun Yatsen's theories of political economy in the post-Mao years lends support to the idea that Deng Xiaoping's reforms are influenced by, and perhaps modelled on, Sun's 'Three Principles'.

Chapters 8 and 9 attempted to contribute to recent studies on Chinese new authoritarianism by suggesting that the NA debates were influenced by historical precedent far more than existing analyses on NA have indicated. Chapter 8 demonstrated that NA proponents believed a union of certain elements from OA and NA to be the best way to guide and strengthen China. They claimed that old forms of authority were familiar, practicable and therefore suited to mass industrialization, and that this was apparent in modern China's history, where attempts to implement political systems that were not based on indigenous authoritarian structures had clashed with, and destroyed, Chinese reform measures. They also supported a gradual reform programme. They said that late Qing reforms as well as Mao's attempt to complete socialist transformation in haste failed because of a desire to bring about change too quickly. Sun Yatsen's politics and Mao Zedong's New Democracy, on the other hand, are defended because they were similar to NA. Each represented a system of authority that advocated incremental reforms, that relied on the vitality and success of capitalism in order to shore up legitimacy and that rejected multiparty democracy because of a shared belief that it would hinder development, exacerbate poverty and provoke chaos.

NA opponents believed that an OA–NA synthesis was unwise because previous attempts to modernize indigenous political authority in China had failed in their view. They said that this was apparent in Yuan Shikai's monarchical revival, which led to warlordism; in Sun

Yatsen's 'Three Principles', which led to civil war under Chiang Kaishek and in Mao Zedong's totalitarianism, which led to the Cultural Revolution. They claimed that this disproved the NA proponents' argument that NA was a transitional political authority. However the chapter suggested that the alternatives that NA opponents recommended did not reflect Western liberal democratic principles. They spoke of a democracy that is 'Chinese' in substance, of 'state democracy' and of a democracy that would sustain centralized political power and the role that it plays in modernization. The chapter concluded that there was a greater similarity in the view on political authority between the opposing sides in the NA debates than previous analyses of the debates suggest.

Chapter 9 demonstrated that the Tiananmen crisis may not have affected the tendency in the NA debates to support varying degrees of authority if this was the best assurance of security. The chapter surveyed the views of the three main groups involved in the debates in the pre-Tiananmen period: NA supporters, elite democrats and democrats. It found that elite democrats did not reject the role of strong leadership that NA proponents were defending. But elite democrats believed that the authority of democratic institutions, especially a legal system, should play a more important role. The democrats followed a similar argument, that 'democracy does not reject or exclude authoritarian elements', and that it may make political authority more rational. The main difference was that the democrats of both distinctions proposed the strengthening of the Chinese legal system and a more efficient National People's Congress (NPC) as well as greater accountability of its members.

Chapter 9 also showed that in the post-Tiananmen period, the democratic argument did not attack the idea of strong authority directly, but was concerned that highly centralized authority would be less capable of dealing with social and economic disorder than a redistributed authority. It was likewise evident during this phase of the debate that when democrats referred to democracy, its scope was almost entirely economic in nature. Despite the Tiananmen crisis, the democrats did not show a profound concern with human rights. The authoritarians' main argument was that China should not leap from a totalitarian regime to democracy without first going through an intermediary authoritarian period. The chapter concluded by suggesting that there might have been greater support overall for authoritarian rule in post-Tiananmen China if this could assure security and continued economic growth.

10.2   AUTHORITY, WELFARE AND DEMOCRACY IN CHINA

Defenders of political authoritarianism in China have argued that centralization is the 'lesser of two evils' when a nation first begins to develop, and that without state-orchestrated reforms there can be no rapid development. But they have also argued that political authoritarianism is not the solution to development over the long-term. In this respect, they believe that the authoritarianism they describe is a 'transitional authoritarianism'. However, there is a wealth of literature on development theory that argues authoritarian rule is not always transitional and that authoritarianism can simultaneously lead to increased levels of industrialization as well as greater centralization and higher levels of inequality.[2] Others argue that in East Asia, Confucian-inspired development strategies are intrinsically anti-democratic.[3] In the case of China, a comparative study between dynastic administrations and modern authoritarian regimes has asserted that China has not, and therefore cannot, function in any other way except according to autocratic practices.[4] Where authoritarian regimes have been seen as capable of transition elsewhere in East Asia, it is suggested that this may operate quite effectively in a small territory such as the Four Dragons (South Korea, Taiwan, Singapore and Hong Kong) but not in a large country like China. Among other reasons, it is argued that the Four Dragons emerged out of harsh colonial traditions that bequeathed political quiescence along with substantial investment in infrastructure.[5] These views have been summed up in the early 1990s on the assumption that there is no guarantee that democracy will be able to overcome the authoritarian alternative even when posed as a transitional and circumscribed authoritarianism.[6] To defend new authoritarianism in China, it is argued, is merely a convenient rationalization for indefinitely forestalling meaningful democratization.[7]

Of course there are no guarantees that China will move towards democracy as China's defenders of authoritarian rule have suggested. But at the same time moralizing about democracy in an abstract way when conditions may not be right for democratic institutions could pose a threat to the stability that is so deeply cherished in China. Perhaps the best test case of political transition is to be found historically, in the West itself. MacPherson's belief that the market economy in Western nations was 'an enormously liberalizing force' that preceded, but which was also the main influence on, the democratic franchise that was introduced into the liberal state,[8] bears similarities with a widely held view in China that economic liberalization can and should precede democratic liberalization. It may be too that in their attempts to rationalize and legitimate this approach to development, modern China's reformers have sought indigenous symbols from China's past such as *li, ren qun, gong* and *wang dao*. Although politicizing these symbols has yet to prove their capabilities in a modern setting, so too has the ancient Greek *demos* yet to be realized fully in Western nations. The belief among NA proponents in the late 1980s that Confucian authority has been profoundly internalized in the Chinese mind, and is therefore worthy of renewal, is a proposition that now seems to be shared by the Secretary General of the CCP, Jiang Zemin, who feels at ease speaking openly, and fondly, of his Confucian upbringing.[9] This, and an acceptance that there is not a fundamental cultural obstacle to the democratization of contemporary Confucian societies, as has been proved by the introduction of successful democratic elections in Taiwan, may suggest that an authoritarian framework is best suited to modelling this course for China.

Notes and References

Chapter 1   Introduction

1. Montesquieu discusses Chinese despotism at some length in *The Spirit of Laws*. See especially pp. 126–8, 315 and 317 of the 1989 edition cited.
2. For further analyses of pre-twentieth century Western perceptions on China, see Dawson, 1964, pp. 1–23 and MacKerras, 1989, pp. 15–65.
3. For a thorough study of the events surrounding the Great Leap Forward and the Cultural Revolution, see MacFarquhar's *The Origins of the Cultural Revolution* (2 vols), especially Parts One and Two of Volume One, pp. 15–165.
4. A Weberian framework is also used to characterize the differences between Mao Zedong and Deng Xiaoping. This is discussed further in Chapter 7 on Deng.
5. There are a number of scholars whose writings could be said to fall within a 'culturalist' framework. De Bary's studies over the decades on the relationship between Confucian ideals and Chinese despotism, as well as his general surveys of Confucian influences on East Asian civilizations, are most instructive. See especially De Bary (1995) for the former and (1988) for the latter. De Bary's classic *Chinese Despotism and the Confucian Ideal* (1957) is also worth recalling in the post-Mao years. Pye's *Asian Power and Politics* (1985) is an incisive account of cultural elements in Asian societies that Pye believes are influential on elite power structures. For Pye's views on the interaction between traditional culture and state–society relations in China, see Pye (1991). A more widely known scholar in recent years, Francis Fukuyama, has also contributed to the culturalist debate. See Fukuyama (1995b). For his views on the ability of Confucianism to transform authoritarian politics to democratic politics, see Fukuyama (1995a). Fei Xiaotong's work (1992) provides an account from mainland China of contemporary China's cultural foundations. For a discussion about cultural influences on Chinese modernization, see Metzger (1987). For discussions on the relationship between Chinese political culture and compliance ideologies, as well as Asian-Western comparative perspectives on culture and selfhood, see Wilson (1992), and Marsella *et al.* (1985).
6. Johnson was critical of Myers and Metzger's 'Sinological Shadows: The state of modern China studies in the United States', *The Washington Quarterly*, 3 (Spring, 1980), pp. 87–114; and of Pye's 1981 work *The Dynamics of Chinese Politics* (Cambridge, Mass.: Oelgeschlager, Gunn & Hain).
7. Virtually all political studies on China in the post-Mao years make reference to Leninism either directly or by implication when discussing

China's elite power structure. For some of the best studies in this area see Friedman (1995, 1991 and 1989b), Baum (1994, 1992, 1989, 1986) and Schram (1993, 1987, 1985).

8. Those who discussed Deng Xiaoping's reforms within a Leninist framework are Schram (1985, 1987), Billeter (1985), Von Senger (1985), Goodman (1987) and Tsou (1987).

9. Those who believed that Deng Xiaoping's reforms might have been influenced by pre-revolutionary cultural antecedents are Bünger (1985) and Schwartz (1987).

10. Andrew Nathan has made significant contributions to discussions on Chinese democracy and welfare. See Nathan (1986a, 1986b, 1990 and 1994). Also see Bedeski (1989). For analysis of cultural influences on authority and welfare theories in republican China, see Chin (1982). For a similar analysis of these influences on Maoist China, see Gong (1989). More general works like Elvin's *The Pattern of the Chinese Past* (1973) and Fairbank's *Chinese Thought and Institutions* (1957) also touch on the authority–welfare nexus.

11. It is the difference between the political hierarchy that *li* creates and 'individual rights' that gets considerable attention in the West. See Hulsewé, 1987, pp. 74, 81, Bastid, 1987, pp. 153, 169, and Tsou, 1987, p. 314.

12. The *Zhouli* is an account of the early Zhou Dynasty (*c.* 1122–771 BC) as an ideal state. Its descriptions of the ideal hierarchy have been used as a blueprint by successive reformers in China's Han, Tang and Song dynasties. The *Liji* is a collection of treatises on ritual matters that were brought together in the Former Han period (202 to *c.* 135 BC). See Hook (1991), p. 344.

13. The analyses of the NA debates to which I refer are the following: Perry (1993), Sautman (1992), Ting and Feng (1991), Ma (1990), Petracca and Mong (1990), Xiu (1990) and Sullivan (1989).

Chapter 2 Xunzi and Ancient Chinese Authority

1. Fung Yu-lan (Feng Youlan), contemporary China's most eminent philosopher, now deceased, expressed these sentiments after receiving an honorary doctorate at Columbia University, 10 September, 1982.

2. Analyses of moral regeneration and social change in the *Lunyu* can be found in Hao Chang's discussions about 'Axial-Age breakthroughs' in relation to classical Confucianism (Chang, 1990, pp. 17–31). Cho-yun Hsu suggests that these same principles apply to Confucian ethics in the modern era (Hsu, 1991, pp. 15–31).

3. *Ren* is most often written as *'jen'*, using the Wade–Giles system of Chinese. I have chosen to use Pinyin throughout this book, and therefore am using the less common romanized spelling of the word.

4. A classic discussion of *ren* and *li's* influence on Confucianism is Fingarette's *Confucius: The Secular as Sacred* (1972). De Bary also explains the important role of both concepts in *The Trouble with Confucianism* (1991). Neville's outline of the Confucian basics in his 1994 article 'Confucianism as a world philosophy' is also useful.

5. There are of course other concepts of philosophical importance in the *Lunyu*, *yi* ('righteousness') and *zhengming* ('rectification of names') to name two. But these, and others, get far less consistent academic coverage than *ren* and *li*.

6. See Roetz, 1993, p. 47. Cua's discourse on *li* in Confucian moral theory is evidence of the ambiguity of the term (Cua, 1989, p. 209). Schwartz's discussion on the 'polarities in Confucian thought' is also instructive (Schwartz, 1964b, pp. 3–15).

7. See Shun, 1993, pp. 457–8, De Bary, 1991, p. 30, Hsu, 1991, p. 19, Ivanhoe, 1990, p. 26, Hall and Ames, 1987, pp. 85, 110–11, 114.

8. See Shun, 1993, pp. 457–8, Ivanhoe, 1990, p. 24, Hall and Ames, 1987, pp. 85, 110–11, 114, Cua, 1989, pp. 214–15, Gong, 1989, p. 369.

9. The idea that Confucius might have made *ren* the general virtue from which all others were to be understood in the *Lunyu* was first brought to my attention in an interview with Professor Zhu Buokun at Beijing University in 1992. This point has also been argued by the following: Fung, 1991, p. 237, Tu, 1985, pp. 86–8, Hsiao, 1979, p. 101 and Chan, 1975, p. 107.

10. See Bloom's 1994 work 'Mencian arguments on human nature', pp. 19–53, and Graham's *Studies in Chinese Philosophy and Philosophical Literature*, especially Chapter 1.

11. For additional references to the Mencian link between benevolence and welfare, see the *Mencius*, 1988, pp. 58–9, 65, 97, 121–2, 186.

12. See Bloom, 1994, pp. 19–53 and Graham, 1990, Chapter 1.

13. Williams also argues that it would be wrong to ascribe any real political role to the common people in the *Mencius* because their actions are determined by the authority of the ruler. See Williams, 1994, p. 115.

14. In 1982, Goh Keng Swee, the architect of much official policy in Singapore at the time, announced that Confucian ethics would (from 1984) be taught in schools. He said that the economic successes of Taiwan, South Korea, Hong Kong and Singapore were possible because of the Confucianist tradition of these countries (see Rodan, 1989, pp. 27, 172). Although 'Confucianism' has become a broad term encompassing several schools of thought, when it is used in this context, it is usually in reference to the principal figure of Confucius himself, rather than his disciples. Li notes that in the case of Taiwan, Confucius may have influenced the importance policymakers placed on 'economic equity' in their development goals (Li, 1988, p. 9). Popular journals which attribute the economic successes of East and Southeast Asia to Confucianism are usually referring to the man, not his followers. See, for example, Ching's 'Confucius the New Saviour' in *Far Eastern Economic Review*, 10 November, 1994, p. 37, and the article in *Asiaweek*, 'Confucian Comeback', 26 October, 1994, pp. 21–2.

15. See Jenner's comments on Confucius's distaste for those who seek profit (Jenner, 1992, p. 173).

16. There are other translations of the *Xunzi*, for example, Homer H. Dubs, 1928, *The Works of Hsuntzu* (London: Probsthain Publishers) and Burton Watson, 1963, *Hsün Tzu: Basic Writings* (New York: Columbia University Press). But these are incomplete, and do not rely

on the extensive critical exegesis from Chinese and Japanese sources that Knoblock provides.

17. For more on Xunzi's belief in the relationship between scarcity and disorder, see Schwartz, 1985, pp. 291–2, and De Bary, 1988, p. 9.

18. For more on Xunzi's criticism of Mozi and of what Xunzi saw as the failure of Mozi's egalitarian beliefs to promote wealth, see *Xunzi*, Vol. 1, pp. 194–5, and Vol. 2, p. 104.

19. It should again be made clear that although Xunzi believed man to be inherently evil, he did not think that there was no hope for mankind. He was optimistic that man could become good through the nurturing of society. As for Li Si's association with the destruction of ancient texts, Knoblock argues that though the burning of some books did occur, the connection between this event and the autocratic ways of the first emperor and his associates has been grossly exaggerated, because any books that were thought to contain practical knowledge were not destroyed (See Knoblock's commentary in the *Xunzi*, Vol. 1, pp. 36–7).

20. The *Ru* school was known for its adherence to regulations. Xunzi argues, however, that it was expected of the *Ru* to support a ruler who applied regulations flexibly and who adapted them according to the demands of particular situations. Knoblock adds that Xunzi's examination of a country's prosperity and the techniques for increasing its wealth are unusual for a *Ru* philosopher (see Knoblock's commentary in the *Xunzi*, Vol. 2, pp. 79, 113).

21. For views on Xunzi as China's great philosophical pragmatist, see especially Cua's 1985 work *Ethical Argumentation: A study of Hsün Tzu's moral epistemology*. Chang, 1990, p. 25, Cotterell, 1988, p. 71 and Tillman, 1982, p. 207 also refer to Xunzi's pragmatism.

22. Xunzi's support for what might be termed accountable institutions is discussed in Roetz (Roetz, 1993, p. 223). The flexibility of Xunzi's political system is discussed in Creel's chapter 'The role of compromise in Chinese culture' (Creel, 1987, pp. 135–51, especially p. 146).

23. Farmer discusses dynastic successions that followed principles similar to Xunzi's orthodoxy (see Farmer, 1990, pp. 105–6, 112, 125).

24. A useful starting point to understanding the adaptation of *li* to post-1949 China is Gong's 'The legacy of Confucian culture in Maoist China' (Gong, 1989, pp. 363–70). De Bary has suggested that *li's* basic purpose, '... demand for compliance with or conformity to direction from above ...' may also be providing the stability needed for economic progress in the post-Mao years (De Bary, 1995, p. 182). Further assessments of *li's* influence in the post-Mao era can be found in Watson's 'The renegotiation of Chinese cultural identity in the post-Mao era' (Watson, 1992, pp. 74–5).

25. For more on Wang Yangming's theory of 'knowledge-for-action', see Ihlan, 1993, pp. 455–6, 458, 461. Cheng's comparative survey 'Practical learning in Yen Yüan, Chu Hsi and Wang Yang-ming' is also instructive (Cheng, 1979, pp. 37–65).

26. Xunzi's *qun* was not so prominent in the *Xunzi* itself, but later became so in a work entitled the *Qunshu Zhiyao* (roughly translated as the *Book of Group Regulations*), which was completed during the Tang dynasty in

the year 631. Knoblock notes that Chapter 38 of the work is an extended excerpt from the *Xunzi*. The *Qunshu Zhiyao* declined in significance in China by the twelfth century. However, it continued to have considerable prestige in Japan well into the twentieth century, where it was printed for the Japanese Imperial Library as late as 1940. Greater contact between Japan and China in the nineteenth century led to the *Qunshu Zhiyao's* reprinting in China in 1857 (see Knoblock's commentary in the *Xunzi*, Vol. 1, pp. 109–10 and 265ff). The *Qunshu Zhiyao* seems to have been a major influence on Liang Qichao and Sun Yatsen, though they do not acknowledge it directly. The influence of *qun* ('grouping') on their political theory is discussed in Chapters 4 and 5.

27. Deng's views on material, ideological and cultural progress could have been derived from his reading of Marxist texts, but it seems more likely that they were influenced by indigenous sources. Long before Deng made this comment in 1983, discussions at the Twelfth Party Congress, in September 1982, deliberated over the special characteristics of China's 'spiritual civilization', which included the relevance to China of what was termed the 'foreign concept' of 'universal humanism' *(rendao zhuyi)*, a concept which, if embraced, was considered by party members to be potentially unsettling to stability. See Baum, 1993, pp. 340–1.

28. For more on Deng's views about egalitarianism, incentives to labour, emolument for work done and uneven economic growth for common prosperity, see Deng, 1987, pp. 55, 57, 96, 101–2, 104, 106, 113, 135, 188.

29. Salisbury has indicated that both Mao's and Deng's periods of political tenure were preceded not by their reading of Marxist works but of Chinese historical texts, one of which, Sima Qian's *Records of the Historian (Shiji)*, includes entries on Xunzi's student, Li Si, Chief Minister at the beginning of the Qin dynasty (Salisbury, 1992, pp. 8–9, 53, 325–6).

30. In 1950, a year after the CCP came to power in China, a concordance to Xunzi's writings was published in Beijing (*Xunzi Yinde*. Beijing: Harvard-Yenching Institute Sinological Index Series Supplement No. 22). I have not come across a similar work published on Confucius or Mencius in China at this time.

31. This standpoint may also have been assisted by Mao's condemnation in 1964 of Confucius and the tradition of *ren* (benevolence), when Mao said, 'Confucius said: "Benevolence is the characteristic element of humanity. The benevolent man loves others." Whom did he [Confucius] love? All men? Nothing of the kind. Did he love the exploiters?' (see Schram, 1974, p. 214).

32. The thoughts of Xunzi's student, Han Feizi, were also considered important during the anti-Confucian campaign of the early 1970s. (see Louie, 1987, pp. 155, 178–88).

Chapter 3   Kang Youwei

1. Tan Sitong (1865–98), a follower of Kang Youwei, was the most audacious critic of Chinese patriarchal authority in the 1890s. This was

reflected in his *Exposition of Benevolence (Ren Xue)*, which Tan believed could provide a democratic alternative to the entrapment Chinese people felt because of 2000 years of feudal ethical codes (see Hook, 1991, p. 320). Tan's determination to adapt *ren* to modern China's political doctrines is a reminder of the ongoing interest among the Chinese literati of the day in this ancient concept and its relationship to *li* on which the feudal ethical codes were based. Tan derided the authoritarian tradition of *li* when he said that 'The teaching of the last two thousand years has been the teaching of [Xunzi]'. But in doing so, he also expressed a view that may have been agreed upon by his contemporaries but not willingly expressed, as even a criticism of Xunzi's influence on the Chinese state system would undermine the prominence given to Confucius in China over the centuries. Tan's excerpt is taken from Chan Sin-Wai's *An Exposition of Benevolence:The Jen-Hsüeh of T'an Ssu-t'ung* (1984), p. 149.

2. Liang Qichao (1873–1929) was a student of Kang Youwei, who went into exile in Japan after the conservative coup of 1898. While in Japan, and during his travels in the West, Liang used his writings to raise support for the reformers' cause among overseas Chinese and foreign governments (see Spence, 1990, p. 798). Liang's excerpt is taken from Hsiao, 1975, p. 207).

3. Although Kang's reform proposals in the late 1890s were pre-dated by figures from the 'Self-strengthening Movement' 30 years earlier, Kang's proposals, it is often agreed, ensured that the political landscape of China was forever changed (interviews, Zhu Buokun and Zhang Dainian, 1992, and Wang Xiaoqiu, 1993). This view is supported by historical works on modern China, which devote considerable space to Kang. See He, 1991, Hu, 1991 and Yü, 1994 as well as Wang Gungwu, 1991, Mu, 1982, and Michael and Taylor, 1964. A more specific work on Kang himself is Jung-pang Lo's *K'ang Yu-wei: A biography and a symposium* (1967). For additional coverage of Kang's impact on the ongoing debates about Chinese authority and democracy, see Chi's *Ideological Conflicts in Modern China: Democracy and authoritarianism* (1992), and Andrew Nathan's *Chinese Democracy: The individual and the state in twentieth century China* (1986a). Revisionist historians have argued that Kang's role in the Reform Movement of 1898 has been exaggerated and that reforms would have taken place without him. Kwong's 1984 work is instructive in this respect, as is Chan's 1992 article 'The reformer as conspirator: K'ang Yu-wei versus the empress Dowager, 1904–1906'. The Revisionists have been criticized by those who continue to think that Kang was fundamental to change in 1898. See especially Young-Tsu Wong's 'Revisionism reconsidered: Kang Youwei and the Reform Movement of 1898' (Wong, 1992, pp. 513–44).

4. See Hook, 1991, pp. 218–20 for details of these conflicts.

5. Yan Fu (1854–1921), also described as a 'reformer', was a Confucian scholar–official in China who was sent to England in 1877 to study naval science. While there, he took a deep interest in Western political theory, translating into Chinese influential works by Huxley, Spencer,

Adam Smith and Charles Darwin. He also made French Enlightenment thought and nineteenth-century socialism accessible to China through his adaptations of Japanese translations. He became the first president of the modernized Peking University in 1912. See Spence, 1990, pp. 239, 302–3, 313–14 and 808, and Hook, 1991, p. 320.

6.   Li Hongzhang (1823–1901), known as the most important figure among the Self-strengtheners, was a Chinese general, provincial official and diplomat in China. In the 1870s and 1880s, he assisted in the development of China's railways, telegraph lines, shipping companies and arms manufacturers. See Spence, 1990, pp. 187–8, 799, and Hook, 1991, pp. 223–5.

7.   These views were expressed most vehemently by Yan Fu in a series of articles written in 1895, which often include the phrase 'freedom is the substance, democracy is the application.' Also see Yan Fu, 1895a, pp. 78–82, 1895b, pp. 71–7. The most frequently cited Western source on Yan Fu is Schwartz's *In Search of Wealth and Power: Yen Fu and the West* (see Schwartz, 1964a).

8.   Tan Sitong's criticisms of *li* can be found in his book *Ren Xue (An Exposition of Benevolence)*. See Chan's 1984 translation, pp. 55–9 and pp. 67–156, where Tan frequently reiterates his criticisms of *li*. Specific Western influences on Tan are difficult to pin down. Shek's article 'Some western influences on T'an Ssu-T'ung's thought' seems the best account to date (Shek, 1976, pp. 194–207).

9.   These views are taken from Zhang Zhidong's *Quan Xue Pian (Exhortation on Learning)*, which is considered a key work from the 1898 reform period. Zhang Zhidong (1837–1909) was a civil servant who was the governor-general of Hunan and Hubei provinces for nearly 20 years. He built up China's first coal iron and steel complex in Hubei. See Spence, 1990, pp. 225–6, 252–3, 810, and Hook, 1991, p. 231. Li Huaxin's 1988 work, *An Intellectual History of Modern China* also provides a useful account of the clash between the Conservative defence of the *sangang* and their fear that support for *minquan* would lead to disorder and the collapse of the government. For the most comprehensive Western account of Zhang's contributions to these debates, see Bays's 1978 work *China Enters the Twentieth Century: Chang Chih-tung and the issues of the new age, 1895–1909*.

10.   This marked the beginning of the '*ti-yong* dichotomy' or '*ti-yong* rationalization' that Levenson has highlighted. *Ti* and *yong* stand for 'substance' and 'function'. These underlay the Self-strengtheners' view that an ideal Chinese modernization would combine Chinese ethics *(ti)* with Western science and technology *(yong)*. As Levenson describes it, '... the way to stay Chinese was to stay Chinese in all aspects of culture [the *ti*]', whereas the utility of Western learning [the *yong*] would be used for Chinese development (see Levenson, 1958, pp. 56–62).

11.   A strong account in Chinese of what the Self-strengtheners' solutions were can be found in Fu Keqing's brief article 'Ten differences between the reformist and Westernization groups' *(Tian reng weixing qiyu yangwu pai de shida fengqi)* (see Fu, 1984, pp. 61–6). The journal *Chinese Studies in History* also contributes a number of articles on the

      late Qing period and this area of enquiry. See, for example, Lü Xiaobo's 'Court sponsored reforms, 1895–1898' (Lü, 1995, pp. 49–66), and Liu Kwang-Ching's article 'The beginnings of China's modernization' (Liu, 1991, pp. 7–18). Hsü's *The Rise of Modern China*, 1970, also comments on the Self-strengtheners' solutions, p. 348, as does Teng and Fairbank's *China's Response to the West*, 1954, p. 86.

12.   One cannot neglect, for example, the important role that the Self-strengtheners played in importing Western political ideas to China in their translations of works by Adam Smith, J. S. Mill, Charles Darwin and Aldous Huxley, to name a few. In addition, the Self-strengtheners' use of *ti-yong* is said to remain important to modernization in China to this day (see Pye, 1993b, p. 128). Moreover, the Conservatives continued to be a significant force into the early twentieth century because of the failure of the 1898 reforms. At this time, the Qing court returned to a more conservative line, which was influenced by Zhang Zhidong, until the demands of China's rapidly deteriorating situation called on the monarchy to initiate wider reforms after the Boxer Rebellion (see Gasster, 1969, pp. 15–16).

13.   On the short-sightedness of the Conservatives' and Self-strengtheners' approaches to reform, see Sun's 1992 article 'The relationship between Chinese traditional culture and Westernization', pp. 374–94. This problem is also commented on by Lü, 1995, pp. 50, 52 as well as a number of Western critics, including Gasster's 1969 work, pp. 5, 7, Twitchett and Fairbank, 1978, pp. 497–9, 511 and Feuerwerker *et. al.*, 1967, pp. 8–9.

14.   This has also been suggested by the majority of scholars included in footnote 3 of this chapter.

15.   Scholars, including Hsiao, argue, however, that *ren* was more important to Kang than *li*, and that *ren* was the basis of Kang's reforms. See Hsiao, 1975, pp. 94, 160, and Chan, 1967, pp. 355–74.

16.   Although Xunzi also referred to *datong*, Kang's 'Three Ages' *(San Shi)*, the 'Age of Disorder', the 'Age of Approaching Peace' and the 'Age of Universal Peace', seem to be based on Confucius's 'Two Ages', *Xiaogang* ('Small Tranquillity') and *Datong* ('Great Community').

17.   Kang's views on the 'educative function' of local self-government are the same as Tocqueville's, who said in *Democracy in America*, 'Town meetings are to liberty what primary schools are to science: they teach men how to use and how to enjoy it. A nation may establish a free government, but without the spirit of municipal institutions it cannot have the spirit of liberty.' (Tocqueville, 1952, p. 57).

18.   For discussions on conservative reaction to the 1898 reforms, see Bays, 1978, pp. 43–6, Wong, 1986, p. 11 and Chi, 1992, p. 13.

Chapter 4   Liang Qichao

1.   Huang also defines *minquan* as 'the "right" of the people to a voice in government.' (Huang, 1972, pp. 28–9).

2.   *Gong* appears in the classic *Liji (Record of Rites)* (see De Bary, 1991, pp. 100–1), which, as was noted in Chapter 2, was highly influential on the *Xunzi*.

3. Chang notes that *qun* became so important to Liang that he tended to '... drift away from the moral ideal of *[ren]*, which had also played a major part in his intellectual background.' (Chang, 1971, p. 99) This again suggests the unimportance of *ren*, and its chief advocate Mencius, to late Qing reformers. It also goes against Nathan's view that Mencian dictates were a crucial part of reformers' attempts to define new approaches to state-society relations in the late Qing (Nathan, 1986b, pp. 148–51).

4. Liang's grasp of Marx and Nietzsche was not as strong as his understanding of Western liberalism.

5. This is also in evidence in Liang's translation of Rousseau's 'general will' as 'national will' *(guomin zhongyi shuo)*.

6. Also see Nathan, 1986b, pp. 155–6 on this point.

7. Liang's criticisms of American democratic institutions are surveyed in Grieder's *Intellectuals and the State in Modern China: A narrative history*, pp. 161–7, as well as in Spence's *Gate of Heavenly Peace: The Chinese and their revolution, 1895–1980*, pp. 42–4.

8. These conclusions bear striking similarities to Tocqueville's observations in America that democracy did not represent an appropriate system for taking collective, future-oriented decisions: 'A democracy finds it difficult to coordinate the details of a great undertaking and to fix on some plan and carry it through with determination in spite of obstacles. It has little capacity for combining measures in secret and waiting patiently for the result.' (quoted in Elster, 1988, pp. 94–5).

9. Gasster claims that the Japanese '... had been intensely interested in German constitutionalism', and that their own constitution of 1889 was modelled on that of Prussia. Gasster cites Ike's work *The Beginnings of Political Democracy in Japan* as proof of this. See Gasster, 1969, p. 109, and Ike, 1950, pp. 174–8.

10. Liang was interested in Bluntschli's ideas as they appeared in the German theorist's work, *Public Law*, published in 1872, which was widely read by Japanese theorists. See Grieder, 1981, pp. 141, 168.

11. I have found the clearest explanation of these points in *Min Bao*, the journal of Sun Yatsen's revolutionary party, published in Tokyo. The views noted were written by one of Sun's followers, Wang Jingwei, who included Liang's points in order to criticize them. See Wang, 1906b, pp. 459–64.

12. Elsewhere, Liang refers specifically to the instability of Brazil and Peru. See Levenson, 1959, pp. 69–70.

13. The recency to Liang's writings of the Boxer Rebellion (1900), the occupation of Beijing by the various colonial powers, including Japan, and the indemnity required, all provided good cause for his fears and thinking on the issue of partition. Liang notes that during the Boxer Rebellion, the Russian government sent its troops to northeast Manchuria, saying that the purpose was 'to safeguard Russian citizens.' But the troops did not retreat until the end of the Russo-Japanese War in 1905 (see Liang, 1906a, p. 285). Japan's annexation of Korea in 1910 must have confirmed Liang's views further.

14. Fairbank and Feuerwerker add more definitively that Sun Yatsen's

vision of a democratic China, embodied in his *Fundamentals of National Reconstruction* (1918), is remarkable for how little it reflects the views of the Guomindang left. They add that Sun's idea of 'self-government' was a model of political development that he had derived from Kang Youwei and Liang Qichao (Fairbank and Feuerwerker, 1986, p. 344). Also see Dirlik, 1988 on this point and Grieder, 1981, p. 187.

15. Along with his writings on the Western theorists we have noted, Liang wrote, though more briefly, on Descartes, Spinoza, Hobbes, Cromwell, Cavour, Mazzini and Kossuth. Between 1903 and 1906, he also introduced his students in China to Platonic philosophy, Kantian liberalism, Hegelian idealism and the works of Kropotkin (see Grieder, 1981, p. 159 and Wakeman, 1975, p. 239).

16. See Liang's book, *History of Chinese Political Thought During the Early Tsin Period* (1930), which has been translated into English.

17. For more on Liang's criticism of Mencius, see Chang, 1971, p. 172, and Hsü, 1970, p. 600.

18. For details of Kang Youwei's and Liang Qichao's influences on Mao Zedong, see Chi, 1992, p. 270, and Huang, 1972, p. 7. For details of Liang's influence on Deng Xiaoping, see Fewsmith, 1991, pp. 25, 30–1, 45–7, and Schell, 1988, p. 199.

Chapter 5   Sun Yatsen

1. After publication in 1924, Sun's *Three People's Principles* was by law the chief textbook in all Nationalist schools in China. See E. G. Chapman's Introduction in Sun, 1928, p. 12. Citations from Sun's *Three People's Principles* are taken from Chapman's 1928 translation of the work.

2. The 'Three People's Principles' is seen as Sun's most important work by scholars in Taiwan (see Shih, 1977, Sun, 1977, and Ma, 1975); by Western Sinologists who have done research on Sun (see Chang, 1989, Cheng, 1989, Godley, 1987, Chin, 1982, Gregor *et al.*, 1981b, and Hana, 1982); and even by Mao and Deng, who, when referring to Sun, usually make reference to his 'Three Principles', rather than to his other writings (see Chapter 6, and Deng, 1987, pp. 50, 65, 75). Other important works of Sun's include *Memoirs of a Chinese Revolutionary: A Programme of National Reconstruction for China* (1918), and *The International Development of China* (1922), to which the chapter will also refer. The chapter does not discuss Sun's 'Five Power Constitution' because it has never been relevant to the politics of post-1949 China.

3. Meisner speaks of the 'extraordinarily influential' role of Li Dazhao and Chen Duxiu (contemporaries of Sun Yatsen's) on the CCP (Meisner, 1994, pp. 182–4). Yet, as Chapters 6 and 7 illustrate, Li and Chen seemed to play no role whatever in Mao's or Deng's development strategies. In fact, Deng spoke with absolute derision about Chen, as do other current Chinese Party members about Hu Shi, a Chinese liberal, and also a contemporary of Sun's (see Chapter 7). The exclusion of these important figures, plus the fact that Li Dazhao is rarely, if ever,

mentioned as significant to present-day Chinese politics, suggests that Sun, whose theoretical contributions to China have been acknowledged frequently in the post-Mao years (see Chapter 7), remains the most important pre-revolutionary figure to the CCP.

4. A substantial amount of research has been done on Sun's nationalism. See in particular Townsend's article 'Chinese nationalism', and pages 97–8, 103, 127, 129 for Townsend's view on Sun's 'ethnic-state' (1992), as well as Jan's 1989 article 'The doctrine of nationalism and the Chinese revolution' (pp. 141–58), and Chan, 1987, pp. 121–38. For the opposing view, that Chinese nationalism prompted a decay of the 'ethnic–state' and a transformation to a more highly politicized nation–state, see Duara's article 'Deconstructing the Chinese nation' (1993) and Bedeski, 1981, p. 154.

5. Gregor and Chang suggest that Sun's thinking about 'knowledge-for-action' drew its inspiration from the neo-Confucian scholar Wang Yangming (Gregor and Chang, 1980, pp. 388–404). As was noted in Chapter 2, Wang Yangming was in this respect influenced by Xunzi. For more on the five ancient concepts that figure prominently in Sun's political doctrines, see Metzger, 1992, p. 22, Yü, 1989, pp. 96–7, Zhang, 1987, p. 49, Kindermann, 1982, p. 83, Nivison, 1953, p. 137, and Linebarger, 1937, pp. 33–4, 54, 71–2, 85. Linebarger's father was a personal adviser to Sun Yatsen. He was also a legal adviser to the Guomindang in its early years. Linebarger's 1937 work, *The Political Doctrines of Sun Yat-sen*, partly relies on his father's notes from interviews with Sun over a three year period (1919–22), and remains a rich and incisive work on Sun's basic outlook.

6. Sun does not use the terms *qun* and *gong* in the *Three People's Principles*, but his lectures on 'nationalism' express a regular concern with the necessity of 'grouping' and 'public-mindedness' to Chinese nationalism. See in particular Sun's first three lectures on 'Nationalism' in Sun, 1928, Volume 1. For further discussion on the historical relevance of the *Qunshu Zhiyao* to Chinese and Japanese theorists, see footnote 26 of Chapter 2.

7. Also see Linebarger, 1937, pp. 71–2 on this point about *wang dao*. Chang and Gordon claim that Japanese scholars and political figures with whom Sun associated while in Japan in the early 1900s believed that *wang dao* was necessary to a full understanding of Sun's policies (Chang and Gordon, 1991, p. 156).

8. Historical details of Sun's 'knowledge-for-action' dictum and what Sun viewed as its opposite, 'knowledge is easy and action is difficult', can be found in Hu and Lin, 1931, pp. 46, 49. For more current appraisals of these in relation to Sun's theories, see Kindermann, 1982, p. 83, and Nivison, 1953, p. 137.

9. Sun also devotes two chapters to the problem of knowledge and action in his *Memoirs of a Chinese Revolutionary*. In this, he says that Japan's transformation was favourably affected by its acceptance of 'action is easy and knowledge is difficult', and that China should follow this example if it wished to be saved from poverty (Sun, 1918, pp. 103–4).

10. These views were expressed by prominent members of Sun's revolu-

tionary party. See Wang Dong's 1907 article *Geming jingshi lun* ('The trend of the revolution') (Wang, 1907a, pp. 791–2), and Wang Jingwei's denunciation of Liang Qichao's writings in his article 'Zai buo "Xinmin Congbao" zhi zhengzhi geming lun' ('A second denouncement on "Xinmin Congbao's" theory of political revolution') (Wang, 1906c, pp. 471–3). These articles are from the journal *Min Bao*, which was inaugurated by Sun Yatsen in November 1905 and published monthly in Tokyo until 1908. After a two year absence, two final issues were published by Wang Jingwei in 1910. All 26 issues were later published in Beijing in 1957. Further analysis of the conflict between the revolutionaries and the reformers over the Manchu aristocracy can be found in Zhang, 1984, pp. 39–40.

11. See footnote 6 of this chapter.
12. See Wang, 1907a, pp. 791–2, Wang, 1906c, pp. 471–3, and Teng and Fairbank, 1954, p. 264.
13. Key figures in the revolutionary movement discuss the importance of national liberation ahead of individual liberties. See in particular Hu Hanmin's article *'Min Bao' zhi liu da shuyi* ('Six Doctrines of "Min Bao"') (Hu, 1906, p. 376). For similar discussions, see Wang, 1906a, pp. 521, 526, and Wang, 1906c, p. 476.
14. Sun's views on 'natural rights' versus 'natural obligations' are analyzed in Chang and Gordon, 1991, p. 109. For the relationship between Sun's understanding of the *Social Contract* and the traditional elements from his Confucian upbringing that may have influenced this interpretation, see Gregor, 1981a, p. 63.
15. Metzger argues that Mill, '... viewing China in similar terms during the nineteenth century, would have agreed with Sun in the early twentieth century that [China] still was not ready for a political system centered on liberty' (Metzger, 1992, p. 33). Metzger quotes from Mill's *On Liberty* to illustrate this point:

> Liberty, as a principle, has no application to any state of things anterior to the time when mankind has become capable of being 'improved by free and equal discussion'. Until that time, there is nothing for them but implicit obedience to an Akbar or a Charlemagne, if they are so fortunate to find one (Metzger, 1992, p. 28).

16. Sun's view seems to be confirmed by Shaffer's study, which notes that '[Even] [w]hile the May Fourth Movement was at the peak of its popularity, its advocates still were shy about asserting individual interest against group interest ... [and often spoke of the individual's] higher obligation, such as dedicated service to the nation.' (Shaffer, 1990, pp. 7–8).
17. Also see Kindermann, 1982, p. 65, and Hsü, 1933, pp. 312, 318.
18. This echoes Kang Youwei's and Liang Qichao's questioning the purpose of the French Revolution, the demand for freedom and equality, when, to Kang's and Liang's minds, the main problems in France after the Revolution were poverty and hunger (see Chapters 3 and 4).
19. Here, Sun's views resemble those of Lee Kuanyu's, spoken several decades later. Lee said that the type of people who should command

Singapore's government were only those who were genuinely talented, of whom, he said in 1982, they '... amounted to only twelve to fourteen persons a year' (quoted in Milne and Mauzy, 1990, p. 110).

20.	Gregor and Chang suggest that Sun's hierarchical system has parallels in Western political theory. They cite John Locke, whose defence of 'natural equality' also acknowledged inequalities of merit and virtue in every society (Gregor and Chang, 1989, p. 128).

21.	This resembles Deng Xiaoping's reason for rejecting multiparty democracy, that it 'hamstrings' a government's ability to get things done (see Chapter 7).

22.	Also see Sun, 1928, Vol. 2, pp. 120–1, 133–5, and Leng and Palmer, 1961, p. 24. The degree to which Sun rejected Marxism can also be seen in his words about communism. He said that communism was a 'good ideal', but not one that people would be ready for '... for another "one or two million years".' (see Friedman, 1974, p. 26).

23.	Leong also disputes the argument that Sun's tightly-knit revolutionary vanguard was based on Leninism, saying that a vanguard party was an idea that had already come to Sun as early as 1914 with the establishment of the Zhonghua Gemindang, independently of any Leninist inspiration (Leong, 1987, p. 69).

24.	Sansom's analysis of Sun's speeches to Chinese labourers and peasants found him to be '... embarrassingly forthright in expressing to their faces his low opinion of [their] political understanding and capacity for political action without the direction and indoctrination of the central government.' (Sansom, 1988, p. 127).

25.	For further views on the insignificance of Leninism to Sun Yatsen's theories, see Gregor and Chang, 1989, p. 117, Friedman, 1989, pp. 253–4, Chan, 1987, p. 129, Chang, 1982, pp. 4, 6, 11–15, and Scalapino and Schiffrin, 1959, p. 333. The idea of a Leninist-style political revolution is also condemned in post-Mao China as 'evil', and as something which must be replaced by '... peaceful transformation based on presumed real national essences.' (see Friedman, 1993, p. 6).

26.	For views on the influences of German and Japanese social reforms on Sun, see Chang, 1985, p. 90, Friedman, 1974, p. 25, and Scalapino and Schiffrin, 1959, pp. 325, 333.

27.	As a child who was educated in the Chinese classics, Sun was expected to read the *Liji* (see Gregor, 1981a, p. 56).

28.	Sun outlined his development plans in the *Programme of National Reconstruction for China* and the *International Development of China*. Analyses of these works can be found in Kindermann, 1982, and Hsü, 1933. For summaries on Sun's plans for local self-government, see Chang and Gordon, 1989, pp. 120–1, and Teng and Fairbank, 1954, pp. 228–9.

29.	It may also be for this reason that Deng Yangda, a prominent member of the Guomindang, who had spent two years studying economics in Europe (1928–30), had familiarized himself with, and seemed to support, the writings of Keynes (Sansom, 1988, pp. 360–1).

30.	For analyses of Sun's view that the long-term goal of Chinese socialism was to begin with a period of capitalist development that was guided by the state, see in particular Chan, 1987, 'The historical significance of Sun Yatsen's career and ideology in twentieth century Chinese politics', pp. 122, 131, 133–5, but also Sansom, 1988, p. 62, Kindermann, 1989, p. 68, Jin, 1987, p. 158, and Hana, 1982, p. 130. For the relationship between Sun's socialism and Chinese Marxism, see Gregor and Chang, 1982, 'Marxism, Sun Yat-sen and the concept of imperialism', pp. 72, 75, 77. For the relationship between Sun's socialism and mainland China's politics in the Deng era, see Wu, 1994, 'Possible political developments in mainland China following the Third Plenum of the CCP's Fourteenth Central Committee', pp. 3, 14, and Godley, 1987, 'Socialism with Chinese characteristics: Sun Yatsen and the international development of China', p. 118. Gregor argues that '... the readiness with which Taiwan accepted foreign concessional and non-concessional aid and foreign loans and investment was a direct result of Sun's conception of international economic relations.' Gregor adds that 'Had Sun's anti-imperialism entailed withdrawal from the international market economy ... the development of [Taiwan] would possibly have been like Castro's Cuba.' (Gregor, 1981b, pp. 92–3).

31. According to Chang and Gordon, the future leadership of mainland China may accept the 'Three People's Principles' (or a modified version of it) 'simply because it is primarily a Chinese creation and attuned to Chinese preferences' (Chang and Gordon, 1991, pp. 166–7). Cheng notes that because 'Sun remains the only political leader honored on both sides of the Taiwan Strait, many of his proposals are now considered the best solutions for China's modernization and industrialization' (Cheng, 1989, pp. 1–2).

Chapter 6   Mao Zedong

1. Quotations from Mao's writings are taken from his *Selected Works*, 1975–77 (5 volumes) (Oxford: Pergamon Press).

2. An understanding of Leninist influences on Mao's thought would be incomplete without a reading of Schram's books and articles. See in particular Schram's *Mao Tse-tung Unrehearsed: Talks and letters, 1956–1971* (1974), and *The Thought of Mao Tse-Tung* (1989). The dramatic economic changes that occurred in post-Mao China make Schram's *The Scope of State Power in China* (1985) and *Foundations and Limits of State Power in China* (1987), as well as his commemorative article on the centenary of Mao's birth, 'Mao Zedong, a hundred years on: The legacy of a ruler' (1994), extremely valuable reading. For more about Leninist influences on Mao, see Schurrmann (1969), Schurrmann and Schell (1967), and Goldstein (1991).

3. One study that does compare Mao's political theory to Sun Yatsen's theories, rather than to Marxism–Leninism, is Bedeski's analysis of the state under Sun and Mao. See Bedeski, 1977, pp. 338–54.

4. In an interview with Edgar Snow in 1936, Mao spoke about the compatibility of Chinese Communism with the 'Three People's Principles'. Mao said that '... in the proposed anti-Japanese united front the Communists would support a parliamentary form of representative

government, *which should restore and once more realize Sun Yat-sen's final will and his three 'basic principles'*. (Snow, 1938, Quoted in Leng and Palmer, 1961 p. 96) (Emphasis added.)

5. Also see Bedeski, 1977, pp. 352–3 on this point.

6. According to one historian at Beijing University, the theme of transition from democratic revolution to socialist revolution embodied in Mao's speech *On New Democracy* relied much more on indigenous political thought than on Marxist–Leninist imports (Rong, 1992, interview).

7. Mao's writings often support the view that the CCP's democratic centralism was the best way to ensure individual initiative, the growth of private capital and the protection of private property. See Mao, Vol. 1, pp. 291–2, Vol. 2, pp. 204–6 and Vol. 3, pp. 230–1.

8. Yuan Shikai (1859–1916), leader of the powerful Beiyang (North China) army and initially loyal to the empress dowager Cixi, later played an important role in arranging the abdication of the Qing in 1912, at which time Sun Yatsen offered Yuan the presidency of the new republic. Yuan abused the office in many ways, but principally when he proclaimed himself emperor in 1915, He died six months later, in 1916 (see Spence, 1990, p. 809).

9. For more on Mao's discussions about productive relations versus productive forces, see his speech 'On the Correct Handling of Contradictions Among the People' (1957), Vol. 5, p. 393.

10. Mao wrote extensively about the need to shift from democratic centralism to mass democracy from as early as 1953. See Mao, Vol. 5, pp. 92, 172, 484–5, 499, 503. These writings are an ominous sign of the chaos that was to follow in China.

11. For critical views on Mao's shift to Marxist–Leninist theory in the late 1950s, see especially Womack, 1986, 'Where Mao went wrong: Epistemology and ideology in Mao's Leftist politics', Meisner, 1982, *Marxism, Maoism, and Utopianism: Eight essays* and Teiwes, 1984, pp. 99–100.

12. Ruan says that Mao's preparations for de-Stalinization and a greater openness to Western capitalist nations are apparent in Mao's speeches 'On the Ten Major Relationships' and the 'Double Hundred Policy'. See Ruan, 1994, pp. 2–5.

13. John Service was a political officer at the American Embassy in the wartime capital of Chongqing, 1941–5.

14. Service and five other Americans were later arrested (December 1951) during the McCarthy purges, on charges of conspiring to commit espionage. According to Sheng, top CCP members at Yan'an considered the six as 'friendly Americans sympathetic to China's cause of resistance and democracy.' See Sheng, 1993, p. 157. Theodore White, an American journalist who was in China from 1938–45, has commented on the great loss of Service as an adviser to American policymakers: 'Service had wined, befriended and spent countless hours of both purposeful and aimless conversation with the same Chinese Red leaders we now confronted across guns. They had respected and had liked him. But the terrorism of Joe McCarthy prevented the use of

either Service ... or anyone who knew anything about Asia, to help us address our problems in Asia.' (White, 1983, p. 515).

15. Mao's view of President Roosevelt as an 'enlightened bourgeoisie' may be an echo of Liang Qichao's belief about the importance of an enlightened leadership (Chapter 4). Mao was so convinced about the possibility of negotiating with Roosevelt that he had a message transmitted, through the American military stationed in China, that he and Zhou Enlai wanted to talk to the President in person (see Sheng, 1993, p. 154).

16. Much of this could also have been influenced by Roosevelt's 'strong China' policy. Roosevelt believed that in the post-War years China could, and should, become strong through American assistance. See Xiang, 1995, Chapter 1.

17. The original quotation of Mao's statement about better economic relations with capitalist countries is from Sun Gang and Sun Dongsheng, 'An important meeting at a turning point in history', *Dangde wenxian*, No. 3 (1991), p. 14. See He, 1994, p. 151ff. This quotation may suggest that Mao was less isolated from other Party members at the Eighth Party Congress in 1956 than is generally assumed. The contents of the Congress, especially in the speeches of Deng Xiaoping and Liu Shaoqi, are notable for their promotion of market forces as the path to greater socialism. Liu in particular reiterated Sun Yatsen's view that the state should use, but also restrict, capitalism for the sake of 'national welfare' and 'people's livelihood' (see *Eighth National Congress*, 1981, pp. 16, 28, 30, 34–5, 37, 53–4).

18. The original citations of Mao's challenge to Dulles's 'Three Principles' and Mao's assertion of an independent development strategy are taken from the article 'Chen Yi's speech discussing the world situation', 17 June 1958 (Archives of the Chinese Foreign Ministry). See He, 1994, p. 152ff. Contemporary historians in China also see 1958 as the year in which the influence of Sun Yatsen's policies had ended in China. Until that time, they suggest that land reform was being carried out in accordance with 'New Democratic' principles and that public ownership was just getting under way, but that the national bourgeoisie was still in charge of economic developments (Rong, 1992, interview).

19. The Sino-Soviet dispute that began in the early 1960s was no doubt exacerbated in 1959, when Khrushchev showed his support for the Indian side in the Sino-Indian border dispute.

20. Deckers notes that despite the 'Great Leap Forward' and other movements of dislocation, growth of GNP per head in China had been around 5 per cent from 1957 to 1979, and that basic literacy reached approximately 65 per cent in the late 1970s. Deckers believes that without Mao's strategy, as he has described it, 'China would be no different from Brazil or India today, and that World Bank statistics on absolute poverty would shoot up by 50 per cent to incorporate the Chinese living in poverty.' (Deckers, 1994, p. 223) Admittedly, statistics do not generally agree with Deckers's proposition. For very different figures on the high incidence of poverty in China in the late 1970s, see the 1992 World Bank report, *China: Strategies for reducing poverty in the 1990s*, pp. ix–xviii, and pp. 1–5.

21. Frakt (1979) argues that Maoist authority comprised elements of Rousseau's 'general will' and Burke's 'national interest'. According to Frakt's argument, Mao, like Burke, was inclined to believe that an educated, rational elite was the best source of political representation because it could find correct solutions for the whole nation. On the other hand, like Rousseau, Mao was critical of the corruptibility of small groups making decisions for the entire nation. Mao attempted to counterbalance this through the 'mass line', which Frakt suggests was similar to Rousseau's 'voluntaristic strain' of the 'virtuous mass' (see Frakt, 1979, pp. 687–8, 698–9). The problem with Frakt's analysis is that it assumes Mao accepted both practices at the same time. If such a comparison is to be made, it is perhaps more accurate to say that Mao only turned to a system of political authority similar to Rousseau's once his 'Burkian' efforts proved unsuccessful. The comparison between Mao and Burke is also one that has been made between Burke and Xunzi (Chapter 2), and Burke and Liang Qichao (Chapter 4).

22. Mao wrote, in a letter of August 1917, that there were only three people in China capable of ruling an elite political system: Yuan Shikai, Sun Yatsen and Kang Youwei (see Fairbank and Feuerwerker, 1986, pp. 795–6). Mao later contradicted his support for Yuan Shikai when he said in the 1940s that political tutelage had proved ineffective in China and that Yuan Shikai's failures as president of the new republic (1912–16) had confirmed this.

23. Discussions about Mao's view that Marxism must acquire a nationalist form in China were put forward in my interview with Rong Tianlin in Beijing (1992). For further discussions about this, see Bedeski, 1977, 'The concept of the state: Sun Yat-sen and Mao Tse-tung', pp. 338–54. Also see Dittmarr, 1993 and Starr, 1979.

24. The Autumn Harvest Uprisings of September 1927 were a series of unsuccessful attacks by peasant forces on a number of small towns near Changsha, Hunan Province. These were led by Mao (see Spence, 1990, p. 789).

25. This quotation is not in the Oxford edition of Mao's *Selected Works* that I used.

26. This argument may even be supported in Russia, where Sun's 1911 Revolution is said to have '... served as an extremely important fermenting function in China's political development.' At the 'First All-Russian Conference on Republican China' in Moscow (4–5 December, 1991), papers that were presented did not only focus on the 1911 Revolution and Sun Yatsen's ideology, but also on the significance of Yan'an to the CCP and of the dialogue between Mao and Stalin in the late 1940s and early 1950s (see Ivanov, 1992, pp. 131–6). It was in Yan'an, and in his first meetings with Stalin, that Mao continued to adhere most closely to Sun Yatsen's principles, as noted in Section 6.4.

27. As disastrous as the Great Leap Forward was, Mao's purpose in launching it had a rational basis. In an interview with Anna Louise Strong in March, 1959, Mao said, 'The greatest difficulty ... [is] the lack of steel in China.... If the steel goal for 1959 is met then in following years it should be possible to give as many as six million tons a year to

farm implements and machinery. In that case, farming should be fairly well mechanized in three or four years.' (see Strong and Keyssar, 1985, p. 497).

Chapter 7 Deng Xiaoping

1. This has been encapsulated in the Chinese metaphor, popularized in China in the 1980s, that Chinese development is analogous to 'stepping gingerly from stone to stone in a stream' rather than 'leaping forward' (Dittmarr, 1993, p. 3).
2. The Weberian analysis of charismatic versus rational-legal authority in Deng's China can be found in Teiwes, 1984, *Leadership, Legitimacy and Conflict in China: From a charismatic Mao to a politics of succession*, Robinson, 1988, 'Mao after death: Charisma and political legitimacy', O'Brien, 1989, 'Legislative development and Chinese political change'. Also see Sullivan (1987) and Baum (1986). Among the scholars who fall within this group, it is Harding (1987) who questions the view that Deng has dispensed fully with using charismatic authority (Harding, 1987, p. 187).
3. For discussions on Deng's elite–party politics versus Mao's mass–line, see Gu, 1991, 'China beyond Deng: Reform in the PRC', p. 77. Also see Bonavia, 1989, p. 106, and Schram, 1987, pp. 248–9. A more general Leninist framework for analyzing post-Mao China was mentioned in Chapter 1, and is also used by principal China specialists such as Baum and Schram, noted here and in footnote 2 of this chapter.
4. For further discussions of Deng's pragmatism, see Hsü, 1990, *China without Mao: The search for a new order*, p. 168, Bachman, 1992, 'The limits on leadership in China', p. 1049, and Lee, 1985, pp. 201–2, 216.
5. Kristof and Wudunn (1994, p. 378) and Xiang (1993, pp. 109, 113) compare Deng's reforms to the economic strategies of Friedrich List and to the politics of Bismarck. Friedman makes the comparison between Burke and Deng on the basis of Burke's view that however despotic a government, if it is 'regular' and 'orderly', and if it delivers the nation from 'anarchy', and if it is judged by its successful ability to produce food for the people, then its despotic nature should remain unchallenged. Friedman, 1995, pp. 286–7.
6. Cohen's view, cited at the beginning of this chapter, that Deng's 'authoritarian modernization' is precisely the ideology of his non-Communist predecessors, best summarizes the views of this group (Cohen, 1988). For further comparisons between Deng's reform programme and the reforms of figures like the Empress Dowager, Yuan Shikai, Chiang Kaishek and Sun Yatsen, see Perry, 1992, pp. 151–2, Young, 1992, p. 15, Hsueh, 1983, pp. 3–4, Shambaugh, 1993a, p. 409 and Shambaugh, 1993b, p. 458.
7. It was Mao who first used the expression *shishi qiushi* but Deng who gave prominence to the expression in the post-78 reform period.
8. For speeches of Deng's which centre on the 'truth from facts' theme, see Deng, 1984, pp. 59, 71, 81, 90, 130, 132, 141, 143.
9. These are the years that Hook has designated as the new democratic

period (Hook, 1991, p. 261), though, as Chapter 6 suggested, elements of new democracy may have governed Mao's thinking until 1958.

10. Deng's support for Mao's Yan'an period (1937–47), and the Rectification Campaign (1942–5), sometimes referred to as the 'sinification of Marxism', also fall within, and are directly related to, the theories found in Mao's speech on 'New Democracy'. See Deng, 1987, pp. 3, 24, and 1984, pp. 24, 57, 154, 277, 287, 326, 358.

11. The dual concerns of socialism's ability to eliminate poverty and create wealth can be seen in Deng's lines, 'Socialism means eliminating poverty. Pauperism is not socialism, still less communism' (Deng, 1987, p. 55), and 'There is some justification for rejecting being rich under capitalism. But how can we advocate being poor under socialism and communism?' (Deng, 1987, p. 176). Other examples of this view can be found in Deng, 1984, p. 173, Deng, 1987, pp. 49, 55, 107–8, 176, 178, 182, 184, 188, and Deng, 1994, pp. 230, 232–3, 245–6, 250–1, 256, 259, 261, 273, 321, 347.

12. This interview with Deng Xiaoping was conducted in Beijing by the 'Oxford University China Study Group' (21 June 1979). The group consisted of Keith Griffin, Roger Hay, Marsh Marshall, Neville Maxwell, Peter Nolan and Ashwani Saith. My thanks to Peter Nolan for allowing me to use his interview notes from this meeting.

13. For Deng's view that a strong state will prevent the polarization of wealth in China, see Deng, 1994, p. 351, Deng, 1987, pp. 12, 55, 57, 96, 102, and Deng, 1984, p. 244.

14. Deng's words remind one of De Bary's descriptions of Xunzi's outlook, '[For Xunzi], [i]ntuition, improvisation, and moral detachment are no substitutes for systematic study, refined judgment, and informed decision making when one faces critical junctures in life.' (De Bary, 1988, p. 10).

15. Next to his concern with poverty, the enhancement of technical expertise comes into Deng's speeches more frequently than any other issues. See Deng, 1984, pp. 66, 105, 107, 214, 217, 247, 308, 342, and Deng, 1987, pp. 4, 8, 81.

16. In this case, an even closer comparison may be between Deng and Xunzi. Xunzi also said that it is impossible for a very able person to be 'universally skilled' and '... impossible for an individual to hold every office' (Chapter 2).

17. This was especially true in 1981 and 1986, the 70th and 75th anniversary of the 1911 Revolution. See, as examples, Mao, 1981, p. 13, He, 1986, pp. 19–22, Chen, 1986, pp. 33–4 and Wang and Chen, 1986, pp. 33–4.

18. Studies on the Reform Movement of 1898 and on historical figures like Kang Youwei and Liang Qichao were also being published in China in the 1980s and 1990s. This was true of research on Sino-American relations between 1945–50 as well, the period when Mao seemed to accept Sun Yatsen's 'Three Principles' (Chapter 6). But none of these studies has reached the extensive number of publications on Sun in the post-Mao years (see Zeng, 1991, pp. 53–64).

19. These summaries are taken from *Historical Abstracts*, and are as follows: Zhang Lei (1992) 'The universal significance of Sun Yatsen's

theory and practice', *Historical Abstracts*, Vol. 46, Part A, No. 1 (1995), Abstract 958; Shi, Bo (1992) 'The 1911 Revolution and the development of the Chinese capitalist economy', *Historical Abstracts*, Vol. 45, Part A, No. 1 (1994), Abstract 1041; Wu, Yannan, (1991), 'Sun Yatsen and the ending of the traditional idea of a universal commonwealth with comments on the feasibility for its attainment', *Historical Abstracts*, Vol. 43, Part B, No. 3 (1992), Abstract 8409; Zhang, Haipeng (1991) 'Comments in the studies in Dr Sun Yatsen's socialist thought'. *Historical Abstracts*, Vol. 44, Part A, No. 2 (1993), Abstract 4929; Liu, Tianchun (1991) 'Sun Yatsen and China's modernization: The 80th anniversary of the 1911 Revolution'. *Historical Abstracts*, Vol. 44, Part A, No. 3 (1993), Abstract 8889; Yu, Xintun (1990) 'Reevaluation of Sun Yatsen's attitude toward Japan', *Historical Abstracts*, Vol. 43, Part B, No. 3 (1992), Abstract 8417; Yeh, George K (1990) 'A study in trends in research on Sun Yatsen' (Taiwan), *Historical Abstracts*, Vol. 44, Part A, No. 1 (1993), Abstract 1050.

20. For Deng's criticisms of Chen Duxiu, see Deng, 1992, pp. 306–7, and Deng, 1994, pp. 232, 290, 300. For details of Chen's role in CCP history, see Spence, 1990, pp. 314–15.

21. It is obvious that some Chinese students share a similar admiration for Sun. In a survey of 80 students who were asked in November 1989 which Chinese figure made the greatest contributions to modern China, Sun topped the list. See Rosen, 1990, p. 227.

22. For a detailed account of the Chinese work-study programme in France, see Bailey, 1988, pp. 441–61, and Levine's chapter 'The Rise of the Work-Study Movement' in Levine, 1993.

23. Franz has documented Deng's opposition to the so-called *Etatists*, Chinese students in France who were also on work-study programmes and whose membership of the GMD had been revoked because of their opposition to Sun Yatsen's desire for a united front with the Communists. In one instance, Deng and other CCP members arrived to disrupt a Chinese national day celebration organized by the *Etatists* in Paris (10 October 1923). One account suggests that Deng himself loudly demanded that the flag of the military Beiyang government (a powerful northern warlord government) '... be taken down and replaced with that of the revolutionary Canton government of Sun Yatsen.' (see Franz, 1988, pp. 46, 48). Because of Deng's disruptive activities, the French authorities began to track his movements in Paris. Aware of this, and of possible arrest, he fled Paris for Moscow in early January 1926. Among his personal belongings left behind after his departure and which were later discovered by the French authorities in his room, was a copy of the *Testament* of Sun Yatsen, written less than a year earlier and shortly before Sun's death in March 1925 (see Wang, 1982, pp. 703–4).

24. There are numerous accounts of Deng's early years. Franz's 1988 biography *Deng Xiaoping* remains especially informative, as does Goodman's *Deng Xiaoping and the Chinese Revolution: A political biography*. For further details of Deng's time in France and Moscow, see Franz, 1988, pp. 59–60, 64, 66–7, and Goodman, 1994, pp. xv, 28.

Chapter 8 The 'New Authoritarian' Debates

1. An account of the NA debates can be found in Xiu Haitao, 1990, *Xin Quanwei Zhuyi Lunzhan Shuping* ('Remarks on the Debate about New Authoritarianism'). Xiu is a teacher at the Central Party University in Beijing. He presented this summary of the NA debates at a conference in Germany entitled the 'European Project on China's Modernization: Contemporary Patterns of Cultural and Economic Change', held at Ruhr University in 1990. My thanks to Professor Luo Rongqu of Beijing University for lending me his copy of Xiu's work while I was in Beijing. Other articles that have recounted the NA debates and the events surrounding them are Petracca and Mong (1990), and especially Sautman's very thorough analysis (1992). Zhang examines briefly ideological influences on the NA debates. See Wei Zhang, *Ideological Trends and Economic Reform in China, 1978–1993*, unpublished PhD Thesis, University of Geneva, 1994, pp. 230–1, 235–6. Zhang is the former director of the Tianjin Economic Development Zone Management Committee and current director of the Tianjin Commission on Foreign Economic Relations and Trade. My thanks to Professor Peter Nolan for lending me his copy of Zhang's dissertation. Where it is available, the background of contributors to the NA debate will be provided.

2. The emphasis here is especially on the CCP's Thirteenth Party Congress (1987), where Zhao made his report on the 'primary stage of socialism', a programme which embodied two fundamental principles that ran parallel to the basic foundation of NA: anti-liberalism in politics and reform and greater openness in economics (see Ruan, 1994, p. 53). For further support for the view that NA is inspired by Zhao Ziyang's theories, see Baum, 1994, p. 18, and Bachman and Yang, 1991, p. 150.

3. Further support for the view that NA originated with Deng can be found in Selden, 1993, p. 111. This view was also put forward by Hua Sheng during my interview with him in March 1992. Hua said that among all the Party members, Deng should be seen as the 'real' new authoritarian. Hua is an economist from mainland China who completed a D.Phil at Oxford and was on a post-doctoral fellowship at Cambridge at the time of our interview.

4. This view was especially prominent in the Hong Kong and Taiwan press. It followed an alleged conversation between Deng Xiaoping and Zhao Ziyang, in which Zhao said, 'There is a theory prevalent in the outside world, called neo-authoritarianism. Our theorists are discussing it heatedly, too. The gist of the theory is that in the process of modernization in the third world countries, authoritative supermen are needed to push the country forward, not democracy.' Deng is said to have responded by saying, 'That is my opinion too. But we need to deliberate carefully as to how to put it forth.' The conversation allegedly occurred on 6 March 1989, and was printed by the 'China News Agency' in Hong Kong on 8 April 1989. See Ruan and Dai, 1990, pp. 3–4. Ruan's reporting of this, and his later view that NA fell within

the domain of Zhao Ziyang's theories (Ruan, 1992, p. 53, and Ruan, 1994, p. 194), suggests that he did not see a great difference in the political orientation of Deng and Zhao. My thanks to Peter Nolan, who loaned me his copy of the Ruan and Dai article.

5. Sautman argues that Su Shaozhi, a well-known radical reform theoretician from Beijing, launched the debate on NA in the winter of 1986, when he said during an interview with an American political scientist that China needed a 'strong liberal leader'. See Sautman, 1992, pp. 73–4.

6. The 'Princelings', or the influential sons of high-ranking leaders, headed by Chen Yuan, a son of top party member Chen Yun, had hoped, but failed, to be elected deputies to the Fourteenth Party Congress in October 1992. See Lu, 1992, pp. 27–9.

7. As noted in Chapter 1, the major surveys on NA to date are Ma (1990), Perry (1993), Petracca and Mong (1990), Sautman (1992), Sullivan (1989), Ting and Feng (1991) and Xiu (1990).

8. See De Bary, 1995, pp. 178–9 for further details of 'The China Confucius Foundation'.

9. Among other posts held, Gu Mu was a Member of the Presidium of the Twelfth and Thirteenth Party Congresses (1982, 1987), and the Presidium executive chairman and National Committee vice chairman, of the Seventh Chinese People's Political Consultative Conference (1988). He accompanied Zhao Ziyang on his eleven-nation African tour in 1982. He also led several government delegations to Western Europe and Latin America in the late 1980s. See MacKerras and Yorke, 1991, p. 82.

10. One of the participants of the 'Positive School', Feng Youlan, noted at the beginning of Chapter 2 for his view that the 'ancient nation' should serve the 'new mission' of China's modernization, evidently put great store in *li's* ability to assist this process.

11. The Cultural Debates continued after the NA debates began. The number of participants in the Cultural Debates grew, eventually dividing into four groups. These were still represented by the two main groups, the Positive School, which included Zhang Dainian, Li Zehou and Tang Yijie, and the Negative School, which included Fang Lizhi, Lü Xiaobo and Bao Zunxin. But a further debate developed between the proponents of New Conservatism (Xiao Gongqin and members of the Southern School in Shanghai) and opponents of New Conservatism (Gan Yang, Chen Lai). For further discussion of these groups, see Hicks (1990).

12. The 'Southern School' distinguishes itself from the 'Northern School' (Beijing) by supporting stronger state guidance in the economy and slower-paced economic reforms. Xiao Gongqin is an Associate Professor in the History Department of Shanghai Normal University.

13. Dr Lin Shengli is a Lecturer in the Politics Department, Fudan University, Shanghai.

14. Professor Luo Rongqu is a senior professor in the History Department, Beijing University, and Member of the Chinese People's Political Consultative Conference.

15. Dr Ren Xiao is a Lecturer in the Department of International Politics, Fudan University, Shanghai.
16. The failings of earlier attempts at 'enlightened despotism' in China are recounted by Qin Xiaoying (1989, p. 132), Huang Wansheng (1989, p. 148), and Yu Haocheng (1989, p. 162). Qin Xiaoying is a researcher affiliated with the Department of Propaganda of the Central Committee of the Chinese Communist Party. Huang Wansheng is a faculty member of the history department of Shanghai's East China Normal University. He believes that there is nothing new about new authoritarianism because the 'new authority' is not based on a democratic system but on the old dictatorship that was defended by supporters of enlightened despotism. Yu Haocheng is a professor at the Chinese Institute of Studies in the Legal System and Social Development. Previously, he had been the president of the Chinese Legal Academy, as well as the director of the Masses Publishing House. He has been criticized by the Chinese leadership on several occasions because of his denunciation of China's authoritarian political system. He strongly supported the student demonstrations of 1989. Also see Rosen and Zou, 1991, Vol. 23, No. 2, p. 6, and Vol. 23, No. 4, p. 4.
17. See Ding Xueliang (1990, p. 32), Fan Zhongxin (1989, p. 5), Gao Yu (1989, p. 1). Ding Xueliang was a former student of Su Shaozhi's in the Marxism–Leninism Institute of the Chinese Academy of Social Sciences, where Ding completed an MA. He was a PhD candidate at Harvard University when he wrote this article. Fan Zhongxin is a researcher at the Taiwan Studies Institute of the Chinese Academy of Social Sciences in Beijing.
18. See Wu Jiaxiang (1989a, p. 36, 1989b, p. 45, 1989c, p. 49). Wu Jiaxiang worked in the General Office for the Central Committee of the Communist Party. There is much speculation that he was close to Deng Xiaoping before the Tiananmen crisis in 1989. The reason for this is that Wu wrote a biography about Deng, which was widely distributed in China in 1988. After this, Wu's opinions, for many, personified the thoughts of Deng himself. Whether Deng wished to distance himself from the increased boldness of Wu's views around the time of Tiananmen is difficult to say, but Wu was imprisoned after Tiananmen. See Luo, 1989, pp. 9–11.
19. Jiang Yihua is a professor in the History department of Fudan University, Shanghai.
20. Kong Jongyuan is an associate professor and Miao Zhuang a Deputy Director of the Research Department, Institute of Economics, Chinese Academy of Social Sciences (CASS) in Beijing. Neither Kong nor Miao took part in the official NA debates of 1988–9, but they, like many academics at CASS, participated in similar discussions at the time.
21. Admittedly, Rong's view is excessively general. For an analysis of the different characteristics of absolutist states in Western and Eastern Europe, see Perry Anderson's *Lineages of the Absolutist State* (1974).
22. Xiao Gongqin's argument about the influence of *fen* on China's 'homogeneous individualities' can be found in his 1992 article 'Duerkaimu,

Makesi yu Xunzi dui tongzhigeti shehui de yanjiu ji qi qishi' ('The research and inspiration of Durkheim, Marx and Xunzi on societies of homogeneous individuality'). Xiao's views on 'transformative authority' were expressed in his 1989 article (pp. 65–7). He expanded on the relationship between *fen* and transformative authority during our second interview in Shanghai (1 March 1993). Along with Durkheim's conceptualizations, Xiao relies on Marx's argument that oriental despotism may have established itself naturally on the basis of homogeneous groups (Xiao, 1992, pp. 10, 12).

23.   Xiao has acknowledged the influence of Durkheim's concept of *anomie* on his own work.

24.   See footnote 22 of this chapter.

25.   Professor Yang Xinyu is the Vice-Dean of the Law Department at Fudan University, Shanghai. He wrote a number of articles that opposed NA during the debates of the late 1980s. None of these was published because of his strong support for the implementation of democratic reforms in China. He was also an adamant opponent of the Southern School of NA supporters. He expressed the views noted during our interview on 3 March 1993.

26.   Professor Hu Shoujun is a faculty member of the Sociology Department, Fudan University, Shanghai. Like Yang Xinyu, Hu was particularly critical of the Southern School of NA supporters. He expressed the views noted during our interview on 2 March 1993.

27.   Dai Qing became a Red Guard activist during the Cultural Revolution in the 1960s. In the early 1980s, she was a journalist at the *Enlightenment Daily* and initiated investigative reporting of intellectual persecution in the history of the CCP. She is a strong advocate of freedom of the press and environmental protection and has collected documents from many scientists and economists opposed to the Three Gorges dam project. In 1989 Dai was imprisoned after the June 1989 crackdown as her book on the Three Gorges dam, *Yangtze! Yangtze!* was banned for allegedly contributing to the Tiananmen crisis. Later released, Dai has since been a Nieman Fellow at Harvard University and a fellow at the Freedom Forum, School of Journalism, Columbia University (see Ruan, 1994, p. 254).

28.   Chen Yizi, director of the Chinese Economic System Reform Research Institute (CESRRI) and co-authors, Wang Xiaoqiang and Li Jun, deputy directors of CESRRI, are said to have acted as the 'brain and legs' of the State Council Commission established in 1982, and first headed by Zhao Ziyang. Chen and others at the Institute are said to have 'had direct access to Zhao through his secretary Bao Tong as well as through normal channels.' In June 1989, Chen fled to Paris and became the deputy head of the Democratic Alliance, an exile organization. See Hamrin, *China and the Challenge of the Future*, pp. 229–30, 238 (quoted in Sautman, 1992, p. 77). Zhang Bingjiu was at the time of writing this article a doctoral student in the Philosophy Department of Beijing University. It appears that Zhang's essay was the earliest contribution to the NA debate (written in April, 1986). His discussion of what he terms a 'semiauthoritarian system' departs from the decade-

long argument in China over centralization by arguing that the decentralization of political power is not the immediate solution to overcoming problems with China's economic reforms. Instead, Zhang believed that a semiauthoritarian system could coordinate economic and political reforms in the transition from a traditional planned economy to a fully developed commodity economy (see Rosen and Zou, 1991, Vol. 23, No. 2, p. 5).

29. Here, Xiao is referring to Benjamin Schwartz's *In Search of Wealth and Power: Yen Fu and the West*. See Schwartz, 1964a. Xiao's views on Yan Fu as a 'new conservative' are also cited in Gu and Kelly, 1994, pp. 222–4.

30. Xiao also refers to Yan Fu as a 'gradualist' *(jianjin zhuyi)*. Additional support for this view can be found in Yü, 1994, who refers to Yan Fu as an 'evolutionary gradualist' (p. 128).

31. According to one source, by 1915, 12 of China's provinces were under Yuan Shikai's administration and many others acquiesced to his directives. His death in 1916 is said to have 'inaugurated the grim era of warlords'. See Hook, 1991, pp. 234–5.

32. Each of these scholars agrees with Jiang's view, though none draws as many parallels with the Qing.

33. This view is also supported by Xiu Haitao, 1990, p. 18.

34. Professor Yin Xuyi is a member of the Institute for the Compilation and Translation of the Works of Marx, Engels, Lenin and Stalin, and Member of the National Committee, Chinese People's Political Consultative Conference, Beijing. He expressed these views during our interview on 19 February 1993.

35. Dong Zhenghua was a PhD candidate in the History Department at Beijing University at the time of our interviews. He is a close associate of Liu Jun and Li Lin, who compiled and published a number of the articles that were printed at the time of the NA debates. He expressed this view during our second interview on 9 March 1993.

36. Yang Baikui was at the time of writing this article the director of the Division of Public Administration Research at the Institute of Political Science, Chinese Academy of Social Sciences. Yang first became known in 1980 when, along with Hu Ping and Wang Juntao, he ran in county-level elections as a representative of Beijing University. He was a close assistant to Yan Jiaqi of the Institute of Political Science and now one of the leaders of the democracy movement in exile. Yang was arrested after 4 June 1989.

37. Su goes so far as to say that without the sort of transitional period that New Democracy advocates, developing countries cannot reach socialism (Su, 1993, p. 11).

38. The hierarchical function of *fen* is in any case the same as that of *li*. Knoblock notes that 'In the *Xunzi, fen* regularly has the technical sense of the divisions or distinctions that characterize the hierarchal society the Ru thinkers advocated'. (Knoblock, Vol. 1, p. 251) *Li's* similar influence on Xunzi's hierarchical society can be seen in Chapter 2.

Chapter 9   The Impact of Tiananmen

1. See especially Xiao and Zhu's 1989 article, p. 55 for this view, but also Chen *et. al*, 1989, pp. 55–6 and Xiu Haitao's summary (1990, pp. 39–40).
2. See Chen *et al.*, 1989, pp. 47–8, 53–5, Wu, 1989a, pp. 36–7, Wu, 1989c, p. 49, and Xiu, 1990, pp. 1, 3.
3. Wu Jiaxiang referred to this stage of development as a 'semi-market economy'. See Wu, 1989c, pp. 47–8. Also see Wang and Zhang, 1989, pp. 8–10.
4. Wu Jiaxiang argued that '… as soon as the new authoritarianism is produced, it becomes an absolute necessity to maintain the pressure of frequent and regular democratic activity.' See Wu, 1989b, p. 45.
5. Chen *et al.* compared 'hard government, soft economy' with what they saw as the negative examples of 'hard government, hard economy' (the Stalinist model), and 'soft government, hard economy', or a political system which relies on a parliamentary democracy but which also promotes a planned economy (India, for example).
6. For an analysis of the argument that authoritarian rule is capable of transforming itself to a constitutional democracy, see Ting and Feng, 1991, p. 93.
7. The elite democrats' view that strong political leadership must be combined with stronger political institutions can be found in Zhang Zhonghou's 1989 article *Xin quanwei heshi fali quanwei* ('New authority or legal authority?'), especially pp. 172–4, as well as in Gao Gao, 1989, p. 5, Wu Haijing, 1989, p. 4, and Rong Jian and Sun Hui, 1989, p. 3. Rong Jian was a doctoral student in the philosophy department of the People's University in Beijing at the time of writing the article with Sun Hui. Rong is considered to be the most important critic of NA in China (see Rosen and Zou, 1991, Vol. 23, No. 2, p. 6).
8. Yue Linzhang and Zheng Yongnian were scholars in the Department of Public Administration at Beijing Youth Political Science College at the time of writing this article (see Rosen and Zou, 1991, Vol. 23, No. 4, p. 4).
9. Cao Yuanzheng graduated with a PhD in economics from the People's University in Beijing. When the NA debates began, he was deputy chief of the Division of Comparative Economic Studies at the Chinese Economic System Reform Research Institute (CESRRI), Beijing (see Rosen and Zou, 1991, Vol. 23, No. 3, p. 4).
10. According to Waterman, the group's origins go back to the 'Democracy Wall' period of 1978–9. The group includes the most prominent figure from that period, Wei Jingsheng, who has only recently been released from serving a prison sentence that has run almost continuously since 1979.
11. Hu Ping's article, 'The Chinese Dream of the New Authoritarianism' was written in 1989 but not published until 1991 (in the United States) (see Rosen and Zou, 1991, Vol. 24, No. 1, pp. 28–46). Hu Ping was the president of the Chinese Democratic Alliance at the time.
12. Ruan's article is taken from Su Shaozhi (ed.) (1990b) *Weilai Zhongguo*

Xueshe Xueshu Taolun Huei Wenji ('On the Selection of a System: A Collection of Papers Presented at a Symposium by the Future China Society'), Columbia University, 11–12 November 1990. My thanks to Peter Nolan for lending me his copy of this collection of papers.

13.   Yan Jiaqi was a Director of the Institute of Political Science at the Chinese Academy of Social Sciences in Beijing. He was also an adviser to Party chief Zhao Ziyang before Zhao was ousted from his position in 1989. Yan is said to have provided considerable inspiration to the 1989 Democracy Movement. He fled China after the Tiananmen crisis, becoming an exile and dissident (see Han, 1990, pp. 154, 208, 217, 309, 372). Yan's quotation is taken from *In Quest of a Better China: Selected Essays, Discussions and Comments from an International Conference at Imperial College, London* (12–13 September 1992). My thanks to Peter Nolan for lending me his copy of this text.

14.   Liu Binyan was an investigative journalist and an outspoken liberal intellectual who was expelled from the CCP in the 'Anti-Bourgeois Liberalism' campaign of 1987. Liu is best known for his pioneering pieces of 'reportage literature', candid exposés of Party corruption and malfeasance, published in the late 1970s and early 1980s. He is currently residing in the United States, and in 1989 was one of the founding members of the Federation for Democratic China (see Han, 1990, p. 53).

15.   My thanks to Peter Nolan for lending me his copy of this paper.

16.   These ideas are also included in Nolan's book *China's Rise, Russia's Fall: Politics, Economics and Planning in the Transition from Stalinism* (1995).

17.   For an expanded analysis of this issue, see Chang and Nolan's chapter, 'Europe versus Asia: Contrasting paths to the reform of centrally planned systems of political economy', in Chang and Nolan, 1995, pp. 3–45.

18.   These views were put forward in two symposia, one in Vancouver (6 December 1992), and the other at Berkeley (no date is given). Each is documented in *In Quest of a Better China*, 1992, pp. 214, 223–4.

19.   Dong's views on Keynesian economics seem to accord with China's Vice Premier Zhu Rongji's views. Zhu said that some Chinese economists' tendency to characterize Western economies as completely unregulated economies was a misrepresentation. As Zhu said, 'After the Second World War, many Western economies had promoted Keynes' ideas that governments must intervene in labour, currency and commodity markets when necessary ...' (quoted in Walker, 1995, p. 8).

20.   Ren Wanding, founder of the China Human Rights League, was one of the most visible student leaders at Tiananmen Square during the Democracy Movement of 1989. He was among the first group of people arrested after 4 June (on 10 June). Ren was later cited in an official report as a major influence on the students. But according to Han (1990), '... it appears that [Ren] and other Democracy Wall activists may not have been as influential on the 1989 protesters as the government has contended: some students reportedly found their views, particularly their call for a multiparty system to challenge the Party's supremacy, too radical.' (pp. 23–4, 120–1).

21. Wang Dan was in the late 1980s a history undergraduate at Beijing University and a son of a Beijing University professor, who became a top leader in the Democracy Movement. Along with Wuer Kaixi (see footnote 23), Wang was one of few student leaders who met with Premier Li Peng (18 May 1989) during the student demonstrations in an attempt to resolve the situation in Tiananmen and end the hunger strike. In the weeks following 4 June, Beijing Security Police issued a most-wanted list of 21 student leaders on which Wang was included. Wang was imprisoned shortly afterwards, but released in 1993 (see Han, 1990, pp. 15, 241–2, 372).

22. Among the scholars who launched this appeal were the NA participants Dai Qing, Yu Haocheng and Yan Jiaqi.

23. Wuer Kaixi was at the time of the Tiananmen demonstrations a first-year student in education at Beijing Normal University as well as chairman of the Beijing Students' Federation. Wuer was included on the most-wanted list of 21 student leaders following the Tiananmen crisis. He escaped to southern China and across the border to Hong Kong, where he defiantly renewed the call for the struggle for democracy in a videotape shown on Hong Kong television (see Han, 1990, pp. 111, 135, 375).

24. Discussions of the 1989 student demonstrations as an elite movement that excluded workers can be found in Chan and Unger, 1990a, 'China after Tiananmen', pp. 79–81, and 1990b, 'Voices from the Protest Movement', p. 273, as well as Walder and Gong, 1993, pp. 23–7, Perry and Fuller, 1991, p. 668, and Feignon, 1990, p. 203.

25. A total of 150 students participated in this survey.

26. This survey was conducted by the Public Opinion Research Institute at the Chinese People's University in the summer of 1987 (1240 surveyed).

27. This survey was conducted in February 1988 (3200 surveyed).

28. This survey included 3200 Beijing residents. The other countries involved in the survey were the US, scoring 35 per cent on the first question and 41 per cent on the second; the UK, 23 per cent and 33 per cent; Germany, 33 per cent and 38 per cent; Italy, 19 per cent and 23 per cent; and Mexico, 6 per cent and 7 per cent. Only in this last example of Mexico did the influence of national government on daily life score slightly lower than in China.

29. US (21.0 per cent, 7.2 per cent); UK (17.5 per cent, 8.0 per cent); Germany (24.8 per cent, 13.1 per cent); Italy (15.0 per cent, 6.6 per cent) Mexico (5.4 per cent, 1.5 per cent) (see Nathan and Shi, 1994, pp. 107–8).

30. For coverage of demonstrations in Fujian, Hangzhou, Shanghai, Tianjin, Xi'an, Shenyang and Chongqing, see *The Australian Journal of Chinese Affairs*, January 1990, Issue 23, pp. 97–160, and July 1990, Issue 24, pp. 181–314.

31. This conclusion stands in opposition to the views expressed in Zha's research that the cause of reform was set back by Tiananmen (Zha, 1995, pp. 204–5; cf 107–8, 113, 192, 202).

32. For a summary of Jiang Zemin's political report to the Fourteenth

Party Congress, see Li, 1992, pp. 5-6.
33. For views that support China's 'evolutionary authoritarian' route, see especially Chao's 1990 article 'Transition from authoritarian rule: Is Eastern Europe's today mainland China's tomorrow?', Sun's 1994 article 'The Chinese and Soviet Reassessment of Socialism: The theoretical bases of reform and revolution in Communist regimes'. Also see Pei (1992).

Chapter 10 Conclusion

1. Nathan has discussed Mencius's influence on the connection between Confucianism and welfare that seems apparent in modern China's constitutions. See Nathan (1986b).
2. Perhaps the best counter example to the Chinese defence of new authoritarianism is Collier's *The New Authoritarianism in Latin America*. See Collier (1979).
3. See Samuel Huntington's article 'Democracy's Third Wave' (1991).
4. See Zhengyuan Fu's book *Autocratic Tradition and Chinese Politics* (1993).
5. See Perry, 1993, pp. 20–1.
6. See McCormick, 1994, pp. 95–110.
7. See Whyte, 1992, p. 70.
8. See C. B. MacPherson (1987) *The Real World of Democracy*, pp. 6, 7 and 9.
9. De Bary comments on Jiang's appearance at the conference on Confucianism that was mentioned at the beginning of Chapter 8, at which the Chinese leader spent two hours discussing his interest in Confucianism. See De Bary, 1995, p. 187.

Bibliography

AI, K. (1989) 'Controversial new authoritarianism', *Joint Publications Research Service – CAR-89-047*, p. 12.

ALLINSON, R. E. (ed.) (1989) *Understanding the Chinese Mind: The philosophical roots* (Oxford: Oxford University Press).

ANDERSON, P. (1974) *Lineages of the Absolutist State* (London: NLB).

AYERS, W. (1971) *Chang Chih-tung and Educational Reform in China* (Cambridge, Mass.: Harvard University Press).

BACHMAN, D. and YANG, D. (trans and eds) (1991) *Yan Jiaqi and China's struggle for democracy* (Armonk: M. E. Sharpe, Inc.).

BACHMAN, D. (1992) 'The limits on leadership in China', *Asian Survey*, Vol. 32, No. 11, pp. 1046–62.

BAILEY, P. (1988) 'The Chinese "Work-Study Movement" in France', *China Quarterly*, No. 115, pp. 441–61.

BASTID, M. (1987) 'Official conceptions of imperial authority at the end of the Qing dynasty', in Schram (1987).

BAUM, R. (1986) 'Modernization and legal reform in post-Mao China: The rebirth of socialist legality', *Studies in Comparative Communism*, Vol. 19, No. 2, pp. 69–103.

BAUM, R. (1989) 'Beyond Leninism? Economic reform and political development in post-Mao China', *Studies in Comparative Communism*, Vol. 22, No. 2, pp. 111–23.

BAUM, R. (ed.) (1991) *Reform and reaction in post-Mao China: The road to Tiananmen* (London: Routledge).

BAUM, R. (1992) 'Political stability in post-Deng China: Problems and prospects', *Asian Survey*, Vol. 32, No. 6, pp. 491–505.

BAUM, R. (1993) 'The road to Tiananmen: Chinese politics in the 1980s', in MacFarQuhar (1993b).

BAUM, R. (1994) *Burying Mao: Chinese politics in the age of Deng Xiaoping* (Princeton: Princeton University Press).

BAYS, D. H. (1978) *China Enters the Twentieth Century: Chang Chih-tung and the issues of a new age, 1895–1909* (Ann Arbor: University of Michigan Press).

BEDESKI, R. (1977) 'The concept of the state: Sun Yat-sen and Mao Tse-tung', *China Quarterly*, No. 70, pp. 338–54.

BEDESKI, R. (1981) *State Building in Modern China: The Kuomintang in the Prewar Period* (Berkeley: University of California Press).

BEDESKI, R. (1989) 'State building and ideology in China: Agendas for unification in the former Han dynasty and the People's Republic', *Crossroads*, No. 27, pp. 43–54.

BENEWICK, R. and WINGROVE, P. (eds) (1995) *China in the 1990s* (London: Macmillan Press Ltd).

BERGÈRE, Marie-Claire (1992) 'Tiananmen 1989: Background and consequences', in Dassù and Saich (1992).

Berkeley Symposium (nd), in *In Quest of a Better China* (1992).

BERNAL, M. (1968) 'The triumph of anarchism over Marxism, 1906–1907', in Wright (1968).

BILLETER, J. F. (1985) 'The system of "class status"', in Schram (1985).

BLOOM, I. (1994) 'Mencian arguments on human nature', *Philosophy East & West*, Vol. 44, No. 1, pp. 19–53.

BODDE, D. (1953) 'Harmony and conflict in Chinese philosophy', in Wright (1953).

BONAVIA, D. (1989) *Deng* (Hong Kong: Longman Publishers).

BÜNGER, K. (1985) 'The Chinese state between yesterday and tomorrow', in Schram (1985).

BURTON, C. (1986) *Political Authority and Value Change in Post-Mao China* Unpublished PhD dissertation, University of Toronto.

CAMERON, M. E. (1931) *The Reform Movement in China, 1898–1912* (Stanford: Stanford University Press).

CAO, Y. (1989) 'The model of the market economy under a "hard government"', in Rosen and Zou (1991), Vol. 23, No. 3, pp. 24–31.

CHAN, A. and UNGER, J. (1990a) 'China after Tiananmen', *The Nation*, No. 22 (New York), 22 January 1990, pp. 79–81.

CHAN, A. and UNGER, J. (1990b) 'Voices from the Protest Movement,' *The Australian Journal of Chinese Affairs*, No. 24, pp. 259–79.

CHAN, A. and UNGER, J. (1991) 'The social origins and consequences of the Tiananmen Crisis', in Goodman and Segal (1991).

CHAN, F. G. (1987) 'The historical significance of Sun Yatsen's career and ideology in twentieth century Chinese politics', in Wong (1987).

CHAN, H. Y. S. (1992) 'The reformer as conspirator: K'ang Yu-wei versus the empress Dowager, 1904–1906,' *Chinese Studies in History*, Vol. 25, No. 4, pp. 38–49.

CHAN, S. W. (tran.) (1984) *An Exposition of Benevolence: The Jen-Hsüeh of T'an Ssu-t'ung* (Hong Kong: The Chinese University Press).

CHAN, W. T. (1967) 'K'ang Yu-wei and the Confucian doctrine of humanity *(Jen)*', in Lo (1967).

CHAN, W. T. (1975) 'Chinese and Western interpretations of *Jen*', *Journal of Chinese Philosophy*, Vol. 2, No. 2, pp. 107–29.

CHANG, C. (1982) 'Dr Sun Yat-sen's "Principle of Livelihood" and "American Progressivism"', *Chinese Studies in History*, Vol. 15, No. 3, pp. 4–19.

CHANG, D. W. (1984) *Zhou Enlai and Deng Xiaoping in the Chinese Leadership Succession Crisis* (New York: University Press of America).

CHANG, D. W. (1989) 'Sun Yatsen's doctrine and the future of China', in Cheng (1989).

CHANG, D. W. (1990) 'Confucianism, democracy and communism: The Chinese example in search of a new political typology for systematic integration', *Issues and Studies*, Vol. 26, No. 11, pp. 53–74.

CHANG, H. J. and NOLAN, P. (eds) (1995) *The Transformation of the Communist Economies: Against the mainstream* (London: Macmillan Press Ltd).

CHANG, H. J. and NOLAN, P. (1995) 'Europe versus Asia: Contrasting paths to the reform of centrally planned systems of political economy', in Chang and Nolan (1995).

CHANG, H. (1971) *Liang Ch'i-ch'ao and Intellectual Transition in China, 1890–1907* (London: Oxford University Press).

CHANG, H. (1987) *Chinese Intellectuals in Crisis: Search for order and meaning (1890–1911)* (Berkeley: University of California Press).

CHANG, H. (1990) 'Some reflections on the problems of the Axial-Age breakthrough in relation to classical Confucianism', in Cohen and Goldman (1990).

CHANG, M. H. (1985) *The Chinese Blue Shirt Society: Fascism and Developmental Nationalism* (Berkeley: University of California Press).

CHANG, M. H. (1992) 'What is left of Mao-Tse-tung thought', *Issues and Studies*, Vol. 28, No. 1, pp. 18–38.

CHANG, S. H. and GORDON, L. H. D. (1991) *All Under Heaven: Sun Yat-sen and his revolutionary thought* (Stanford: Hoover Institution Press).

CHAO, C. M. (1990) 'Transition from authoritarian rule: Is Eastern Europe's today mainland China's tomorrow?', *Issues and Studies*, Vol. 26, No. 11, pp. 33–52.

CHEEK, T. (1992) 'From priests to professionals: Intellectuals and the state under the CCP', in Wasserstrom and Perry (1992).

CHEN, Y. *et al.* (1989) 'The deep-seated questions and the strategic choice China's reform faces', in Rosen and Zou (1991), Vol. 23, No. 3, pp. 39–60.

CHEN, Z. (1986) 'Sun Yatsen's *Complete Works* published', *Beijing Review*, 17 November 1986, pp. 33–4.

CHENG, C. Y. (1979) 'Practical learning in Yen Yüan Chu Hsi and Wang Yang-ming', in De Bary and Bloom (1979).

CHENG, C. Y. (ed.) (1989) *Sun Yat-sen's Doctrine in the Modern World* (Boulder: Westview Press).

CHENG, C. Y. (1991) *New Dimensions of Confucian and Neo-Confucian Philosophy* (Albany: State University of New York Press).

CHERRINGTON, R. (1991) *China's Students: The struggle for democracy* (London: Routledge Publishers).

CHI, W. S. (1992) *Ideological Conflicts in Modern China: Democracy and authoritarianism* (London: Transaction Publishers).

CHIANG, Kaishek (1947) *China's Destiny and Chinese Economic Theory* (London: Dennis Dobson Publishers).

CHIN, H.Y. (1982) 'The influence of Chinese Confucian political theory and cultural tradition on Sun Yat-sen's ideology of synthesis', in Kindermann (1982).

CHING, F. (1994) 'Confucius, the new saviour', *Far Eastern Economic Review*, 10 November 1994, p. 37.

CHUNG, J. H. (1991) 'The politics of prerogatives in socialism: The case of the *Taizidang* in China', *Studies in Comparative Communism*, Vol. 24, No. 1, pp. 58–76.

COHEN, P. A. (1967) 'Wang T'ao and incipient Chinese nationalism', *Journal of Asian Studies*, Vol. 26, No. 4, pp. 559–74.

COHEN, P. A. (1988) 'The post-Mao reforms in historical perspective', *The Journal of Asian Studies*, Vol. 47, No. 3, pp. 518–40.

COHEN, P. A. and GOLDMAN, M. (eds) (1990) *Ideas Across Cultures: Essays in honor of Benjamin I. Schwartz* (Cambridge, Mass.: Harvard University Press).

COHEN, P. A. and SCHRECKER, J. E. (1976) *Reform in Nineteenth-Century China* (Cambridge, Mass.: Harvard University Press).

COLLIER, D. (ed.) (1979) *The New Authoritarianism in Latin America* (Princeton: Princeton University Press).

'Confucian comeback: The master's teachings are a boon to the modern world', *Asiaweek*, 26 October, 1994, pp. 21–2.

CONFUCIUS (1971) *Analects*, first translated into English by James Legge in 1893 (English edition, New York: Dover Publications).

COTTERELL, A. (1988) *China: A concise cultural history* (London: John Murray Publishers).

CRAIG, A. M. *et al.* (1978) *East Asian Tradition and Transformation* (New York: Houghton Mifflin).

CREEL, H. G. (1970) *The Origins of Statecraft in China, Vol. 1: The Western Chou Empire* (Chicago: University of Chicago Press).

CREEL, H. G. (1987) 'The role of compromise in Chinese culture', in Le Blanc and Blader (1987).

CUA, A. S. (1985) *Ethical Argumentation: A study of Hsün Tzu's moral epistemology* (Honolulu: University of Hawaii Press).

CUA, A. S. (1989) 'The concept of *li* in Confucian moral theory', in Allinson (1989).

DASSÙ, M. and SAICH, T. (1992) *The Reform Decade in China: From hope to dismay* (London: Kegan Paul International).

DAWSON, R. (1964) *The Legacy of China* (Oxford: Oxford University Press).

DE BARY, W. T. (1957) 'Chinese despotism and the Confucian ideal: A seventeenth century view', in Fairbank *et al.* (1957).

DE BARY, W. T. (1988) *East Asian Civilizations: A dialogue in five stages* (Cambridge, Mass.: Harvard University Press).

DE BARY, W. T. (1991) *The Trouble with Confucianism* (Cambridge, Mass.: Harvard University Press).

DE BARY, W. T. (1995) 'The new Confucianism in Beijing', *The American Scholar*, Vol. 64, No. 2, pp. 175–89.

DE BARY, W. T. and BLOOM I. (eds) (1979) *Principle and Practicality: Essays in neo-Confucianism and practical learning* (New York: Columbia University Press).

DECKERS, W. (1994) 'Mao Zedong and Friedrich List on de-linking', *Journal of Contemporary Asia*, Vol. 24, No. 2, pp. 217–26.

DENG, Xiaoping (1979) Interview (conducted by the 'Oxford University China Study Group' in Beijing, 21 June 1979).

DENG, Xiaoping (1984) *Selected Works of Deng Xiaoping* (Beijing: Foreign Languages Press).

DENG, Xiaoping (1987) *Fundamental Issues in Present-Day China* (Beijing: Foreign Languages Press).

DENG, Xiaoping (1992) *Selected Works of Deng Xiaoping, 1938–1965* (Beijing: Foreign Languages Press).

DENG, Xiaoping (1994) *Selected Works of Deng Xiaoping, Vol. 3 (1982–1992)* (Beijing: Foreign Languages Press).

DES FORGES, R. (1993) 'Democracy in Chinese history', in Des Forges *et al.* (1993).

DES FORGES, R. *et al.* (eds) (1993) *Chinese Democracy and the Crisis of*

1989: Chinese and American Reflections (Albany: State University of New York Press).
DICKSON, B. J. (1992) 'What explains Chinese political behavior?: The debate over structure and culture', *Comparative Politics* Vol. 25, No. 1, pp. 103–18.
DIRLIK, A. (1988) 'Socialism and capitalism in Chinese socialist thinking: the origins', *Studies in Comparative Communism*, Vol. 21, No. 2, pp. 131–52.
DITTMARR, L. (1993) 'Chinese reform socialism under Deng Xiaoping: Theory and practice', in Kau and Marsh (1993).
DITTMARR, L. (1994) *China under Reform* (Boulder: Westview Press).
DONG, Dr Zhenghua (1993) History Department, Beijing University (Interview One, 6 March 1993; Interview Two, 9 March).
DOW, T. I. (1979) 'Mao Tse-tung and Marxism', *Asian Profile*, Vol. 7, No. 2, pp. 97–118.
DUARA, P. (1988) *Culture, Power, and the State: Rural north China, 1900–1942* (Stanford: Stanford University Press).
DUARA, P. (1993) 'Deconstructing the Chinese nation', *The Australian Journal of Chinese Affairs*, No. 30, pp. 1–28.
EDWARDS, R. R. *et al.* (eds) (1986) *Human Rights in Contemporary China* (New York: Columbia University Press).
Eighth National Congress of the Communist Party of China (1981), first published in Chinese in 1956. (English edition, Beijing: Foreign Languages Press).
ELSTER, J. (1988) 'Consequences of constitutional choice: reflections on Tocqueville', in Elster and Slagstad (1988).
ELSTER, J. and SLAGSTAD, R. (eds) (1988) *Constitutionalism and Democracy* (Cambridge: Cambridge University Press).
ELVIN, M. (1973) *The Pattern of the Chinese Past* (London: Eyre Methuen).
ESHERICK, J. W. (ed.) (1974) *Last Chance in China: The World War Two despatches of John S. Service* (New York: Random House).
ETO, S and SCHIFFRIN, H. (eds) (1984) *The 1911 Revolution in China: Interpretive Essays* (Tokyo: University of Tokyo Press).
FAIRBANK, J. K. (1992) *China: A new history* (Cambridge, Mass.: Harvard University Press).
FAIRBANK, J. K., *et al.* (eds) (1957) *Chinese Thought and Institutions* (Cambridge: Cambridge University Press).
FAIRBANK, J. K. and FEUERWERKER, A. (1986) *The Cambridge History of China, Vol. 13, Republican China, 1912–1949, Part 2* (Cambridge: Cambridge University Press).
FAIRBANK, J. K. and LIU, K. C. (1980) *The Cambridge History of China, Vol. 11, Late Ch'ing, 1800-1911, Part 2* (Cambridge: Cambridge University Press).
FAIRBANK, J. K. and REISCHAUER, E. O. (1989) *China: Tradition and transformation.* (London: Allen and Unwin).
FANN, K. T. (1979) 'Mao's revolutionary humanism', *Studies in Soviet Thought*, Vol. 19, No. 2, pp. 143–54.
FARMER, E. L. (1990) 'Social regulations of the first Ming emperor: Orthodoxy as a function of authority', in Liu (1990).

FATHERS, M., and HIGGENS, A. (1989) *Tiananmen: The rape of Peking* (London: Transworld Publishers).

FEI, X. (1992) *From the Soil: The foundations of Chinese society* (Berkeley: University of California Press).

FEIGNON, L. (1990) *China Rising: The meaning of Tiananmen* (Chicago: Ivan R. Dee Publishers).

FENG, Q. (1990) 'The Liberal Teachings of the Young Liang Qichao', *Chinese Studies in Philosophy*, Vol. 22, No. 1, pp. 32–57.

FEUERWERKER, A. (1958) *China's Early Industrialization: Sheng Hsuan-Huai (1844–1916) and Mandarin enterprise* (Cambridge, Mass.: Harvard University Press).

FEUERWERKER, A. *et al.* (1967) *Approaches to Modern Chinese History* (Berkeley: University of California Press).

FEWSMITH, J. (1991) 'The Dengist reforms in historical perspective', in Womack (1991).

FEWSMITH, J. (1995) 'Neoconservatism and the end of the Dengist era', *Asian Survey*, Vol. 35, No. 7, pp. 635–51.

FINCHER, J. (1968) 'Provincialism and the devolution of 1909–1913', in Wright (1968).

FINGARETTE, H. (1972) *Confucius: The secular as sacred* (New York: Harper Torchbooks).

FINGARETTE, H. (1991) 'Reason, spontaneity, and the *li*: A Confucian critique of Graham's solution to the problem of fact and value', in Rosemont (1991).

FRAKT, P. M. (1979) 'Mao's concept of representation', *American Journal of Political Science*, Vol. 23, No. 4, pp. 684–704.

FRANZ, U. (1988) *Deng Xiaoping* (Boston: Harcourt Brace Johanovich Publishers).

FRIEDMAN, E. (1974) *Backward Toward Revolution: The Chinese revolutionary party* (Berkeley: University of California Press).

FRIEDMAN, E. (1989a) 'Democratization and re-Stalinization in China', *Telos*, No. 80, pp. 27–36.

FRIEDMAN, E. (1989b) 'Modernization and democratization in Leninist states: The case of China', *Studies in Comparative Communism*, Vol. 22, No. 3, pp. 251–64.

FRIEDMAN, E. (1991) 'Permanent technological revolution and China's tortuous path to democratizing Leninism', in Baum (1991).

FRIEDMAN, E. (1993) 'A failed Chinese modernity', *Daedalus*, Vol. 122, No. 2, pp. 1–17.

FRIEDMAN, E. (1995) *National Identity and Democratic Prospects in Socialist China* (Armonk: M. E. Sharpe).

FRISINA, W. G. (1989) 'Are knowledge and action really one thing? – a study of Wang Yang-ming's doctrine of mind', *Philosophy East & West*, Vol. 39, No. 4, pp. 419–47.

FU, Z. (1993) *Autocratic Tradition and Chinese Politics* (Cambridge: Cambridge University Press).

FUKUYAMA, F. (1995a) 'Confucianism and democracy', *Journal of Democracy*, Vol. 6, No. 2, pp. 20–33.

FUKUYAMA, F. (1995b) *Trust: The social virtues and the creation of prosperity* (London: Hamish Hamilton).

FUNG, Y. L. (1991) *Selected Philosophical Writings of Fung Yu-Lan* (Beijing: Foreign Languages Press).

GANGULEE, N. N. (ed.) (1945) *The Teachings of Sun Yatsen: Selections from His Writings* (London: The Sylvan Press).

GASSTER, M. (1968) 'Reform and revolution in China's political modernization', in Wright (1968).

GASSTER, M. (1969) *Chinese Intellectuals and the Revolution of 1911: The birth of modern Chinese radicalism* (Seattle: University of Washington Press).

GERNET, J. (1987) 'Introduction', in Schram (1987).

GITTINGS, J. (1992) 'How best to achieve democracy in China?', in *In Quest of a Better China* (1992).

GODLEY, M. (1987) 'Socialism with Chinese characteristics: Sun Yatsen and the international development of China', *Australian Journal of Chinese Affairs*, No. 18, pp. 109–25.

GOLD, T. B. (1991) 'Autonomy versus authoritarianism', in Hicks (1991).

GOLDMAN, M. (1994) *Sowing the Seeds of Democracy in China: Political reform in the Deng Xiaoping era* (Cambridge, Mass.: Harvard University Press).

GOLDSTEIN, A. (1991) *From Bandwagon to Balance-of-Power Politics: Structural constraints and politics in China, 1949–1978* (Stanford: Stanford University Press).

GONCHAROV, S. N. *et al.* (1993) *Uncertain Partners: Stalin, Mao, and the Korean War* (Stanford: Stanford University Press).

GOODMAN, D. S. G. (1987) 'Democracy, interest, and virtue: The search for legitimacy in the People's Republic of China', in Schram (1987).

GOODMAN, D. S. G. (1990) *Deng Xiaoping* (London: Sphere Books).

GOODMAN, D. S. G. (1994) *Deng Xiaoping and the Chinese Revolution: A political biography* (London: Routledge).

GOODMAN, D. S. G. and HOOPER, B. (1994) *China's Quiet Revolution: New interactions between state and society* (New York: St. Martin's Press).

GOODMAN, D. S. G. and SEGAL, G. (eds) (1991) *China in the Nineties: Crisis management and beyond* (Oxford: Clarendon Press).

GONG, W. (1989) 'The legacy of Confucian culture in Maoist China', *The Social Science Journal*, Vol. 26, No. 4, pp. 363–74.

GRAHAM, A. C. (1990) *Studies in Chinese Philosophy and Philosophical Literature* (Albany: State University of New York Press).

GREGOR, A. J. (1981a) 'Confucianism and the political thought of Sun Yatsen', *Philosophy East & West*, Vol. 31, No. 1, pp. 55–70.

GREGOR, A. J. *et al.* (1981b) *Ideology and Development: Sun Yat-sen and the economic history of Taiwan* (Berkeley: University of California Press).

GREGOR, A. J. and CHANG, M. H. (1980) 'Wang Yang-ming and the ideology of Sun Yat-sen', *Review of Politics*, No 42, pp. 388–404.

GREGOR, A. J. and CHANG, M. H. (1982) 'Marxism, Sun Yat-sen and the concept of "imperialism"', *Pacific Affairs*, Vol. 55, No. 1, pp. 54–79.

GREGOR, A. J. and CHANG, M. H. (1989) 'The Thought of Sun Yat-sen in Comparative Perspective', in Cheng (1989).

GRIEDER, J. B. (1981) *Intellectuals and the State in Modern China: A narrative history* (London: Collier Macmillan).

GU, Dr Xin (1995) Sinological Institute, Leiden University (Personal Interview, Cambridge, England, 11 July 1995).

GU, X. and KELLY, D. (1994) 'New conservatism: intermediate ideology of a "new elite"', in Goodman and Hooper (1994).

GU, Z. (1991) *China Beyond Deng: Reform in the PRC* (Jefferson, Missouri: McFarland & Company Inc. Publishers).

HALL, D. L. and AMES, R. T. (1987) *Thinking Through Confucius* (Albany: State University of New York Press).

HAN, M. (ed.) (1990) *Cries for Democracy: Writings and speeches from the 1989 Chinese Democracy Movement* (Princeton: Princeton University Press).

HANA, C. (1982) 'The development of the *San-min Chu-i* during the "May Fourth Movement"', in Kindermann (1982).

HANSEN, C. (1983) *Language and Logic in Ancient China* (Ann Arbor: University of Michigan Press).

HAO, W. (1993) Personal Correspondence, 25 April 1993.

HARDING, H. (1987) *China's Second Revolution: Reform after Mao* (Washington: The Brookings Institution).

HE, B. (1991) 'Democracy as viewed by three Chinese liberals: Wei Jingsheng, Hu Ping, and Yan Jiaqi', *China Information*, Vol. 6, No. 2, pp. 23–43.

HE, B. (1992) 'Democratisation: Antidemocratic and democratic elements in the political culture of China', *The Australian Journal of Political Science*, Vol. 27, No. 1, pp. 120–36.

HE, D. (1994) 'The most respected enemy: Mao Zedong's perception of the United States', *China Quarterly*, No. 137, pp. 144–58.

HE, Z. (1986) 'Sun Yatsen: Initiator of China's democracy', *Beijing Review*, 10 November 1986, pp. 19–22.

HE, Z. (tran.) (1991) *An Intellectual History of China* (Beijing: Foreign Languages Press).

HEALY, P. (1990) 'Reading the Mao texts: The question of epistemology', *Journal of Contemporary Asia*, Vol. 20, No. 3, pp. 330–58.

HEGEL, G. W. F. (1980) *Lectures on the Philosophy of World History, Introduction: Reason in History* (translated by H. B. Nisbet) (Cambridge: Cambridge University Press).

HEGEL, G. W. F. (1995) *Lectures on the History of Philosophy, Vol. 1: Greek Philosophy to Plato* (translated by E. S. Haldance) (Lincoln: University of Nebraska Press).

HICKS, G. (1991) *The Broken Mirror: China after Tiananmen* (London: Longman Publishers).

Historical Abstracts, Vol. 46, Part A, No. 1 (1995), pp. 85–6; Vol. 45, Part A, No. 1 (1994), p. 84; Vol. 44, Part A, No. 3 (1993), p. 722; Vol. 44, Part A, No. 2 (1993), pp. 389, 403; Vol. 44, Part A, No. 1 (1993), p. 87; Vol. 43, Part B, No. 3 (1992), pp. 665–6 (Oxford: ABC Clio Publications).

History of the Chinese Communist Party: A chronology of events, 1919–1990 (1991) (Beijing: Foreign Languages Press).

HOOK, B. (ed.) (1991) *The Cambridge Encyclopedia of China, 2nd edn* (Cambridge: Cambridge University Press).

HOU, H. (1990) 'Montesquieu and China', *Chinese Studies in Philosophy*, Vol. 22, No. 1, pp. 11–31.

HOWELL, J. (1995) 'Civil society', in Benewick and Wingrove (1995).

HSIAO, K. C. (1959) 'K'ang Yu-wei and Confucianism', *Monumenta Serica*, No. 18, pp. 96–212.

HSIAO, K. C. (1965) 'The Case for Constitutional Monarchy: K'ang Yu-wei's Plan for the Democratization of China', *Monumenta Serica*, No. 24, pp. 1–83.

HSIAO, K. C. (1975) *A Modern China and a New World: K'ang Yu-Wei, reformer and utopian, 1858–1927* (Tokyo: University of Tokyo Press).

HSIAO, K. C. (1979) *A History of Chinese Political Thought, Vol. 1: From the beginnings to the sixth century A.D.* (Princeton: Princeton University Press).

HSU, C. Y. (1991) 'Applying Confucian Ethics to International Relations', *Ethics and International Affairs*, No. 5, pp. 15–31.

HSÜ, I. C. Y. (1970) *The Rise of Modern China* (London: Oxford University Press).

HSÜ, I. C. Y. (1990) *China Without Mao: The search for a new order* 2nd edn (Oxford: Oxford University Press).

HSÜ, L. S. (tran.) (1933) *Sun Yatsen: His political and social ideals* (Los Angeles: University of Southern California Press).

HSUEH, C. T. (1983) 'An Essay on Huang Hsing, with a commentary on the Revolution of 1911', *Chinese Studies in History*, Vol. 16, No. 3, pp. 36–77.

HU, P. (1989) 'The Chinese dream of the new authoritarianism', in Rosen and Zou (1991), Vol. 24, No. 1, pp. 28–46.

HU, S. (1991) *From the Opium War to the May Fourth Movement, Vol. 1* (Beijing: Foreign Languages Press).

HU, S., and LIN Y. (1931) *China's Own Critics: A selection of essays* (Tianjin: China United Press).

HU, Professor Shoujun (1993) Sociology Department, Fudan University, Shanghai (Personal Interview, 2 March 1993).

HUA, S. (1992) 'On democracy and economic progress in China', in *In Quest of a Better China*, pp. 133–8.

HUA, Dr Sheng (1992) Research Fellow, Corpus Christi College, University of Cambridge (Personal Interview, Cambridge, 4 March 1992).

HUANG, P. C. (1972) *Liang Ch'i-ch'ao and Modern Chinese Liberalism* (Seattle: University of Washington Press).

HUANG, W. (1989) 'A dialogue on the critiques of the new authoritarianism', in Rosen and Zou (1990), Vol. 23, No. 2, pp. 77–93.

HUANG, Y. (1995) 'Why China will not collapse', *Foreign Policy*, No. 99, pp. 54–68.

HULSEWÉ, A. (1987) 'Law as one of the foundations of state power in early imperial China', in Schram (1987).

HUNTINGTON, S. P. (1991) 'Democracy's Third Wave', *Journal of Democracy*, No. 2, pp. 17–31.

IHLAN, A. (1993) 'Wang Yang Ming: a philosopher of action', *Journal of Chinese Philosophy*, No. 20, pp. 451–63.

IKE, N. (1950) *The Beginnings of Political Democracy in Japan* (Baltimore: Johns Hopkins Press).

In Quest of a Better China: Selected essays, discussions and comments from an international conference at Imperial College, London (12–13 September 1992) (London: Global Publishing Co. Inc).

'Interview with Wuer Kaixi', in Yu and Harrison, 1990, pp. 147–54.

IRIYE, A. (ed.) (1980) *The Chinese and the Japanese: Essays in political and cultural interactions* (Princeton: Princeton University Press).

IVANHOE, P. J. (1990) 'Reweaving the "one thread" of the *Analects*', *Philosophy East & West*, Vol. 40, No. 1, pp. 17–33.

IVANOV, P. (1992) 'Russian studies on Republican China in 1991', *Republican China*, Vol. 17, No. 2, pp. 131–6.

JAN, G. P. (1989) 'The doctrine of nationalism and the Chinese revolution', in Cheng (1989).

JENNER, W. J. F. (1992) *The Tyranny of History: The roots of China's crisis* (London: Penguin Books).

JIANG, Professor Yihua (1993) History Department, Fudan University, Shanghai (Personal Interview, 2 March 1993).

JIN, C. (1987) 'Sun Yatsen's world-view', in Wong (1987).

JOHNSON, C. (ed.) (1973) *Ideology and Politics in Contemporary China* (Seattle: University of Washington Press).

JOHNSON, C. (1982). 'What's wrong with Chinese political studies?', *Issues and Studies*, Vol. 18, No. 6, pp. 12–28.

KAU, M. Y. M. and MARSH, S. H. (eds) (1993) *China in the Era of Deng Xiaoping: A decade of reform* (Armonk: M. E. Sharpe).

KELLY, D. (ed. and tran.) (1996) 'Realistic responses and strategic options: An alternative CCP ideology and its critics', *Chinese Law and Government*, Vol. 29, No. 2.

KINDERMANN, G. K. (ed.) (1982) *Sun Yat-sen: Founder and symbol of China's revolutionary nation-building* (Munich: Günter Olzag Verlag München Wien).

KINDERMANN, G. K. (1989) 'An overview of Sun Yat-sen's doctrine', in Cheng (1989).

KISSINGER, H. (1979) *The White House Years* (London: Wiedenfeld & Nicolson Ltd).

KLAITS, J, and HALTZEL, M. (eds) (1994) *The Global Ramifications of the French Revolution* (Cambridge: Cambridge University Press).

KNIGHT, N. (1990) 'Soviet philosophy and Mao Zedong's sinification of Marxism', *Journal of Contemporary Asia*, Vol. 20, No. 1, pp. 89–109.

KONG, Professor Jongyuan (1992) Institute of Economics, Chinese Academy of Social Sciences, Beijing (Personal Interview, 7 October 1992).

KRISTOF, N. D. and WUDUNN, S. (1994) *China Wakes: The struggle for the soul of a rising power* (London: Nicholas Brealey).

KWONG, L. S. K. (1984) *A Mosaic of the Hundred Days: Personalities, politics, and ideas of 1898* (Cambridge, Mass.: Harvard University Press).

LAWRENCE, S. (1994) 'Democracy Chinese Style', *The Australian Journal of Chinese Affairs*, No. 32, pp. 55–69.

LE BLANC, C. and BLADER, S. (eds) (1987) *Chinese Ideas about Nature and Society: Studies in honour of Derk Bodde* (Hong Kong: Hong Kong University Press).

LEE, B. (1995) 'Critical Internationalism', *Public Culture*, Vol. 7, No. 3, pp. 559–92.

LEE, C. H. (1985) *Deng Xiaoping: The Marxist road to the Forbidden City* (Princeton: The Kingston Press, Inc.).

LENG, S. C. and PALMER, N.D. (1961) *Sun Yat-sen and Communism* (London: Thames and Hudson).

LEONG, S. T. (1987) 'Sun Yatsen's international orientation: The Soviet phase, 1917–1925', in Wong (1987).

LEVENSON, J. R. (1958-65) *Confucian China and its Modern Fate* (3 vols) (London: Routledge and Kegan Paul).

LEVENSON, J. R. (1959) *Liang Ch'i-ch'ao and the Mind of Modern China* (London: Thames and Hudson).

LEVINE, M. A. (1993) *The Found Generation: Chinese communists in Europe during the twenties* (Seattle: University of Washington Press).

LI, H. (1992) 'Party congress introduces market economy', *Beijing Review*, 19 October 1992, pp. 5–6.

LI, J. (1991) 'On the historical status of Confucianist humanistic thought', *Chinese Studies in Philosophy*, Vol. 23, No. 1, pp. 34–56.

LI, K. T. (1988) *The Evolution of Policy Behind Taiwan's Development Success* (New Haven: Yale University Press).

LI, X. J. (1989) *The Long March to the Fourth of June* (Worcester: Billing & Sons Ltd).

LIANG, Chi-Chao (Qichao) (1930), *History of Chinese Political Thought During the Early Tsin Period* (trans. by L. T. Chen) (London: Kegan Paul, Trench, Trubner & Co. Ltd).

LIN, Dr Shengli (1993) Politics Department, Fudan University, Shanghai (Personal Interview, 3 March 1993).

LINEBARGER, P. (1937) *The Political Doctrines of Sun Yatsen: An exposition of the San Min Chu I* (Baltimore: Johns Hopkins Press).

LINK, P. (1992) *Evening Chats in Beijing: Probing China's predicament* (London: W. W. Norton & Company).

LINK, P. (1994) 'China's "Core" Problem', in Tu (1994).

LIU, B. (1990) *China's Crisis, China's Hope* (Cambridge, Mass.: Harvard University Press).

LIU, K. C. (1990) *Orthodoxy in Late Imperial China* (Berkeley: University of California Press).

LIU, K. C. (1991) 'The beginnings of China's modernization', *Chinese Studies in History*, Vol. 25, No. 1, pp. 7–18.

LO, J. P. (ed.) (1967) *K'ang Yu-wei: A biography and a symposium* (Tucson: University of Arizona Press).

LOUIE, K. (1986) *Inheriting Tradition: Interpretations of the classical philosophers in communist China, 1949–1966* (Oxford: Oxford University Press).

LU, W. (1992) 'How the princelings launched their political platform', in Kelly (1996).

LUO, Professor Rongqu (1993) History Department, Peking University (Personal Interview, 18 January 1993).

LUO, Y. (1989) 'Star of the CPC's think tank, Wu Jiaxiang – Deng Xiaoping's policy interpreter', *Guang Jiao Jing (Wide Angle)*, Hong Kong, 16 January 1989, pp. 22–4, in Joint Publications Research Service (JPRS) – CAR-89-028, 31 March 1989, pp. 9–11.

LÜ, X. (1995) 'Court sponsored reforms, 1895–1898', *Chinese Studies in*

History, Vol. 28, No. 4, pp. 49–66.

MA, C. H. (1975) 'An explication of the *San-Min-Chu-I* system: A systems analytical review', *China Forum*, Vol. 2, No. 2, pp. 129–59.

MA, L. E. A. (1983) 'A Chinese statesman in Canada: translated from the travel journal of Liang Ch'i-ch'ao', *BC Studies*, No. 59, pp. 28–43.

MA, S. Y. (1990) 'The rise and fall of neo-authoritarianism in China', *China Information*, Vol. 5, No. 3, pp. 1–18.

MACFARQUHAR, R. (1974, 1983) *The Origins of the Cultural Revolution* (2 vols) (Oxford: Oxford University Press).

MACFARQUHAR, R. (1993a) 'Comments on Hong Yung Lee's chapter, "Political and administrative reforms of 1982–1986: The changing Party leadership and state bureaucracy"', in Kau and Marsh (1993).

MACFARQUHAR, R. (ed) (1993b) *The Politics of China, 1949–1989* (Cambridge: Cambridge University Press).

MACKERRAS, C. (1989) *Western Images of China* (Oxford: Oxford University Press).

MACKERRAS, C. and YORKE, A. (eds) (1991) *The Cambridge Handbook of Contemporary China* (Cambridge: Cambridge University Press).

MACPHERSON, C. B. (1987) *The Real World of Democracy*, first published in 1965. (This edition: Toronto: CBC Enterprises).

Major Documents of the People's Republic of China (1991) (Beijing: Foreign Languages Press).

MAO, Z. (1981) 'In commemoration of Sun Yatsen', *Beijing Review*, 19 October 1981, p. 13.

MAO, Zedong (1975–7) *Selected Works of Mao Tsetung* (5 vols) (Oxford: Pergammon Press).

MARSELLA, A. J., *et al.* (1985) *Culture and Self: Asian and western perspectives* (London: Tavistock Publishers).

MARTIN, B. and SHUI, C. T. (1972) *Makers of China: Confucius to Mao* (Oxford: Basil Blackwell).

MARX, K. (1986) *Collected Works, Vol. 15 (1856–58)* (London: Lawrence & Wishart).

MARX, K. and ENGELS, F. (1975) *Collected Works, Vol. 1 (1835–43)* (London: Lawrence & Wishart).

MATHEWS, R. H. (1943) *Mathews' Chinese–English Dictionary* (Cambridge, Mass.: Harvard University Press).

McCORMICK, B. L. (1994) 'Democracy or Dictatorship?: a response to Gordon White', *Australian Journal of Chinese Affairs*, 31, pp. 95–110.

MEISNER, M. (1982) *Marxism, Maoism, and Utopianism: Eight essays* (Madison: University of Wisconsin Press).

MEISNER, M. (1994) 'The French Revolution and Chinese socialism', in Klaits and Haltzel (1994).

MENCIUS (1988) *Mencius* (translated by D. C. Lau) (Harmondsworth: Penguin Books).

METZGER, T. A. (1987) 'Developmental criteria and indigenously conceptualized options: a normative approach to China's modernization in recent times' *Issues and Studies*, Vol. 23, No. 2, pp. 19–81.

METZGER, T. A. (1992) 'Did Sun Yat-sen understand the idea of democracy? The conceptualization of democracy in the *Three Principles of the*

People and in John Stuart Mill's *On Liberty, American Asian Review*, Vol. 10, No. 1, pp. 1–41.

MIAO, Professor Zhuang (1992) Institute of Economics, Chinese Academy of Social Sciences, Beijing (Personal Interview, 7 October 1992).

MICHAEL, F. H. and TAYLOR, G. E. (1964) *The Far East in the Modern World* (London: Methuen & Co. Ltd.).

MILL, J. S. (1991) *On Liberty and Other Essays* (edited by John Gray) (Oxford: Oxford University Press).

MILLER, D. (ed.) (1991) *The Blackwell Encyclopedia of Political Thought* (Oxford: Blackwell Publishers).

MILNE, R. S. and MAUZY, D. K. (1990) *Singapore: The legacy of Lee Kuan Yew* (Boulder: Westview Press).

MONTESQUIEU (1989) *The Spirit of Laws* (translated and edited by Anne M. Cohler, Basia Carolyn Miller and Harold Samuel Stone) (Cambridge: Cambridge University Press).

MOODY, P. R. (1984) 'Political liberalization in China: A struggle between two lines', *Pacific Affairs*, Vol. 57, No. 1, pp. 26–44.

MU, C. (1982) *Traditional Government in Imperial China: A critical analysis* (Hong Kong: The Chinese University Press).

NATHAN, A. J. (1976) *Peking Politics, 1918–1923: Factionalism and the failure of constitutionalism* (Berkeley: University of California Press).

NATHAN, A. J. (1986a) *Chinese Democracy: The individual and the state in twentieth century China* (London: I. B. Tauris & Co. Ltd).

NATHAN, A. J. (1986b) 'Sources of Chinese rights thinking', in Edwards, *et al.* (1986).

NATHAN, A. J. (1990) 'The place of values in cross-cultural studies: The example of democracy in China', in Cohen and Goldman (1990).

NATHAN, A. J. and SHI, T. (1994) 'Cultural requisites for democracy in China: Findings from a survey', in Tu (1994).

NAUGHTON, B. (1993) 'Deng Xiaoping: The economist', *China Quarterly*, No. 135, pp. 491–514.

NEVILLE, R. C. (1994) 'Confucianism as a world philosophy', *Journal of Chinese Philosophy*, No. 21, pp. 5–25.

NIVISON, D. S. (1953) 'The problem of "knowledge" and "action" in Chinese thought since Wang Yang-ming', in Wright (1953).

NIVISON, D. S. and WRIGHT, A. F. (eds) (1959) *Confucianism in Action* (Stanford: Stanford University Press).

NOLAN, P. (1990) 'Democracy and China's political economy in the 1990s', Paper presented at the 'Future China Society Symposium', Columbia University, 11–12 November 1990.

NOLAN, P. (1992) 'Remarks on the Chinese Economy', in *In Quest of a Better China* (1992).

NOLAN, P. (1995) *China's Rise, Russia's Fall: Politics, Economics and Planning in the Transition from Stalinism* (London: Macmillan Press Ltd).

O'BRIEN, K. J. (1989) 'Legislative development and Chinese political change', *Studies in Comparative Communism*, Vol. 22, No. 1, pp. 57–75.

PEERENBOOM, R. P. (1993) *Law and Morality in Ancient China: The silk manuscripts of Huang-Lao* (Albany: State University of New York Press).

PEI, M. (1992) 'Societal takeover in China and the USSR', *Journal of*

Democracy, Vol. 3, No. 1, pp. 108–18.

PERRY, E. J. (1992) 'Casting a Chinese "Democracy" movement: The roles of students, workers, and entrepreneurs', in Wasserstrom and Perry (1992).

PERRY, E. J. (1993) 'China in 1992: An experiment in neo-authoritarianism', *Asian Survey*, Vol. 33, No. 1, pp. 12–21.

PERRY, E. J. and FULLER, E. V. (1991) 'China's Long March to democracy', *World Policy Journal*, Vol. 8, No. 4, pp. 663–85.

PETRACCA, M. and MONG, X. (1990) 'The concept of Chinese neo-authoritarianism: An exploration and democratic critique', *Asian Survey*, Vol. 30, No. 11, pp. 1099–117.

PYE, L. W. (1985) *Asian Power and Politics: The cultural dimensions of authority* (Cambridge, Mass.: Harvard University Press).

PYE, L. W. (1991) 'The state and the individual: an overview interpretation', *China Quarterly*, No. 127, pp. 443–66.

PYE, L. W. (1993a) 'An introductory profile: Deng Xiaoping and China's political culture', *China Quarterly*, No. 135, pp. 412–43.

PYE, L. W. (1993b) 'How China's nationalism was shanghaied', *The Australian Journal of Chinese Affairs*, No. 29, pp. 107–33.

QIN, X. (1989) 'Escaping from a historical vicious cycle', in Rosen and Zou (1991), Vol. 23, No. 4, pp. 7–30.

REN, W. (1989a) 'Reflections on the historical character of the Democracy Movement', in Yu and Harrison (1990).

REN, W. (1989b) 'Why did the rally in memory of Hu Yaobang turn into a democracy movement?', in Yu and Harrison (1990).

REN, Dr Xiao, (1993) Department of International Politics, Fudan University (Personal Interview, 3 March 1993).

REN, Dr Xiao, (1995) Personal correspondence, 8 March 1995.

ROBINSON, J. C. (1988) 'Mao after death: Charisma and political legitimacy', *Asian Survey*, Vol. 28, No. 3, pp. 353–68.

RODAN, G. (1989) *The Political Economy of Singapore's Industrialization: National state and international capital* (London: Macmillan Press Ltd).

ROETZ, H. (1993) *Confucian Ethics of the Axial Age: A reconstruction under the aspect of the breakthrough toward postconventional thinking* (Albany: State University of New York Press).

RONG, J. (1991) 'The new authoritarianism: China's error', in Rosen and Zou (1991), Vol. 24, No. 1, pp. 47–64.

RONG, Professor Tianlin (1992) History Department, Peking University (Personal Interview, 26 October 1992).

ROSEMONT, H. (1970) 'State and society in the *Hsün Tzu*: A philosophical commentary', *Monumenta Serica*, No. 29, pp. 38–78.

ROSEMONT, H. (ed) (1991) *Chinese Texts and Philosophical Contexts: Essays dedicated to Angus C. Graham* (La Salle: Open Court).

ROSEN, S. (1990) 'Youth and students in China before and after Tiananmen', in Yang and Wagner (1990).

ROSEN, S. (1992) 'Students and the state in China: The crisis ideology and organization', in Rosenbaum (1992).

ROSEN, S. and ZOU, G. (guest editors) (1990–1) 'The Chinese debate on new authoritarianism', *Chinese Sociology and Anthropology*, Vol. 23, Nos 2–4 and Vol. 24, No. 1.

ROSENBAUM, A. L. (ed.) (1992) *State and Society in China: The consequences of reform* (Boulder: Westview Press).

ROUSSEAU (1938) *The Social Contract* (edited by G. D. H. Cole) (London: J. M. Dent & Sons Ltd).

RUAN, M. (1992) 'From new authoritarianism to new conservatism', in Kelly (1996).

RUAN, M. (1994) *Deng Xiaoping: Chronicle of an empire* (Boulder: Westview Press).

RUAN, M. and DAI, L. (1990) 'New-authoritarianism in contemporary China', Paper presented at the 'Future of China Society Conference', Columbia University, 11–12 November, 1990.

SALISBURY, H. E. (1989) *Tiananmen Diary: Thirteen days in June* (London: Unwin Paperbacks).

SALISBURY, H. E. (1992) *The New Emperors: China in the era of Mao and Deng* (New York: Avon Books).

SANSOM, B. (1988) *'Minsheng' and the national liberation: Socialist theory in the Guomindang, 1919–1931*, unpublished PhD dissertation, University of Wisconsin.

SAUTMAN, B. (1992) 'Sirens of the strongman: Neo-authoritarianism in recent Chinese political theory', *China Quarterly*, No. 129, pp. 72–102.

SCALAPINO, R. and SCHIFFRIN, H. (1959) 'Early socialist currents in the Chinese revolutionary movement: Sun Yatsen versus Liang Qichao', *Journal of Asian Studies*, Vol. 18, No. 3, pp. 321–42.

SCHELL, O. (1988) *Discos and Democracy: China in the throes of reform* (New York: Pantheon Books).

SCHIFFRIN, H. (1957) 'Sun Yatsen's early land policy: The origin and meaning of equalisation of land rights', *Journal of Asian Studies*, Vol. 16, No. 4, pp. 549–64.

SCHIFFRIN, H. (1968) *Sun Yat-sen and the Origins of the Chinese Revolution* (Berkeley: University of California Press).

SCHRAM, S. R. (ed.) (1973) *Authority, Participation, and Cultural Change in China* (Cambridge: Cambridge University Press).

SCHRAM, S. R. (ed.) (1974) *Mao Tse-tung Unrehearsed: Talks and letters, 1956–1971* (Harmondsworth: Penguin Books).

SCHRAM, S. R. (ed.) (1985) *The Scope of State Power in China* (London: School of Oriental and African Studies).

SCHRAM, S. R. (ed.) (1987) *Foundations and Limits of State Power in China* (London: School of Oriental and African Studies).

SCHRAM, S. R. (1989) *The Thought of Mao Tse-Tung* (Cambridge: Cambridge University Press).

SCHRAM, S. R. (1993) 'Deng Xiaoping's quest for "modernization with Chinese characteristics" and the future of Marxism–Leninism', in Kau and Marsh (1993).

SCHRAM, S. R. (1994) 'Mao Zedong a hundred years on: The legacy of a ruler', *China Quarterly*, No. 137, pp. 125–43.

SCHRECKER, J. E. (1980) 'The Reform Movement of 1898 and the Meiji Restoration as Ch'ing-I movements', in Iriye (1980).

SCHURRMANN, F. (1969) *Ideology and Organization in Communist China* (Berkeley: University of California Press).

SCHURMANN, F. and SCHELL, O. (eds) (1967) *Republican China: Nationalism, war, and the rise of communism, 1911–1949* (Harmondsworth: Penguin Books).

SCHWARTZ, B. (1985) *The World of Thought in Ancient China* (Cambridge, Mass.: Harvard University Press).

SCHWARTZ, B. (1987) 'The primacy of political order in East Asian societies: some preliminary generalizations', in Schram (1987).

SCHWARTZ, B. (1964a) *In Search of Wealth and Power: Yen Fu and the west* (Cambridge, Mass.: Harvard University Press).

SCHWARTZ, B. (1964b) 'Some polarities in Confucian thought', in Wright (1964).

SELDEN, M. (1993) 'The social origins and limits of the democratic movement', in Des Forges, *et al.* (1993).

SHAFFER, L. (1990) 'Marxism enters a Confucian realm: The People's Republic in the perspective of Chinese history', *The Fletcher Forum of World Affairs*, Vol. 14, No. 1, pp. 1–9.

SHAMBAUGH, D. (1993a) 'Assessing Deng Xiaoping's legacy', *China Quarterly*, No. 135, pp. 409–11.

SHAMBAUGH, D. (1993b) 'Deng Xiaoping: The politician', *China Quarterly*, No. 135, pp. 457–90.

SHEK, R. H. (1976) 'Some western influences on T'an Ssu-T'ung's thought', in Cohen and Schrecker (1976).

SHENG, M. M. (1993) 'America's lost chance in China?: A reappraisal of Chinese communist policy toward the United States before 1945', *The Australian Journal of Chinese Affairs*, No. 29, pp. 135–57.

SHIH, C. S. (1977) '*The Min-sheng Chu-I* and the economic modernization of Taiwan', *China Forum*, Vol. 4, No. 2, pp. 79–100.

SHUN, K. L. (1991) 'The self in Confucian ethics', *The Journal of Chinese Philosophy*, Vol. 18, No. 1, pp. 25–35.

SHUN, K. L. (1993) '*Jen* and *li* in the *Analects*', *Philosophy East & West*, Vol. 43, No. 3, pp. 457–79.

SMITH, A. (1990) *An Inquiry into the Nature and Causes of the Wealth of Nations* (Chicago: Encyclopædia Britannica, Inc.).

SOLINGER, D. J. (1989) 'Democracy with Chinese characteristics', *World Policy Journal*, Vol. 6, No. 4, pp. 621–32.

SPECTOR, S. (1964) *Li Hung-Chang and the Huai Army: A study in nineteenth century Chinese regionalism* (Seattle: University of Washington Press).

SPENCE, J. D. (1982) *The Gate of Heavenly Peace: The Chinese and their revolution, 1895–1980* (London: Faber & Faber).

SPENCE, J. D. (1990) *The Search for Modern China* (London: Hutchinson).

STARR, J. B. (1979) *Continuing the Revolution: The political thought of Mao* (Princeton: Princeton University Press).

STRONG, T. B. and Keyssar, H. (1985) 'Anna Louise Strong: Three interviews with Chairman Mao Zedong', *China Quarterly*, No. 103, pp. 489–509.

SU, S. (1993) 'The formation and characteristics of China's existing system', in Des Forges, *et al.* (1993).

SULLIVAN, L. R. (1987) 'The analysis of "despotism" in the CCP: 1978–1982', *Asian Survey*, Vol. 27, No. 7, pp. 800–21.

SULLIVAN, M. J. 'The authoritarian route to reform of Leninist states: The

1988–1989 Chinese neo-authoritarian debate in comparative perspective', paper presented at the Midwest Conference on Asian Affairs, East Lansing, 29–30 October 1989.

SUN, C. (1977) 'A comparison between *Min-Sheng Chu-I* and the collectivism of Chinese communists', *China Forum*, Vol. 4, No. 2, pp. 101–22.

SUN, Y. (1994) 'The Chinese and Soviet Reassessment of Socialism: The theoretical bases of reform and revolution in Communist regimes', *Communist and Post-Communist Studies*, Vol. 27, No. 1, pp. 50–62.

SUN, Yatsen (1918) *Memoirs of a Chinese Revolutionary: A Programme of National Reconstruction for China* (London: Hutchinson & Co. Ltd).

SUN, Yatsen (1928) *The People's Three Principles*, first written in Chinese, 1924 (2 vols). (This edition translated by Elizabeth Goucher Chapman and deposited in the University of Cambridge library, Rare Books room).

SUN, Yatsen (1944) *The International Development of China*, first published in Chinese, 1922. (English edition, London: Hutchinson & Co. Ltd; no translator noted).

TAN, C. C. (1980) 'Tradition and the new culture', *The Tsing Hua Journal of Chinese Studies*, May, 1980.

TAN, Z. (1995) 'The Third Plenum of the Eleventh Central Committee is a major turning point in the history of the Party since the founding of the People's Republic of China', *Chinese Law and Government*, Vol. 28, No. 3, pp. 5–87.

TANG, T. (1991) 'The Tiananmen tragedy: The state-society relationship, choices and mechanisms in historical perspective', in Womack (1991).

TEIWES, F. C. (1984) *Leadership, Legitimacy, and Conflict in China: From a charismatic Mao to a politics of succession* (London: Macmillan Press Ltd).

TENG, S. Y. and FAIRBANK, J. K. (1954) *China's Response to the West: A documentary survey, 1839–1923* (Cambridge, Mass.: Harvard University Press).

The Australian Journal of Chinese Affairs Vol. 23, pp. 97–160, and Vol. 24, pp. 181–314 (special issues on the 1989 Democracy Movements in China's provinces).

THOMPSON, L. G. (1967) *'Ta-t'ung Shu* and *The Communist Manifesto*: Some comparisons', in Lo (1967), pp. 341–54.

TILLMAN, H. C. (1982) *Utilitarian Confucianism: Ch'en Liang's challenge to Chu Hsi* (Cambridge, Mass.: Harvard University Press).

TING, G. and FENG, C. (1991) 'New authoritarian theory in mainland China', *Issues and Studies*, Vol. 27, No. 1, pp. 84–98.

TOCQUEVILLE, A. (1952) *Democracy in America*, first published in French, 1840. (English edition, London: Oxford University Press, translated and edited by H. Reeve).

TOWNSEND, J. (1992) 'Chinese nationalism', *The Australian Journal of Chinese Affairs*, No. 27, pp. 97–130.

TSOU, T. (1987) 'Marxism, the Leninist party, the masses, and the citizens in the rebuilding of the Chinese state', in Schram (1987).

TU, W. (1985) *Confucian Thought: Selfhood as creative transformation* (New York: State University of New York Press).

TU, W. (ed.) (1994) *China in Transformation* (Cambridge, Mass.: Harvard University Press).

TWITCHETT, D. and FAIRBANK, J. K. (eds) (1978) *The Cambridge History of China, Vol. 10, Late Ch'ing, 1800–1911, Part 1* (Cambridge: Cambridge University Press).

Vancouver Symposium, 6 December 1992, *In Quest of a Better China* (1992), pp. 213–14.

VON SENGER, H. (1985) 'Recent developments in the relations between state and party norms in the People's Republic of China', in Schram (1985).

WAKEMAN, F. (1975) *The Fall of Imperial China* (London: Collier Macmillan Publishers).

WAKEMAN, F. and GRANT, C. (eds) (1975) *Conflict and Control in Late Imperial China* (Berkeley: University of California Press).

WALDER, A. G. and GONG, X. (1993) 'Workers in the Tiananmen protests: The politics of the "Beijing Workers' Autonomous Federation"', *The Australian Journal of Chinese Affairs*, No. 29, pp. 1–29.

WALKER, T. (1995) 'China urged to keep up economic reform', *Financial Times*, 18 May 1995, p. 8.

WANG, D. (1989a) 'On freedom of speech for the opposition', in Yu and Harrison, (1990).

WANG, D. (1989b) 'The star of hope rises in Eastern Europe', in Yu and Harrison (1990).

WANG, G. (1991) *The Chineseness of China: Selected essays* (Hong Kong: Oxford University Press).

WANG, N. (1982) 'Deng Xiaoping: The years in France', *China Quarterly*, No. 92, pp. 698–705.

WANG, N. and CHEN, Y. (1986) 'Recollections of Sun Yatsen's life published', *Beijing Review*, 15 December, pp. 33–4.

WANG, Professor Xiaoqiu (1993) History Department, Peking University (Personal Interview, 29 January 1993).

WANG, Y. (1991) 'Why we cannot agree with the new authoritarianism', in Rosen and Zou (1991), Vol. 23, No. 4, pp. 56–66.

WASSERSTROM, J. N. and Perry, E. J. (eds) (1992) *Popular Protest and Political Culture in Modern China: Learning from 1989* (Boulder: Westview Press).

WATERMAN, H. (pseudonym for the mainland Chinese scholar Hao Wang) (1990) 'Which way to go?: Four strategies for democratization in Chinese intellectual circles', *China Information*, Vol. 5, No. 1, pp. 14–32.

WATSON, J. L. (1992) 'The renegotiation of Chinese cultural identity in the post-Mao era', in Wasserstron and Perry (1992).

WEBER, M. (1951) *The Religion of China* (translated and edited by Hans H. Gerth) (London: Collier Macmillan Ltd).

WHITE, G. (1994) 'Democratization and economic reform in China', *The Australian Journal of Chinese Affairs*, No. 31, pp. 73–92.

WHITE, T. H. (1983) *In Search of History: A personal adventure, 2nd ed.* (New York: Warner Books Inc.).

WHYTE, M. K. (1992) 'Prospects for democratization in China', *Problems of Communism*, No. 41, pp. 58–70.

WILLIAMS, D. (1994) *Japan: Beyond the end of history* (London: Routledge Publishers).

WILSON, R. W. (1992) *Compliance Ideologies: Rethinking political culture*

(Cambridge: Cambridge University Press).

WOMACK, B. (1979) 'Politics and epistemology in China since Mao', *China Quarterly*, No. 80, pp. 768–92.

WOMACK, B. (1986) 'Where Mao went wrong: Epistemology and ideology in Mao's leftist politics', *The Australian Journal of Chinese Affairs*, No. 16, pp. 23–40.

WOMACK, B. (ed.) (1991) *Contemporary Chinese Politics in Historical Perspective* (Cambridge: Cambridge University Press).

WONG, D. (1991) 'Is there a distinction between reason and emotion in Mencius?', *Philosophy East & West*, Vol. 41, No. 1, pp. 31–44.

WONG, J. Y. (1986) 'Three visionaries in exile: Yung Wing, K'ang Yu-wei and Sun Yat-sen, 1894–1911', *Journal of Asian History*, No. 20, pp. 1–32.

WONG, J. Y. (1987a) 'Resurrecting Sun Yatsen: The past, present, and future of Sun Yatsen studies', in Wong (1987).

WONG, J. Y. (1987b) 'Sun Yatsen and the British connection, 1896–97 and 1984', in Wong (1987).

WONG, J. Y. (ed.) (1987) *Sun Yatsen, His International Ideas and International Connections: With special emphasis on their relevance today* (Sydney: Wild Peony Publishers).

WONG, Y. T. (1992) 'Revisionism reconsidered: Kang Youwei and the Reform Movement of 1898', *The Journal of Asian Studies*, Vol. 51, No. 3, pp. 513–44.

WOODBRIDGE, S. I. (tran.) (1900) *China's Only Hope* (New York: Fleming H. Revell Company).

World Bank (1992) *China: Strategies for reducing poverty in the 1990s* (Washington, DC: World Bank).

WRIGHT, A. F. (ed.) (1953) *Studies in Chinese Thought* (Chicago: University of Chicago Press).

WRIGHT, A. F. (1964) *Confucianism and Chinese Civilization* (Stanford: Stanford University Press).

WRIGHT, M. C. (ed.) (1968) *China in Revolution: The first phase, 1900–1913* (New Haven: Yale University Press).

WU, A. C. (1993) 'Power and policy orientation in mainland China since the CCP's Fourteenth Congress', *Issues & Studies*, Vol. 29, No. 1, pp. 59–74.

WU, A. C. (1994) 'Possible political developments in mainland China following the Third Plenum of the CCP's Fourteenth Central Committee', *Issues & Studies*, Vol. 30, No. 2, pp. 1–14.

WU, J. (1989) 'The new authoritarianism: An express train toward democracy by building markets', in Rosen and Zou (1991), Vol. 23, No. 2, pp. 36–45.

WU J. and ZHANG, B. (1989) 'Radical democracy or stable democracy', in Rosen and Zou (1991), Vol. 23, No. 2, pp. 7–15.

XIANG, L. (1993) 'Fin de siècle Beijing: Economic nationalism versus political inertia', *Communist and Post-Communist Studies*, Vol. 26, No. 1, pp. 104–19.

XIANG, L. (1995) *Recasting the Imperial Far East* (Boulder: M. E. Sharpe).

XIAO, Professor Gongqin (1993) History Department, Shanghai Normal University (Personal Interviews: Interview One, 28 February 1993; Interview Two, 1 March 1993).

XUNZI, (1988–94) *Xunzi: A Translation and Study of the Complete Works* (translated by John Knoblock) (3 vols) (Stanford: Stanford University Press).

YAN, J. (1992) 'A future federal system for China', in *In Quest of a Better China*, (1992).

YAN, S. (1994) 'The Chinese and Soviet reassessment of socialism: Theoretical bases of reform and revolution in Communist regimes', *Communist and Post-Communist Studies*, Vol. 27, No. 1, pp. 39–58.

YANG, B. (1993) 'The making of a pragmatic communist: The early life of Deng Xiaoping, 1904–49', *China Quarterly*, No. 135, pp. 444–56.

YANG, W. L. Y. and WAGNER, M. L. (1990) *Tiananmen: China's struggle for democracy, its prelude, development, aftermath, and impact* (Baltimore: University of Maryland).

YANG, Professor Xinyu (1993) Vice-Dean, Law Department, Fudan University, Shanghai (Personal Interview, 3 March 1993).

YIN, Professor Xuyi. (1993) Institute for the Compilation and Translation of the Works of Marx, Engels, Lenin and Stalin, and Member of the National Committee, Chinese People's Political Consultative Conference, Beijing (Personal Interview, 19 February 1993).

YOUNG, E. P. (1992) 'Imagining the *Ancien Régime* in the Deng Era', in Wasserstrom and Perry (1992).

YU, H. (1989) 'Does China need new authoritarianism?', in Rosen and Zou (1991), Vol. 23, No. 4, pp. 44–55.

YU, M. C. and HARRISON, J. F. (eds) (1990) *Voices from Tiananmen Square: Beijing Spring and the Democracy Movement* (New York: Black Rose Books).

YÜ, Y. S. (1989) 'Sun Yat-sen's doctrine and traditional Chinese culture', in Cheng (1989).

YÜ, Y. S. (1994) 'The radicalization of China in the twentieth century', in Tu (1994).

ZENG, J. (1991) 'An introduction to development studies of modern Chinese history in the last five years (1986–90)', *Chinese Studies in History*, Vol. 25, No. 2, pp. 53–65.

ZHA, J. (1995) *China Pop* (New York: The New Press).

ZHANG, Professor Dainian (1992) Philosophy Department, Peking University (Personal Interview, 5 October 1992).

ZHANG, Professor Jiqian (1992) History Department, Peking University (Personal Interview, 28 September 1992).

ZHANG, K. (1980) 'A general review of the study of the Revolution of 1911 in the People's Republic of China', *Journal of Asian Studies*, Vol. 39, No. 3, pp. 525–31.

ZHANG, K. (1983) 'Liberate thought, seek truth from facts, and diligently research the history of the 1911 Revolution', *Chinese Studies in History*, Vol. 16, No. 3, pp. 78–103.

ZHANG, K. (1984) 'The slogan "Expel the Manchus" and the Nationalist Movement in modern Chinese history', in Eto and Schiffrin (1984).

ZHANG, K. (1987) 'Sun Yatsen and the Miyazaki brothers', in Wong (1987).

ZHANG, S. (1991) 'The two-tier system of property rights and the transitional situation in China', in Rosen and Zou (1991), Vol. 24, No. 1, pp. 65-85.

ZHANG, W. (1994) *Ideological Trends and Economic Reform in China, 1978–1993* Unpublished PhD dissertation, University of Geneva.
ZHAO, S. (1993) 'Deng Xiaoping's southern tour: Elite politics in post-Tiananmen China', *Asian Survey*, Vol. 33, No. 8, pp. 739–56.
ZHU, Professor Buokun (1992) Philosophy Department, Peking University (Personal Interview, 27 October 1992).
ZHU, J. *et al.* (1990) 'Public political consciousness in China: An empirical survey', *Asian Survey*, Vol. 30, No. 10, pp. 992–1006.
ZHU, Y. (1995) 'On late Qing economic laws and regulations (ca. 1901–1911)', *Chinese Studies in History*, Vol. 28, No. 4, pp. 101–35.
ZI, Z. (1987) 'The relationship of Chinese traditional culture to the modernization of China: An introduction to the current discussion', *Asian Survey*, Vol. 27, No. 4, pp. 442–58.
ZOLOTOW, M. (1948) *Maurice William and Sun Yat-sen* (London: Robert Hale Ltd).

WORKS IN CHINESE

CHEN, Jinsong (1989) *Xunqiu zhengzhi xiandaihua zhi lu: Fang Zheng Yongnian* ('Seeking the road to political modernization: An interview with Zheng Yongnian'), *Guangming Ribao*, 7 April 1989, p. 3.
CHEN, Tianhua (1905) *Lun Zhongguo yi gai chuang minzhu zhengti* ('A Discussion on whether China should change to a democratic system'), *Min Bao*, in Wang and Zhang, 1979 (Vol. 2).
DAI, Qing (1989) *Cong Lin Zexu dao Jiang Jingguo* ('From Lin Zexu to Jiang Jingguo'), in Liu and Li (1989).
DING, Xueliang (1990) *Dong ya mo shi yu xin quanwei zhuyi* ('East Asian development patterns and new authoritarianism'), *Minzhu Zhongguo (Democratic China)* (Paris), April 1990, pp. 29–36.
FAN, Zhongxin (1989) *Xin quanwei zhuyi xi* ('An analysis of new authoritarianism'), *Renmin Ribao*, 6 March 1989, p. 5.
FENG, Ziyou (1906) *'Minsheng Zhuyi' yu Zhongguo zhengzhi geming zhi qiantu* ('"People's Welfare" and the prospects for political revolution in China'), in Wang and Zhang, 1979 (Vol. 2).
FU, Keqing (1984) *Tian reng weixing qiyu yangwu pai de shida fengqi* ('Ten differences between the reformist and westernization groups'), *Tianjin Shehui Kexu Bao*, June 1984, p. 61–6.
GAO, Gao (1989) *Jianquan yi fazhi wei zhuti de shehuikongzhi xitong* ('Improve the social control system taking the rule of law as the main body'), *Jingjixue Zhoubao*, 12 March 1989, p. 5.
GAO, Yu (1989) *Xin quanwei zhuyi shi 'jingling' haishi 'laoshu'?* ('New authoritarianism: Does it represent a "spirit" or a "rat"?'), *Jingjixue Zhoubao*, 12 March 1989, p. 1.
GUO, Sujian (1989) *Ping xin quanwei zhuyi de wuqu* ('Review on the mistakes of new authoritarianism'), in Liu and Li (1989).
HU, Hanmin (1906) *'Min Bao zhi liu da shuyi* ('Six Doctrines of *Min Bao*'), in Wang and Zhang, 1979 (Vol. 2).

HUANG, Shiqing and ZHANG, Dehua (1989) *Xianshi xueyao quanwei, quanwei xueyao zhiyue* – *cong difangzhuyi wenti tanqi* ('Reality needs authority, authority needs restrictions – and this should begin with localism'), in Liu and Li (1989).

JIAN, Buozhan, *et al.* (eds) (1957) *Wu Shu Bien Fa (The 1898 Reforms)* (4 vols), first published in 1898 (This edition: Shanghai: Renmin Chubanshe).

KANG, Youwei (1922) *Kongzi Gaizhi Kao (Confucius as a Reformer)* (21 *quan*), first published in 1897 (This edition: Beijing: Lingnan Library Distribution).

KANG, Youwei (1988) *Xinxue Weijing Kao (The Study of the Forged Classics of the Xin Dynasty)*, first published in 1891 (This edition: Beijing: Zhonghua Shu).

KANG, Youwei and LIANG, Qichao (1906) *Faguo geming lun* ('A discussion about French revolutionary history'), *Xinmin Congbao*, in Wang and Zhang, 1979 (Vol. 2).

LI, An (1911) *Li Wenxiang Gong Quanji (Complete Works of Li An)* (Beijing: Zhengshi Huifu Tang).

LI, Huaxin (1988) *Zhongguo Jindai Sixiang Shi (An Intellectual History of Modern China)* (Zhejiang: Renmin Chubanshe).

LI, Wei (1989) *Xin quanwei zhuyi de qitu* ('New authoritarianism going astray'), *Jingjixue Zhoubao*, 26 March 1989, p. 7.

LIANG, Qichao (1896) *Bien fa tongyi zishu* ('A Comprehensive Survey of Constitutional Reform'), in Jian, *et al.*, 1957 (Vol. 3).

LIANG, Qichao (1898) *Ren jun zhang ming zhang xiang shan zili* ('On the principle of evolution from monarchy to democracy'), in Jian, *et al.*, 1957 (Vol. 3).

LIANG, Qichao (1906a) *Baodong yu waiguo ganshe* ('Insurrection and foreign interference'), *Xinmin Congbao*, in Wang and Zhang, 1979 (Vol. 2).

LIANG, Qichao (1906b) *Kaiming zhuanzhi lun* ('An argument on enlightened despotism'), *Xinmin Congbao*, in Wang and Zhang, 1979 (Vol. 2).

LIANG, Qichao (1906c) *Shehui geming guo wei jinri Zhongguo suo biyao hu?* ('Is social revolution necessary for today's China'?), *Xinmin Congbao*, in Wang and Zhang, 1979 (Vol. 2).

LIANG, Qichao (1906d) *Shenlun zhongzu yu zhengzhi geming zhi deshi* ('Racial revolution and the merits and demerits of political revolution'), *Xinmin Congbao*, in Wang and Zhang, 1979 (Vol. 2).

LIANG, Qichao (1907) *Zai bo moubao zhi tudi guoyoulun* ('Reputing the land nationalization programme of a certain magazine'), *Xinmin Congbao*, in Wang and Zhang, 1979 (Vol. 2).

LIU, Binyan (1990) *Dui xin quanwei zhuyi de piping* ('Criticisms against new authoritarianism'), in Su (1990b)

LIU, Jun and LI, Lin (eds) (1989) *Xin Quanwei Zhuyi: Dui gaige li lun gang ling de lunzheng (New Authoritarianism: The debate on the outline of reform theory)* (Beijing: Beijing Economic Institute Press).

LUO, Rongqu and NIU, Dayong (1992) *Zhongguo Xiandaihua Licheng de Tansuo (Exploration of the Process of Chinese Modernization)* (Beijing: Beijing University Press).

MINYI (pseudonym) (1907) *Gao feinan 'minsheng zhuyi' zhe* ('Words to those who are against the principle of "People's Livelihood"'), *Min Bao*, in

Wang and Zhang, 1979 (Vol. 2).

QIN, Xiaoying (1989) *Tiaochu lishi de exing xuahuan* ('Escaping from a historical vicious cycle'), in Liu and Li (1989).

RISKIN, C. (1990) *Quanwei zhuyi yu Zhongguo de jingji fazhan* ('Authoritarianism and China's economic development'), in Su (1990b).

RONG, Jian (1989) *Zhongguo xiandaihua xuyao jiquan zhengzhi ma?* ('Does China need an authoritarian political system in the course of modernization?'), in Liu and Li (1989).

RONG, Jian and SUN Hui (1989) *Xin quanwei zhuyi: Yizhong weixian de xuanzhe* ('New authoritarianism: A vicious circle'), *Guangming Ribao*, 31 March 1989, p. 3.

RUAN, Ming (1990) *Dangdai Zhongguo xin quanwei zhuyi de lishi fazhan* ('The historical development of new authoritarianism in contemporary China'), in Su (1990b).

SHU, Yu (ed.) (1898) *Yijiao Congbian (Miscellaneous Writings in Defense of Orthodox Confucian Teachings)* (205 *quan*) (Beijing: Beijing University Archives).

SU, Shaozhi (1990a) *Quanwei yu quanwei zhuyi* ('Authority and authoritarianism'), in Su (1990b).

SU, Shaozhi (ed.) (1990b) *Weilai Zhongguo xueshe xueshu taolun huei wenji (On the Selection of a System: A Collection of papers presented at a symposium by the 'Future China Society')* (New York: Columbia University, 11–12 November 1990).

SUN, Guangde (1992) *Zhongguo chuantong wenhua yu xihua huo xiandaihua de guanxi* ('The relationship between Chinese traditional culture and Westernization'), in Luo and Niu (1992).

SUN, Zhongsan (Sun Yatsen) (1905) *Fa Kan Ci* ('Statement of the first issue [of *Min Bao*']), *Min Bao*, in Wang and Zhang, 1979 (Vol. 1).

WANG, Dong (1907a) *Geming jingshi lun* ('The trend of the revolution') *Min Bao*, in Wang and Zhang, 1979 (Vol. 2).

WANG, Dong (1907b) *Zheng 'Minyi' Faguo geming shi lun* ('Rectify the mistakes of Minyi's [Kang Youwei's] comment on the French revolution'), *Min Bao*, in Wang and Zhang, 1979 (Vol. 2).

WANG, Jingwei (1906a) *Buo geming keyi sheng neiluan shuo* ('A denouncement of the theory that revolution will lead to civil riots'), *Min Bao*, in Wang and Zhang, 1979 (Vol. 2).

WANG, Jingwei (1906b) *Buo geming keyi zhao guafen shuo* ('Denouncement of the theory that revolution will result in partition'), *Min Bao*, in Wang and Zhang, 1979 (Vol. 2).

WANG, Jingwei (1906c) *Zai buo 'Xinmin Congbao' zhi zhengzhi geming lun* ('A second denouncement on "*Xinmin Congbao's*" theory of political revolution'), *Min Bao*, in Wang and Zhang, 1979 (Vol. 2).

WANG, Renzhi and Zhang, Nan. (eds) (1979) *Xinhai Geming Qianshi Nian Jian Shilun Xuanji (Selected Works From Ten Years of Debate Before the 1911 Revolution)* (3 vols, 5 books) (Beijing: Sanlian Chubanshe).

WANG, Yizhou (1989) *Wei shenmo buneng zantong xin quanwei zhuyi* ('Why we cannot agree with the new authoritarianism'), in Liu and Li (1989).

WU, Guoguang (1990) *Xin quanwei zhuyi zhenglun san ge wenti* ('Three problems in the debate on new authoritarianism'), in Su (1990b).

WU, Haijing (1989) *Xin quanwei zhuyi zhenglun chengwei xueshujie yi da redian* ('New authoritarianism: A hot topic of discussion in academic circles'), *Jingji Cankao*, 7 March 1989, p. 4.

WU, Jiaxiang (1989a) *Xin quanwei zhuyi shuping* ('A review of new authoritarianism'), in Liu and Li (1989).

WU, Jiaxiang (1989b) *Xin quanwei: Tongguo shichanghu kai wang minzhuhua de tebie kuaiche* ('The new authoritarianism: An express train toward democracy by building markets'), in Liu and Li (1989).

WU, Jiaxiang (1989c) *Xin quanwei zhuyi yanjiu tiqang* ('An outline for studying the new authoritarianism'), in Liu and Li (1989).

XIAO, Gongqin (1989) *Guodu quanweilu yu Zhongguo de gaige yundong* ('The theory of transformative authority and the Chinese reform movement'), in Liu and Li (1989).

XIAO, Gongqin (1992) *Duerkaimu, Makesi yu Xunzi dui tongzhigeti shehui de yanjiu ji qi qishi* ('The research and inspiration of Durkheim, Marx and Xunzi on societies of homogeneous individuality'), *Tianjin Shehue Kexue* (1992), No. 6, pp. 10–15.

XIAO, Gongqin (1993) *Cong langman de minzu zhuyi dao zhengzhi jijinzhuyi dui Zhongguo zhaoqi yihui minzhu sichao de lishi kaocha* ('From romantic nationalism to political radicalism: a historical investigation on parliamentary democratization in the early part of this century in China'), *Zhongguo Shehui Kexue Jikan* (Hong Kong), May 1993, pp 82–7.

XIAO, Gongqin and ZHU Wei (1989) *Tongku de liangnan xuanzhe: Guanyu 'xin quanwei zhuyi' lilun dawenlu* ('A painful dilemma: A dialogue on the theory of "new authoritarianism"'), in Liu and Li (1989).

XIAO, Gongquan (1992) *Xingzheng zhidu xiandaihua – Kang Youwei: zhi zhuzhang ji qi yiqi* ('Kang Youwei and the modernization of administrative institutions'), in Luo and Niu (1992).

XIU, Haitao (1990) *Xin quanwei zhuyi lunzhun shuping* ('Remarks on the debate about new authoritarianism') (Ruhr University: 'European Project on China's Modernization: Contemporary Patterns of Cultural and Economic Change').

YAN, Fu (1895a) *Pi Han* ('In refutation of Han Yu') in Jian, *et al.*, 1957 (Vol. 3).

YAN, Fu (1895b) *Renshi bien ziji* ('On the speed of world change') in Jian, *et al.*, 1957 (Vol. 3).

YAN, Fu (1895c) *Yi ziyou weiti, yi mingzhu weiyong* ('Freedom is the substance, democracy is the application') in Jian, *et al.*, 1957 (Vol. 3).

YANG, Baikui (1989) *Zhengzhi fazhan zhong de minzhu he quanwei*, ('Democracy and authority in the course of political development'), in Liu and Li (1989).

YE, Dehui (1898) *You xuan jing yuping* ('The current analysis of You Xuan'), in Shu, 1898 (Vol. 4).

YU, Haocheng (1989) *Zhongguo xuyao xin quanwei zhuyi ma?* ('Does China need new authoritarianism?'), in Liu and Li (1989).

YUE, Linzhang and Zheng Yongnian (1989) *Xin quanwei zhuyi yu zhengzhi minzhuhua* ('The new authoritarianism and political democratization'), in Liu and Li (1989).

ZHANG, Bingjiu (1989) *Jingji tizhi gaige he zhengzhi tizhi gaige de jincheng yu*

xietiao ('The Progress and Coordination between Economic and Political System Reform'), in Liu and Li (1989).

ZHANG, Zhidong (1898) *Quan Xue Pian (Exhortation on Learning)*, in Shu, 1898, (Vol. 202).

ZHANG, Zhonghou (1989) *Xin quanwei heshi fali quanwei* ('New authority or legal authority?'), in Liu and Li (1989).

ZHU, Zhixin (1906) *Lun shehui geming yu zhengzhi geming bingxing* ('Social revolution should be parallel to political revolution'), *Min Bao*, in Wang and Zhang (Vol. 2).

Index

Note: 'n.' after a page reference indicates the number of a note on that page.

ability (*neng*), 69–70, 71, 105, 106
absolutism, 52, 55
agriculture, 39, 83, 85
Analects, see Lunyu
autarkic development, 87
authoritarianism, 116–19, 151
  Deng Xiaoping's views, 98, 107–9
  Kang Youwei's views, 60
  Liang Qichao's views, 60
  Mao Zedong's views, 127–9
  new, *see* new authoritarianism
  Sun Yatsen's views, 92–4, 107–9,
    125–7
authority (*quan*), 69–70, 71, 105, 106
Autumn Harvest Uprisings, 93, 94

Bachman, D., 148
ba dao ('way of might'), 64–5
Bai Ri Weixin (Hundred Days of
    Reform), 7, 41–2, 44
Bao Tong, 184n.28
Bao Zunxin, 182n.11
Baum, R., 147
Bebel, August, 53
benevolence, *see* ren
Bentham, Jeremy, 50
Bergère, Marie-Claire, 145, 147
Billeter, J. F., 5
Bismarck, Otto von, 37, 53, 73, 74,
    98
Bluntschli, Johann Kaspar, 51–2
Bodde, D., 6
*Book of Group Regulations (Qunshu
    Zhiyao)*, 66, 164–5n.26
Book of Odes (Shijing), 15
Bornhak, Conrad, 51–2
Boxer Rebellion, 168n.12, 169n.13
Brazil, 126
Burke, Edmund
  Deng Xiaoping's views, 98
  Liang Qichao's views, 58
  Mao Zedong's views, 177n.21
  Xunzi's views, 21

Yan Fu's views, 123
Burton, C., 113
Bush, George, 104

Cao Yuanzheng, 186n.9
capitalism, 151
  Deng Xiaoping's views, 102, 103
  Liang Qichao's views, 53–4, 57
  Mao Zedong's views, 81–2, 85, 88
  Sun Yatsen's views, 57, 75–6
Carter, Jimmy, 104
Cavour, Camillo Benso, Conte di,
    37
centralism, 82, 86, 117
Chan, F. G., 84
Chang, Hao, 46–7, 50–1, 59, 162n.2
Chang, M. H., 173n.20
Chang, S. H., 174n.31
chaos, 14–15, 19–20, 147
charismatic authority, 97
Chen Boda, 94
Chen Duxiu, 108, 170n.3
Cheng, C. Y., 174n.31
Chen Lai, 182n.11
Chen Yizi, 184n.28
Chen Yuan, 182n.6
Chen Yun, 87, 182n.6
Chiang Kaishek, 65, 75, 81, 90
Chile, 126
China Confucius Foundation, 114
Chinese Alliance for Democracy
    (CAD), 139
Chinese Communist Party (CCP)
  Chen Duxiu's influence, 170n.3
  Deng Xiaoping's views, 101, 102,
    105, 106, 107
  and Dulles, relations between, 91
  Eleventh Congress, 2
  Li Dazhao's influence, 170n.3
  Mao Zedong's influence, 80–1,
    83–4, 85–6, 87, 95; democrat-
    ic centralism, 82; leadership,
    94; nationalization, 90, 93

Chinese Communist Party –
    continued
    new authoritarianism, 132, 136
        post-Tiananmen debates,
        138, 139, 140
        Tiananmen's impact, 143,
        146
    Sun Yatsen's influence, 63, 107,
        125
    Twelfth Congress, 165n.27
    Western perceptions, 3–4
'Chinese Philosophy' conference
    (Hangzhou, 1980), 114
class struggle, 72
Cohen, P. A., 97, 178n.6
commune system, 85
communication, 37
communism, 173n.22
Communist Party
    Chinese, *see* Chinese Communist
        Party
    Russian, 94
community, great, *see datong*
Complete Works of Xunzi, see
    Xunzi
conflict, 14–15, 19–20
Confucianism and Confucius, 5, 13,
    14, 152, 163n.14
    authority and welfare, 18–19, 27,
        163n.14
    basis, 14–15
    campaign against, 165n.32
    chaos, 14–15, 19
    'conservative' criticism, 27
    ethics and order, search for,
        15–16
    influence: on Jiang Zemin, 159;
        on Kang Youwei, 35, 42, 43,
        168n.16; on Liang Qichao, 7,
        45, 46; on Mao Zedong, 79,
        80; on Sun Yatsen, 76
    institutionalized, 119–22
    Mao's criticism, 165n.31
    modernization attempts, 26
    revival (1980s), 114–16
    Ru school, 25
    Western perceptions, 3
    Xunzi compared to, 21
    see also Lunyu

confused authority, detour toward,
    31–4
Conservatives
    confused authority, 31, 32–3, 34
    opinions on Kang Youwei, 42
    patriarchal authority challenged,
        31
    twentieth century, influence in,
        168n.12
constitutional monarchy, 36–8
constitutions, 48–50
cosmopolitanism, 66–7
Creel, H. G., 6
Cua, A. S., 163n.6
cultural construction 25
Cultural Debates, 113, 115–16,
    129–30
culturalist framework of research, 4,
    5
Cultural Revolution, 4

Dai Qing, 122–3
Darwin, Charles, 168n.12
datong (great community)
    Kang Youwei's views, 36, 39, 43
    Xunzi's views, 23, 71, 168n.16;
        Sun Yatsen's socialism, 75
De Bary, W. T., 161n.5, 164n.24,
    179n.14
Deckers, W., 92
democracy (*minquan*), 158–9
    Deng Xiaoping's views, 104, 107
    Kang Youwei's views, 36
    Liang Qichao's views, 67
    Mao Zedong, 81, 82, 84–6
    new authoritarianism, 117, 118,
        120, 125, 132; institutional-
        ized Confucianism, 121, 122
    parliamentary, 124
    Sun Yatsen's views, 65–6, 67–72,
        107
    Tan Sitong's views, 32
Democracy Wall movement, 140,
    186n.10
democrats, 134–7, 149–50, 157
    elite, 133–4, 135, 136–7
    post-Tiananmen debates, 137–40,
        142, 157
    Tiananmen's impact, 143–4, 145–7

Deng Xiaoping, 9, 97–8, 109–10
  keynote address, Eleventh Party
    Congress, 2
  knowledge-for-action, 65
  Leninist analysis, 5
  Mao Zedong's views, 87, 90, 92,
    161n.4
  multiparty democracy, rejection
    of, 173n.21
  new authoritarianism, 113, 117,
    118
  'open-door policy', 92
  poverty, 26, 99, 101, 152
  socialism, 176n.17
  Sun Yatsen's influence, 63, 67, 77,
    78, 155–6, 170n.2; authori-
    tarianism, 107–9; on
    economic reforms, 100–3; on
    political reforms, 103–6; on
    socialism, 106–7; on theory,
    98–100
  Wu Jiaxiang's biography, 183n.18
  Xunzi's influence, 25, 26
Deng Yangda, 173n.29
despotism, enlightened, 51–2, 57,
  117
Ding Xueliang, 183n.17
disorder, *see* order and disorder
Dong, Zhenghua, 142, 185n.35
Duara, P., 33
Dulles, John Foster, 91
Durkheim, Émile, 184n.22

Eastern Europe, democratization,
  141
economic growth
  Deng Xiaoping's views, 100
  Mozi's views, 21
  Self-strengthening Movement, 32
  Xunzi's views, 21–2
economic reforms, 39–41
education, 83, 105
egalitarianism, 21, 35, 106
elite democrats, 133–4, 135, 136–7
elite hierarchy, 69–71, 93, 105, 106
Engels, Friedrich, 3
England, 37, 38, 46–7
enlightened despotism 51–2, 57, 117
Enlightenment, European, 2

equality, 69, 82, 106, 173n.20
Etatists, 180n.23
ethics, 15–16, 119
ethnic-state thesis, 63–4

Fairbank, J. K., 6, 41
Fang Lizhi, 182n.11
Fan Zhongxin, 183n.17
federalism, 139, 141, 149
Fei Xiaotong, 161n.5
fen (status, social role), 121, 130
Feng Youlan, (Fung Yu-lan), 13,
  162n.1, 182n.10
France
  Kang Youwei's writings, 38,48,
    172n.18
  Revolution, 71; Kang Youwei's
    writings, 48, 172n.18; Liang
    Qichao's writings, 47, 48,
    172n.18; Sun Yatsen's writ-
    ings, 69
  Yang Baikui's writings, 126
Frankt, P. M., 177n.21
Friedman, E., 178n.5
Frisina, W. G., 25
frugality, 21, 22, 35
Fukuyama, Francis, 161n.5
function (*yong*), 167n.10, 168n.12
Fung Yu-lan (Feng Youlan), 13,
  162n.1, 182n.10

Gan Yang, 182n.11
Gasster, M., 33, 66, 169n.9
general will, 47–8
George, Henry, 56, 73, 74
Germany, 37, 73, 74
Goh Keng Swee, 163n.14
gong (public mindedness)
  Liang Qichao's views, 46, 47, 48,
    50, 57, 60
  Sun Yatsen, 64, 65
Gorbachev, Mikhail, 101, 138
Gordon, L. H. D., 174n.31
Great Britain, 30, 126
great community *see datong*
Great Leap Forward, 4, 177–8n.27
Gregor, A. J., 76, 173n.20, 174n.30
grouping, *see qun*
Guangwudi, 25

Guangxu, Emperor, 34
  'Hundred Days of Reform', 7, 41, 42
  Kang Youwei's influence, 7, 41, 122–3
Gu Mu, 114–15, 116
Guomindang (GMD), 81, 84, 128

Hamilton, Alexander, 72
Han Feizi, 24, 165n.32
Han people, 25, 46, 66–7
Hegel, Georg Wilhelm Friedrich, 2–3
hierarchical society, 69–71
Hobbes, Thomas, 21, 58
Hong Kong, 30, 139, 158
Hou, H., 49
household contract system, 87
Hou Shoujun, 130
Howell, J., 148
Hsiao, K. C., 22, 40
Hsu, Cho-yun, 162n.2
Huang, Philip, 7, 45–6, 50, 59
Huang Wansheng, 126, 134–5, 183n.16
Hua Sheng, 141, 181n.3
humane government (*wang dao*), 28, 64
humanism, 17, 165n.27
human rights, 105, 106
Hundred Days of Reform, 7, 41–2, 44
Hu Ping, 185n.36, 186n.11
Hu Shaojun, 122
Hu Shi, 108, 170n.3
Huxley, Aldous, 168n.12

illiteracy, elimination of, 83
India, 176n.19
individualism, 46–7, 50–1, 121
industrialization
  Kang Youwei's views, 39
  Liang Qichao's views, 53–4, 60
  Mao Zedong's views, 88, 92
  Sun Yatsen's views, 75–6
institutionalized Confucianism, 119–22
investment, 40, 73, 76, 77–8, 103

Japan
  annexation of Korea, 169n.13
  German constitutionalism, 51–2
  Meiji restoration, 36, 37, 55
  Qunshu Zhiyao, 165n.26
  Shimonoseki Treaty, 30, 42
  Sino–Japanese War (1894–5), 30
  social reformism, 73
  state socialism, 53, 74
  Sun Yatsen's writings, 73, 74, 108, 171n.9
  zaibatsu, 40
Jefferson, Thomas, 71
Jiang Yihua, 124–5, 130, 183n.19
Jiang Zemin, 147–8, 159
Johnson, C., 4

Kang Youwei, 7, 14, 29–30, 34, 43–4, 153
  authority and welfare, 34–5, 60;
    constitutional monarchy
    supported, 36–8; economic
    reforms, 39–41; titular
    monarchical republic
    supported, 38–9; Xunzi's
    theories revived, 35–6
  elite government, 177n.22
  on French Revolution, 48, 172n.18
  Hundred Days of Reform, 41–2
  influence: on Liang Qichao, 45,
    50, 51, 55, 56, 58; on Mao
    Zedong, 60, 93; on Sun
    Yatsen, 77, 170n.14
  new authoritarianism, 122
Kant, Immanuel, 93
Keynesianism, 142, 173n.29
Khrushchev, Nikita, 87, 176n.19
Kim Il-sung, 90
kings, way of (*wang dao*), 28, 64
Kissinger, Henry, 95
knowledge-for-action
  Chiang Kaishek, 65
  Deng Xiaoping, 65
  Sun Yatsen, 64, 65, 98–9, 110
  Wang Yangming, 25,58, 171n.5
Kong Jongyuan, 183n.20
Korea, annexation by Japan, 169n.13

Korean War, 90

Lafayette, Marquis de, 48
land
    nationalization: Kang Youwei's
        views, 39; Liang Qichao's
        views, 55–6; Mao Zedong's
        views, 81, 83, 85; Sun
        Yatsen's views, 55
    value, 40
landlords, 83, 85
Laozi, 26
Lawrence, S., 148
Lee Kuanyu, 172–3n.19
Legalist school of philosophy, 24
legal system, 138–9, 140
Leninism, 4–5, 39, 57, 173n.25
    Mao Zedong's views, 79, 80, 87,
        94, 95, 128
    Sun Yatsen's views, 72–3, 77
Leong, S. T., 173n.23
Levenson, J. R., 3–4, 167n.10
li (social order), 2, 6–7
    Confucius's views, 15–16, 18
    Cultural Debates, 115–16, 129
    Kang Youwei's views, 35, 43
    Liang Qichao's views, 48, 59, 60
    Qing scholar–officials, 44
    Sun Yatsen, 64, 65
    Tan Sitong's views, 31, 166n.1
    Xunzi's views, 6, 20, 21, 23, 25,
        27–8; emphasis, 31
Liang Qichao, 7–8, 14, 45, 59–60,
    166n.2
    authority and welfare, 56–9
    democracy, 67
    enlightened despotism, 51–2
    French Revolution, 47, 48,
        172n.18
    influence on Mao Zedong, 93
    intellectual journey to the West;
        constitution, problem with,
        48–50; 'general will, prob-
        lems with, 47–8; 'individual
        interests', problem with,
        50–1; utilitarianism and
        'public interest', 50
    on Kang Youwei, 29, 43
    perspectives on, 45–7

revolutionaries, critique of; land
    nationalization and Henry
    George's 'single tax', 55–6;
    Manchu rule vs. partition,
    54–5; social reform vs. social
    revolution, 53–4
Sun Yatsen's views, 52, 55, 56, 57,
    60, 64; socialism, 77; wealth,
    65
Xunzi's influence, 25, 26, 165n.26
Yan Fu's views, 123–4
liberalism
    Confucian, *see* Confucianism and
        Confucius
    Mao Zedong's views, 82
    Western, 3; Liang Qichao's views,
        7, 45, 46–7, 59
liberty, 58, 68
Li Dazhao, 109, 170–1n.3
Li Hongzhang, 31, 34, 167n.6
Li Huaxin, 167n.9
Liji, 6, 23, 75
Li Jun, 184n.28
Li Lin, 185n.35
Linebarger, P., 63, 70, 171n.5
Lin Shengli, 182n.13
Li Peng, 144, 148, 188n.21
Li Ruihuan, 148
Li Si, 24, 164n.19, 165n.29
List, Friedrich, 73, 92, 98
Liu Binyan, 187n.14
Liu Jun, 185n.35
Liu, K. C., 41
Liu Shaoqi, 87, 128, 176n.17
livelihood, *see minsheng*
Li Xiannian, 114
Li Zehou, 182n.11
local self-government, 36, 75, 82
Locke, John, 173n.20
Louie, K., 27
Lunyu (Analects), 19
    authority and welfare, 16–17, 18,
        27
    ethics and order, 14–16
    Xunzi's subordination to, 24
Luo Rongqu, 128, 182n.14
Lü Xiaobo, 182n.11

Ma, S. Y., 133

Macau, 139
MacPherson, C. B., 158–9
Manchu regime, 47, 54–5, 65
Mao Zedong, 8–9, 79–80, 94–6
    Chinese historical texts, reading
        of, 165n.29
    on Confucius and *ren*, 165n.31
    Deng Xiaoping's views, 97,
        161n.4; economic reforms,
        100–1, 102; truth from facts,
        100, 178n.7
    Kang Youwei's influence on, 60
    Liang Qichao's influence on, 60
    new authoritarianism, 118, 122,
        127–9, 157
    Sun Yatsen's influence on, 63, 78,
        80, 154–5, 170n.2; authori-
        tarianism, 92–4; retreat from
        'Three Principles', 83–92;
        'Three Principles' and Mao's
        early years, 80–3
    Western perceptions, 4
market economy, 40
martial law, 106
Marxism and Marx, 3, 4
    Deng Xiaoping's views, 99, 109,
        165n.27
    Liang Qichao's views, 46–7, 53
    Mao Zedong's views, 79, 80, 87,
        93, 94, 95
    new authoritarianism, 184n.22
    Sun Yatsen's views, 72, 77
mass democracy, 86
materialism, Xunzi, 26
May Fourth Movement, 67–8, 108,
    116, 123, 125
McCarthy, Joe, 175–6n.14
McCarthy purges, 175–6n.14
Meiji restoration, 36, 37, 55
Meisner, M., 86, 170n.3
Mencius, 19
    authority and welfare, 16, 17–18,
        27, 152
    'conservative' criticism, 27
    influence, limited, 169n.3
    Kang Youwei's views, 35
    Liang Qichao's views, 58
    new authoritarianism, 122
    Xunzi's views, 20–1, 72

Mencius, 17–18, 19, 24, 27
meritocracy, 23–4
Metzger, T. A,. 172n.15
Miao Zhuang, 183n.20
might, way of (*ba dao*), 64–5
military, 95
Mill, John Stuart, 3, 168n.12
    influence on Liang Qichao, 46, 59
    Mao Zedong's views, 93
    Sun Yatsen's views, 68
    Yan Fu's views, 123
Min Bao, 172n.10
minquan (democracy, popular sover-
    eignty, rights), 31, 36, 45–6, 48
minsheng (livelihood), Sun Yatsen's
    views, 65, 66, 70, 72–6, 108
    influence on Deng Xiaoping,
        106–7
    influence on Mao Zedong, 81
minzu (nationalism), 64–7
modernization, 118, 119, 120, 147
monarchical authority, 120
monarchical republic, Kang
    Youwei's support, 38–9, 42
Montesquieu, Charles Louis, 2, 37,
    49, 93
morals, 14
Mozi, 21–4, 35, 58
multiparty democracy, 104, 105, 106
Muslim rebellions, 30

Nanjing, Treaty of, 30
Nathan, Andrew, 162n.10
nationalism (*minzu*), 64–7, 83, 93
Nationalist Party (Guomindang), 81,
    84, 128
nationalization
    of land: Kang Youwei's views, 39;
        Liang Qichao's views, 55–6;
        Mao Zedong's views, 81, 83,
        85; Sun Yatsen's views, 55, 76
National People's Congress (NPC),
    118, 134, 135, 138, 157
natural equality, 69, 106, 173n.20
Negative School, Cultural Debates,
    115–16, 129
neng (ability), 69–70, 71, 105, 106
new authoritarianism (NA), 9–10,
    113–14, 129–30, 131–2, 156–7

Confucian revival (1980s), 114–16
early debates, 132–7
institutionalized Confucianism,
119–22
late Qing, lessons from, 122–5
and Mao Zedong's authoritarianism, 127–9
and old authoritarianism, 116–19
post-Tiananmen debates, 137–42,
149–50
and Sun Yatsen's authoritarianism, 125–7
Tiananmen's impact, 142–7
transitional, 147–9
New Conservatism, 182n.11
Nian Rebellion, 30
Nietzsche, Friedrich, 46–7
Nixon, Richard, 95
Nolan, Peter, 140–1
Northern School, 182n.12
North Korea, 90
old authoritarianism (OA), 116–19
Opium War, 30
order and disorder, 14–16, 19–20,
21, 22, 23
see also li

parliamentary democracy, 124
partition, 54–5
patriarchal authority, 30–1
patrimony, 120
patriotism, 144–5
People's Political Consultative
Conference, 118, 134
people's rights (*minquan*), 31, 36,
45–6, 48
Perry, E. J., 147–8
Peter the Great, 36, 37, 77
planning bureau (*zhidu ju*), 37–8
political culture school of research,
4, 5
Political Research Institute, 56–7
political rights/popular sovereignty
(*minquan*), 31, 36, 45–6, 48
population levels, 30
Positive School, Cultural Debates,
115, 116, 129–30
post-Mao perceptions of China's
authoritarian politics, 4–5

poverty
Confucius, 18
Deng Xiaoping, 26, 99, 101, 152
Mozi, 21
Sun Yatsen, 99, 106
Xunzi, 21, 22–3
power, 117
pragmatism
Deng Xiaoping, 26, 97–8
Xunzi, 25
'Princelings' (*Taizidang*), 113
production, 56
profit, 18, 50
Progressivists, 73
public interest, 50
public-mindedness (*gong*)
Liang Qichao's views, 46, 47, 48,
50, 57, 60
Sun Yatsen, 64, 65
Pye, L. W., 161n.5, 161n.6

Qiao Shi, 148
Qin dynasty, 13–14
Qing dynasty
confused authority, detour
toward, 32, 34
conservative line, 168n.12
divisions, 43
end of, 38
Han Learning, School of, 46
Hundred Days of Reform, 42
Kang Youwei's influence, 7, 35,
37, 39
Liang Qichao's writings, 55
new authoritarianism, 122–5
patriarchal authority challenged,
30
philosophical sources of traditional
authority explored, 13, 14
revolutionaries, crackdown on,
56–7
Xunzi's influence, 19, 25
Yuan Shikai, 175n.8
Qin Shihuangdi, 24
Qin Xiaoying, 126–7, 128, 130,
183n.16
quan (authority), 69–70, 71, 105, 106
qun (grouping)
Liang Qichao's views, 26, 46, 47,

qun (grouping) – *continued*
  57, 59, 60
  general will, 48
  and individual interests, 51
  utilitarianism, 50
  Sun Yatsen's views, 26, 64, 65
  Xunzi's views, 26, 66
Qunshu Zhiyao (*Book of Group Regulations*), 66, 164–5n.26

rational–legal authority, 97
realism, Xunzi, 26
Record of Rites (*Liji*), 6, 23, 75
Records of the Historian (*Shiji*), 165n.29
Rectification Campaign, 179n.10
Reform Movement
  confused authority, 31, 34
  Deng Xiaoping's views, 98
  Kang Youwei's role and views, 41, 166n.3
  patriarchal authority challenged, 31
regulations, adherence to, 164n.20
ren (benevolence)
  Confucius's views, 15–16, 18
  Kang Youwei's views, 43, 168n.15
  Liang Qichao's views, 50, 169n.3
  Mao Zedong's views, 165n.31
  Mencius's views, 17
  Tan Sitong's views, 166n.1
  Xunzi's views, 20
Renaissance, 17
Ren Wanding, 187n.20
Ren Xiao, 183n.15
republicanism, 38, 43, 52, 54–5, 124
Revisionism, 166n.4
Revolution (1911), 33, 38, 98
rights, people's
  Deng Xiaoping's views, 105, 106
  minquan, 31, 36, 45–6, 48
  new authoritarianism, 138, 142
Rights of Zhou (*Zhouli*), 6
Roetz, H., 14
Rong Jian, 120–1, 139, 186n.7
Roosevelt, Franklin D., 89, 176n.16
Rousseau, Jean-Jacques
  Liang Qichao's views, 47, 49, 52, 169n.5

Mao Zedong's views, 93, 177n.21
Sun Yatsen's views, 68
Ruan, M., 87, 181–2n.4
rulers, 17–18, 23–4
Ru school of Confucianism, 25
Russia
  Boxer Rebellion, 169n.13
  Communist Party, 94
  democratization, 141
  Liang Qichao's views, 51, 77
  Mao Zedong's writings, 84
  Peter the Great, 36, 37, 77

sangang (three bonds), 30–4
Sansom, B., 173n.24
Sautman, B., 182n.5
Scalapino, R., 58
scarcity and disorder, relationship between, 20
Schiffrin, H., 58
Schmoller, 53
Schram, S. R., 4, 5, 6, 174n.2
Schwartz, Benjamin, 123, 163n.6
self-government, local, 36, 75, 82
selflessness, 32
Self-strengthening Movement, 166n.3
  confused authority, 31–2, 34
  Deng Xiaoping's views, 98
  patriarchal authority challenged, 31
  Western political ideas, importation of, 168n.12
semiauthoritarianism, 184–5n.28
Service, John, 88, 92, 93, 175–6n.14
Shaffer, L., 172n.16
Sheng, M. M., 89
Shiji, 165n.29
Shijing, 15
Shimonoseki Treaty, 30, 42
Sima Qian, 165n.29
Singapore, 18, 158, 163n.14
single tax, 56, 74
Sino–Japanese War (1894–5), 30
Sino-Soviet Technological Defense Agreement, 92
'Small Sword Society Uprising', 30
Smith, Adam, 3, 168n.12
social classes, 22–3, 72

socialism
  Deng Xiaoping's views, 99, 100,
    101, 102–3, 106–7
  Liang Qichao's views, 53–4, 57
  Mao Zedong's views, 81–2, 83,
    84–5
  Sun Yatsen's views, 57, 72–6, 77
social order, *see li*
social reform, 53–4
social revolutionaries, 53–4
social role (*fen*), 121, 130
societal pressurists, 135–6
Song dynasty, 19
Southern School, 116–17, 182n.11
South Korea, 90, 158
sovereignty, 52, 70
Soviet Union, *see* Union of Soviet
    Socialist Republics
Spencer, Herbert, 93
spiritual civilization, 165n.27
Stalinism and Stalin 79, 87, 89–90,
    91–2, 94
State Statistical Bureau and
    Auditing Administration, 135
statism, 51, 52, 59
status (*fen*), 121, 130
students, Tiananmen crisis, 143–5,
    149
substance (*ti*), 167n.10
Sun Yatsen, 8, 63, 76–8, 154
  democracy (*minquan*), 65–6,
    67–72
  elite government, 177n.22
  George's 'single tax', 56
  Guangxu's influence, 42
  influence on Deng Xiaoping, 98,
    109–10, 155–6; authoritaria-
    nism, 107–9; economic
    reforms, 100–3; political
    reforms, 103–6; theory,
    98–100
  influence on Mao Zedong, 63, 78,
    80, 94–5, 154–5, 170n.2;
    authoritarianism, 92–4;
    Mao's retreat from 'Three
    Principles', 83–92; 'Three
    Principles' and Mao's early
    years, 80–3
  Kang Youwei's influence, 170n.14

land nationalization, 55
Liang Qichao's views, 52, 55, 56,
    57, 60, 64; socialism, 77;
    wealth, 65
nationalism (*minzu*), 63–7
new authoritarianism, 125–7, 157
self-government, 170n.14
socialism (*minsheng*), 72–6
Xunzi's influence, 25, 26, 165n.26
Su Shaozhi, 113, 185n.37

Taiping Rebellion, 30
Taiwan
  Confucius's influence, 163n.14
  democracy, 159
  federalism proposal, 139
  Sun Yatsen's influence, 78,
    174n.30
  transitional authoritarianism, 158
Taizidang ('Princelings'), 113
Tang Yijie, 182n.11
Tan Sitong, 34, 165–6n.2, 167n.8
  sangang, 31, 32
  on Xunzi, 29, 31
taxation, 32, 56, 74
technical expertise, 105
Technological Defense Agreement,
    Sino-Soviet, 92
technology, 32, 33
Teiwes, F. C., 83
three bonds (*sangang*), 30–4
ti (substance), 167n.10, 168n.12
Tiananmen crisis, 131, 157
  Dai Qing, 184n.27
  demands, 140
  Deng Xiaoping's views, 104–5;
    and Wu Jiaxiang, 183n.18
  impact, 141, 142–7
Tiananmen Event, 139
titular monarchical republic, Kang
    Youwei's support, 38–9, 42
ti-yong dichotomy, 167n.10, 168n.12
Tocqueville, Alexis de, 168n.17,
    169n.8
Traditionalists, *see* Conservatives
Tradition of Zuo (*Zuozhuan*), 66
transitional authoritarianism, 141,
    147–9, 158
Treaty of Nanjing, 30

truth from facts, 99–100, 110

uneven economic development, 100
unification of China, 24
Union of Soviet Socialist Republics
    Deng Xiaoping, 101
    Mao Zedong, 87, 88, 89–90, 91–2,
        94
    see also Russia
United States of America
    Kang Youwei's writings, 37, 38
    Liang Qichao's writings, 50–1
    loyalty towards Guomindang,
        128
    Mao Zedong's attempts at
        improved relations with, 87,
        88–9, 90, 91, 94–5
    Progressivists, 73
    Revolution, 71–2
    Tocqueville's writings, 169n.8
utilitarianism, 50, 73

virtue, 18
virtuocracy, 119
Voltaire, 2

Wagner, Alfred, 53
Wakeman, F., 33–4, 45
Wang Dan, 188n.21
wang dao ('way of kings'), 28, 64
Wang Jingwei, 169n.11, 172n.10
Wang Juntao, 185n.36
Wang Xiaoqiang, 184n.28
Wang Yangming, 25, 58, 171n.5
Warring States period, 19, 43
Waterman, H., 135
wealth
    Confucius's views, 18
    Deng Xiaoping's views, 101, 103
    Kang Youwei's views, 35–6
    Mao Zedong's views, 83
    Mencius's views, 18
    Mozi's views, 21
    Self-strengthening Movement, 32
    Sun Yatsen's views, 63, 65, 68, 74
    Xunzi's views, 21–2
Weber, Max, 3
Weberian framework of research,
    161n.4

Wei Jingsheng, 186n.10
West
    legitimate authority, foundation
        of, 1
    liberalism, 3; Liang Qichao's
        views, 7, 45, 46–7, 59
    perceptions of Chinese authority,
        2–4
    political ideas imported by China,
        168n.21
Westernizers, *see* Self-strengthening
    Movement
White, G., 148
White, Theodore, 91, 175–6n.14
will, general, 47–8
William, Maurice, 73
Williams, D., 163n.13
Wuer Kaixi, 144, 188n.21, 188n.23
Wu Jiaxiang, 123, 183n.18, 186n.3,
    186n.4

Xiao Gongqin, 116–17, 121–2,
    123–4, 128, 129–30
Xidan Democracy Wall movement,
    139–40, 186n.10
Xiu Haitao, 181n.1
Xunzi, 6, 152
    authority and welfare, 19–20,
        27–8; Mencius, critique,
        20–1; Mozi, critique, 21–4
    Deng Xiaoping's views, 110,
        179n.14, 179n.16
    influence on Chinese history and
        politics, 24–7
    influence on Kang Youwei, 29–30,
        34–6, 39–40, 42, 43–4
    influence on Liang Qichao, 7, 45,
        46, 48, 50, 58–9
    influence on Mao Zedong, 93
    influence on Sun Yatsen, 63,
        76–7; democracy, 67, 70–1,
        72; nationalism, 64, 65, 66,
        67; socialism, 75, 76
    new authoritarianism, 121, 123,
        129–30
Xunzi, 6, 19–24, 27

Yan Fu, 31, 123–4, 166–7n.5, 167n.7
Yang Baibang, 148

Yang Baikui, 125–6
Yang Rongguo, 26–7
Yang Xinyu, 122
Yan Jiaqi, 185n.36, 187n.13
Ye Xuanping, 148
Yin Xuyi, 125, 128, 148, 185n.34
yong (function), 167n.10, 168n.12
Yuan Shikai, 84, 124, 156, 177n.22
Yue Linzhang, 186n.8
Yu Haocheng, 128–9, 183n.16

zaibatsu, 40
Zhang Bingjiu, 136, 184–5n.28
Zhang Dainian, 182n.11

Zhang, S., 140, 141
Zhang Wei, 181n.1
Zhang Zhidong, 33, 167n.9, 168n.12
Zhao Ziyang, 113, 144, 182n.9,
    184n.28
Zheng Yongnian, 186n.8
zhidu ju (planning bureau), 37–8
Zhonghua Gemindang, 173n.23
Zhou dynasty, 13, 14, 19, 119
Zhou Enlai, 87, 91, 95
Zhouli, 6
Zhu Rongji, 148, 187n.19
Zou Jiahua, 148
Zuozhuan (*Tradition of Zuo*), 66